W9-CEQ-469

Patterns Plus

A Short Prose Reader with Argumentation

Seventh Edition

Mary Lou Conlin
Cuyahoga Community College

HOUGHTON MIFFLIN COMPANY Boston New York

Senior Sponsoring Editor: Mary Jo Southern
Associate Editor: Kellie Cardone
Editorial Development: Danielle Richardson
Associate Project Editor: Kate Hartke
Senior Production/Design Coordinator: Jill Haber
Manufacturing Manager: Florence Cadran
Marketing Manager: Annamarie Rice

Acknowledgments begin on page 335.

Cover image: © Jane Nelson, Artville 2001.

Copyright © 2002 by Houghton Mifflin Company. All rights reserved.

No part of this work may be reproduced or transmitted in any form or by any means, electronic or mechanical, including photocopying and recording, or by any information storage or retrieval system without the prior written permission of the copyright owner unless such copying is expressly permitted by federal copyright law. With the exception of non-profit transcription in Braille, Houghton Mifflin is not authorized to grant permission for further uses of copyrighted selections reprinted in this text without the permission of their owners. Permission must be obtained from the individual copyright owners as identified herein. Address requests for permission to make copies of Houghton Mifflin material to College Permissions, Houghton Mifflin Company, 222 Berkeley Street, Boston, MA 02116-3764.

Printed in the U.S.A.

Library of Congress Control Number: 2001131487

ISBN: 0-618-12309-1

6789-MV-06-05-04-03

As part of Houghton Mifflin's ongoing
commitment to the environment, this text
has been printed on recycled paper.

Contents

4 Examples *79*

PARAGRAPHS

ESSAYS

5 Classification and Division   *111*

PARAGRAPHS

6 Comparison and Contrast   *143*

PARAGRAPHS

ESSAYS

7 Process   *175*

PARAGRAPHS

ESSAYS

Thematic Table of Contents

3 The Natural Environment

The following selections consider our impact on the environment and its
   impact on us.

4 Animals and Humans

The following readings discuss animal and human behavior, from sports
   fans to human mistreatment of a frog and the sea.

5 Progress

The memorable but sometimes questionable effects of discoveries,
   inventions, and decisions made in the name of "progress," as well as our
   lack of progress in solving some of society's problems, are considered in
   the following readings.

6 Expectations and Reality

In the following readings, the writers show us that expectations, whether
   positive or negative, may not be realized or may turn out differently than
   anticipated.

7   Education and Learning

What we've learned and what we have yet to learn are considered in the
   following selections.

8   Food for Thought

The following readings consider things we like to eat and drink, things we shouldn't drink, and the celebration of the harvest that signals plentiful food for the year ahead.

9   The Working World

The nature of work, the definition of work, and the effect of not working are considered in the following readings.

10   Values

Values associated with a particular culture, race, society, sight, food, piece of clothing, language, and even color are considered in the following readings.

11   The Family

The following readings consider the positive and not-so-positive aspects of family life.

12   Childhood

In the following readings, the writers share their memories, lessons learned, risks taken in childhood and youth, and the significance of early parental involvement with their children.

13   Communication

In the following readings, the writers consider the many ways we
communicate and fail to communicate effectively.

Writing Across the Curriculum
Table of Contents

20   Women's Studies

Preface

Patterns Plus: A Short Prose Reader with Argumentation provides students with an understanding of the thinking process, organizational principles, and rhetorical strategies involved in producing clear and effective writing. In this seventh edition, students are introduced to the uses of freewriting and brainstorming in defining ideas for their writing and to the process of collaborative writing. The study apparatus provides complete and clear explanations of the various rhetorical modes, and the paragraph and essay-length readings provide students with examples of how the modes can be used in organizing and developing their ideas.

New to the Seventh Edition

Patterns Plus, seventh edition, provides students with a variety of models for their own writing and with readings that stimulate lively and thoughtful classroom discussions. Features of the new edition include:

- Selections by such traditional favorites as E. B. White, Jack London, and John Ciardi are joined by new selections by Stephen King, James Baldwin, and Joseph Epstein. Women authors are represented by Anna Quindlen, Nancy Masterson Sakamoto, and Harper Lee, among others, with minority authors represented by Clifton Taulbert, Brent Staples, Martin Luther King, Jr., Magdoline Asfahani, Jeanne Park, and many others.
- An update of the introductory chapter, which provides a fuller treatment of the writing of paragraphs and essays, the need for revising and editing each piece of writing, and the collaborative writing process.
- A new writing review list to assist students in revising and editing their writing.
- A revised Thematic Table of Contents.
- A revised Writing Across the Curriculum Table of Contents.
- New Internet-based writing assignments (look for the globe icon) that ask students to research and write about topics ranging from the effects of air pollution to the effectiveness of college web sites.

An Overview of Patterns Plus

Chapter 1, an introductory chapter, describes the basics of the writing process and the construction of paragraphs and essays. In chapters 2 through 10, the various techniques in developing the main idea—*narration, description, examples, classification and division, comparison and contrast, process, cause and effect, definition,* and *argumentation and persuasion*—are explained. These techniques are the traditional *rhetorical modes*—the strategies for development that have proved effective in providing starting points for many student writers. Chapter 11, "Combining the Strategies," contains essays that illustrate the ways writers combine various modes of development within a single essay.

Professional and student selections in *Patterns Plus* were chosen specifically to build students' confidence by showing them that the writing of short, effective compositions is within their reach. Selections range from simple, accessible paragraphs to longer, more challenging essays. The student writings that are included throughout the text will make students aware of the level of skill they can realistically expect to achieve.

The breadth of reading selections also allows the instructor a wide choice of topics—from serious and timely discussions related to discrimination, cultural differences, and social concerns to lighthearted pieces that reveal human foibles. As a stimulus to discussion, two sides of a controversial subject are sometimes provided. Students will probably respond quite differently to the argumentation and persuasional essays on the death penalty, homosexuality laws, and portrayal of violence in the media.

Apparatus

Patterns Plus offers a full range of study apparatus:

- *Headnotes* provide author information and a context for each reading selection to help students understand and enjoy the selection.
- *Words to Know* define unfamiliar words and clarify allusions that might be unfamiliar or regional.
- *Getting Started* questions prepare students to think critically about the topic presented in the reading selection or about topics for their own writing.
- Exercises promote comprehension and critical skills.
  Questions About the Reading are designed to stimulate thinking about the selection's meaning—expressed and implied—and to help students gain fuller understanding of the writer's message.
  Questions About the Writer's Strategies ask students to discuss the writer's *thesis statement, mode of development, point of view, figurative language*—or whatever strategy is particularly appropriate to

a given selection—and thereby promote critical and analytical thinking.

Writing Assignments are related to the topic and development mode of the reading selection and are designed to encourage the student to generate ideas that can be developed into paragraphs and essays.

- The *Thematic Table of Contents* groups the readings in the text by such themes as "The Individual in Society," "Values," and "The Working World."
- The *Writing Across the Curriculum Table of Contents* arranges the readings by academic discipline, such as biology, education, and history.
- The *Glossary* provides definitions of all writing-process, rhetorical, and literary terms that are boldfaced throughout the chapter introductions and end-of-selection questions.

Support for Instructors

The Instructor's Resource Manual for *Patterns Plus* offers instructors a wide variety of supplemental materials:

- Part One supplies teaching suggestions that will allow flexibility in determining course content and structure.
- Part Two contains questions and their answers about the content of each chapter. The questions can be used as quizzes or to generate class discussion.
- Part Three provides suggested answers to the reading comprehension and Writer's Strategies questions that appear at the end of each reading selection in chapters 2 through 10.
- Part Four offers suggested questions and answers for the extra readings in chapter 11.
- Part Five includes a list of the reading levels according to the Fry and Dale-Chall readability formulas. Reading levels are arranged by chapter and by grade.

Acknowledgments

I would like to thank my good friends Ruth Silon, Cuyahoga Community College, for sharing her student's essay, "Students," and Kim Flachmann, California State University, Bakersfield, for providing "An Intruder in the House." My thanks also to Lynn Schubert, Los Angeles Harbor College, for "My Suit," a paragraph by one of her students, and to George D. Gess, George Fox College, for his student's essay, "Overindulgence."

I am further indebted to the following persons for their help on this seventh edition of the text:

Juanita G. Bass, LeMoyne-Owen College, TN
Juliana F. Cárdenas, Grossmont College, CA
David Elias, Eastern Kentucky University, KY
Louis Gallo, Radford University, VA

Finally, I again extend my appreciation to the people at Houghton Mifflin who worked with me on this book: Mary Jo Southern, Danielle Richardson, Kellie Cardone, and Kate Hartke. No writer could ask for a better team.

                                                        Mary Lou Conlin

The Basics of Writing: Process and Strategies

"A writer is somebody for whom writing is more difficult than it is for other people."

Thomas Mann

THIS BOOK TELLS you about the process and strategies that you can use to produce effective writing. It includes many paragraphs and essays—by both student and professional writers—that you can study as models for your own writing. By understanding and following the process involved in writing, by learning the strategies other writers use to communicate their ideas, and by practicing in paragraphs and essays of your own, you can develop the skill and confidence needed to write effectively on many different subjects.

Purpose and Audience

It is important that you understand the writing process and learn a variety of writing strategies because you will find yourself, in school and afterward, writing for different **purposes,** to different types of **audiences,** and for varied **occasions.** Your purpose might be to persuade (perhaps in a memo recommending a new procedure at work), to instruct (in a description of how to do a lab assignment), or to inform (in a letter to your daughter's teacher explaining her absence from school). Your audience, or reader, may be fellow students or friends, and the occasion may be an informal activity; your audience may be your employer, and the occasion a formal report. In any case, you will need to make choices—as you work through the process of prewriting, drafting, rewriting, revising, and editing your work—about the writing strategies that will most effectively explain your ideas.

As a student, you will often have tests and assignments that require you to write either a **paragraph** or an **essay.** Although such compositions may differ in their length and content, a paragraph and an essay are alike in two important ways. First, each one should have a **main idea.** Second, the main idea should be fully explained or developed. In this book, you will learn the ways in which many writers go about finding a main idea and the strategies they use in explaining or developing it.

Finding a Main Idea

If you are like most writers, you may find it difficult to come up with a main idea of your own. You may stare out the window, get something to eat, play a game on your computer, or in some other way put off starting to write. When you find yourself stalling, you may find it helpful to do some prewriting exercises to generate ideas. One method is to sit down and write without stopping for five or ten minutes. This is called **freewriting,** and its primary purpose is to get you started writing.

As the term implies, freewriting is often disorganized and lacks a clear focus. Your freewriting might look like this:

> I need to go to the grocery store as soon as I get an idea for this assignment. Why is that car parked in the middle of the road? Hope he doesn't get hit by that truck pulling out of my neighbor's. The leaves have already started falling and we haven't really had much summer yet. I wish I'd had more time to go swimming. All the pools are closed now until next summer. Too bad. No more vegetables from the garden either. They're all gone now. I'll have to pull the dead flowers out soon. Hope this winter isn't as bad as last year's. I hate to think of all that snow and ice again.

When you look over your freewriting, you can see that many of the observations you wrote down have to do with the passing of summer. You could write about the things you will miss when summer is over.

Sometimes your instructor will suggest a topic to focus your freewriting. For example, suppose your instructor asks you to write a paragraph describing the room you are in. Your freewriting might then look like this:

> Looks like rain. Wonder if I closed my bedroom windows. What can I say about this classroom except that it's pretty much like all college classrooms. Seats with writing arms, blackboard, teacher's desk, tan walls with lots of dents in them. Have to pick Chad up from the day-care center at 4. Hope he won't be crabby like he was yesterday. What should I say about this classroom?

When you read over your freewriting, underline anything that strikes you as interesting or important. Your freewriting may trigger an idea that will focus your description. For example, you may notice that your classroom is like all classrooms, except that the walls have lots of dents. Choosing this as a main idea, you might then write a paragraph like this:

Main idea

> The classroom is like all college classrooms except for the many dents in its walls. Like all classrooms, it has thirty chairs with writing arms, lined up in five rows with six chairs in each row; a blackboard that still has the assignment on it from the previous class and needs a good washing; the professor's desk, with a podium on it to hold his oft-used lecture notes; and tan, finger-marked walls. But for some unknown reason, chairs have been shoved hard and often against the walls, which have more and deeper dents than

Main idea restated

> those in other classrooms. Only its dented walls make this classroom different from all college classrooms.

Suppose, however, that the assignment is to **collaborate** with one or more of your classmates in writing an essay about the environment. Collaboration means working with others on a project—in this case, writing an essay about the environment. Once the members of your collaborative group are determined, you will need to meet to discuss the assignment, determine each person's responsibilities, and schedule the project. One member of your group may emerge as the leader, or your group may elect a leader. The leader is responsible for coordinating the project and for seeing that each member of the group meets the schedule that is set for drafting, revising, and editing the assignment.

Next, each of you might want to do some freewriting in order to get started, but then you will want to do some **brainstorming** together. Brainstorming, like freewriting, is simply a way of putting your thoughts on paper to help you choose a main idea and develop supporting evidence for a paragraph or an essay. You will need to focus your thinking on words and ideas that relate to the environment, with one of you writing down what each person contributes. Your group's list might look like this:

trees	water
pollution	diapers
landfills	food
harmful	resources
paper	waste disposal
flowers	cars, airplanes—noise
smog	cars, exhaust

plastics   wasting resources—oil, coal, water
land

After your group finishes the brainstorming list, you will need to look for relationships among the words and ideas. For instance, your group could decide that the items can be clustered into two groups or categories: (1) things that the environment provides and (2) things that can harm or damage the environment.

Environment provides:	Environment damaged by:
trees	waste disposal—diapers, plastics
flowers	cars—exhaust fumes, noise
food	airplanes—noise
resources—water, oil, coal	wasting resources—water, oil, coal, trees

Based on these categories, your group may decide that the main idea for the group's essay could be "We depend on our environment for food, water, and other resources, but we are damaging our environment in several ways." Your group could then decide to classify the *ways* we are damaging our food, water, and other resources. After reviewing your brainstorming list and talking it over, your group might decide that the classifications could be *polluting, poisoning,* and *wasting.* You could say, "We are *polluting* the land and our water supply with waste disposal, *poisoning* the air with the exhaust from cars and airplanes, and *wasting* our resources by the overuse of paper and oil."

You might then decide to assign responsibility for providing supporting details for each of the classifications to different members of the group. Thus someone could be responsible for providing examples to support "polluting the land and our water supply with waste disposal"; someone else for "poisoning the air with the exhaust from cars and airplanes"; and someone else for "wasting our resources by the overuse of paper and oil."

Stating the Main Idea

The main idea of a paragraph is called the **topic.** This topic is usually stated in a sentence, called a **topic sentence.** The topic sentence usually expresses a general rather than a specific idea, and it may be placed anywhere within the paragraph. However, you will find that it generally helps to keep your writing clear and focused if you state your main idea at the *beginning* of the paragraph. In the sample paragraph that follows, the main idea (or topic) of the paragraph is stated in the first sentence, followed by the supporting examples. This is called general-to-specific, or deductive, order.

Topic sentence

From George Washington to George Bush, soup has warmed the hearts and stomachs of many of our nation's leaders. Did you know . . . ? The Bush family's favorite soup is clam chowder. The Reagans' favorite soup recipe calls for browned beef patties in beef broth with onions, garlic, carrots, honey, celery, tomatoes and black pepper. President Washington's favorite dish was cream of peanut soup. The recipe was based on chicken stock and flavored with carrots, onions, peanut butter and Tabasco sauce! Hyannis Fish Chowder was, of course, JFK's choice. Eleanor Roosevelt once sent a memo to FDR recommending peanut soup for the Navy and War Department's menus.

Land O'Lakes, Inc., 1995

In the following paragraph, the writer has stated the topic in the first and second sentences.

Topic sentences

A lot of people get married and then are disappointed because marriage turns out to be much different from what they expected it to be. The trouble may be not with their marriages but with their expectations. If men and women were more thoroughly acquainted with the realities of marriage before they walked down the aisle together, and if they accepted those realities, the divorce rate in the United States would probably drop dramatically.

William J. Lederer and Don D. Jackson, M.D.,
"Do People Really Marry for Love?"
Family Circle, August 1973

As you become more experienced, you may sometimes find it effective to place the topic sentence at the *end* of the paragraph. In the following paragraph the writer has stated the topic in the last sentence. This is called specific-to-general, or inductive, order.

We think of an ideal society as being a community—whatever its size—in which the people, the environment, and the institutions are in harmony. No nation, ours included, has ever achieved such a society. In fact, most Americans would say it is not really possible to establish an ideal society. But strangely enough, we keep trying. Time after time, a group of people will drop out of the mainstream of American society to try another "life style" based on the group's concept of an ideal society. Most of these groups have believed in holding their property in common—that is, they believed in a communistic or communal concept of property. Most of the groups have also used the word "family" to refer to all

Topic sentence

> members of the group, rather than to a mother, father, and their children as the family unit. But the groups have differed widely in their attitudes toward sex, marriage, and other values and seldom lasted for very long as a consequence.

As you study the student and professional writings that follow, you will find that writers do not always state the main idea of their paragraphs and essays outright. Instead, they may prefer to suggest or to **imply** the idea. Notice that the writer must provide enough clues to allow the careful reader to **infer** (determine) the main idea. In the following paragraph, for example, the writer implies the idea that the man saw the berries reflected rather than actually floating in the water. The writer provides the clues the reader needs to infer the main idea by saying that the man struck the bottom of the river when he dived in and that he then looked up and saw the berries hanging over him.

> While walking along the river, he saw some berries in the water. He dived down for them, but was stunned when he unexpectedly struck the bottom. There he lay for quite a while, and when he recovered consciousness and looked up, he saw the berries hanging on a tree just above him.
>
> Paul Radin,
> "Manbozho and the Berries"

If you experiment with implying your main idea, be sure to give the reader enough clues to determine your meaning.

In a longer piece of writing, such as an essay, the main idea is called the **thesis** (rather than the topic). The thesis is usually stated in one or more sentences called the **thesis statement.** Like the topic sentence of a paragraph, the thesis statement is often placed near the beginning of an essay. In the essay that follows, the thesis is stated in the opening paragraph.

Thesis statement

> Scientists all agree that packages are very necessary. They also agree that packages are a problem. But they do not agree on what to do about it.

Topic sentence of paragraph 2

> There is the make-it-attractive group. These designers concentrate on making the package so interesting that the buyer cannot bring himself to part with it—thus keeping it out of the trash. . . .

Topic sentence of paragraph 3

> Next there are the no-package-package groups. They have ideas like spraying a protein coating, derived from corn, on foods to protect them against loss of vitamins and spoilage. . . .

Topic sentence of paragraph 4

> In the no-package-package group is a new type of glass that may be the answer to the 26 billion bottles thrown away every year. The glass is coated on the inside as well as on the outside by a water-resistant film. When the bottle is smashed, the glass will dissolve in plain water. . . .

Topic sentence
of paragraph 5

> Another no-package is the plastic bag used to hold laundry bleach or bluing. Tossed into the laundry, it dissolves before the washing is finished. But the prize will go to the scientist who can come up with a container that is as successful as the ice cream cone.
>
> Suzanne Hilton,
> *How Do They Get Rid of It?*

In addition to noting the thesis statement, notice that each paragraph has its own topic sentence.

Experienced writers may place the thesis statement in later paragraphs or at the end of the essay. They may, indeed, only imply the thesis. For your own writing, the important point to remember is that an effective essay has a clear thesis statement, just as a well-made paragraph has a topic sentence. When you are reading, your task is to discover the writer's thesis. When you are writing, your task is to make your own thesis as clear as possible to your reader. And your best strategy, initially, is to *state your thesis at or near the beginning of your essay.*

Developing the Main Idea

The second important way in which paragraphs and essays are alike is that their main ideas must be explained or **developed** by the writer. The strategies used by writers to develop their ideas include:

narration	process
description	cause and effect
examples	definition
classification and division	argumentation and persuasion
comparison and contrast	

These strategies for developing the main idea are called **modes of development.** Although they have different characteristics, the modes of development have a common purpose: to provide the reader with the specific information needed to **support** or clarify the main idea. As stated earlier, the main idea is a general statement; the development provides the details to support or explain the main idea.

In developing a paragraph, the writer usually (1) begins with a topic sentence, (2) develops the main idea (topic) by a series of related sentences that explain the idea fully, and (3) concludes with a sentence that restates or summarizes the main idea. Look at the following paragraph diagram and compare it with the example paragraph about the classroom on page 3. Notice that the example paragraph begins with a topic sentence; develops the main idea (topic) with the sentences about the chairs, blackboard, desk, and walls; and then concludes by restating the topic sentence.

Paragraph

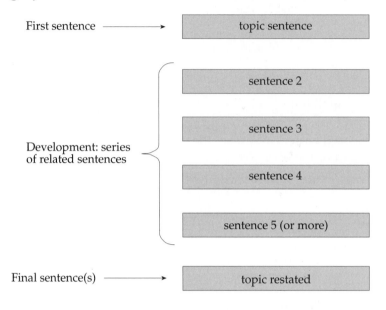

First sentence ⟶ topic sentence

Development: series of related sentences {
sentence 2
sentence 3
sentence 4
sentence 5 (or more)
}

Final sentence(s) ⟶ topic restated

Next, compare the paragraph diagram with the essay diagram that follows. Notice that in developing the essay, the writer starts with a thesis statement, which is generally part of the introduction and may make up the whole first paragraph. Then the writer develops the thesis in a series of related paragraphs, called the **body** of the essay. Usually, each paragraph has its own topic sentence. The conclusion, which may restate the thesis or summarize the essay's important points, is usually found in the final paragraph.

Essay

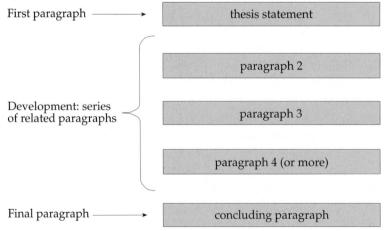

First paragraph ⟶ thesis statement

Development: series of related paragraphs {
paragraph 2
paragraph 3
paragraph 4 (or more)
}

Final paragraph ⟶ concluding paragraph

Now look at the following essay developed by a group of students for the environment assignment. Notice that the thesis is stated in the first paragraph, which is called the **introduction** of the essay. The thesis is developed, or supported, by the next three paragraphs that make up the body of the essay. In these paragraphs, each classification of the ways the environment is being damaged has been used as the topic for a body paragraph and items from the brainstorming lists (see pp. 3–4) have been used as examples to develop the topics. The final paragraph, called the **conclusion** or concluding paragraph, restates the thesis and sums up the main points of the essay.

Thesis statement (introduction)

Modern conveniences have made our lives easier, but often at the expense of our environment. Science and society, which have been so quick to create and adopt new consumer goods, have been slow in creating and adopting practices to protect the environment from the same consumer goods. As a result, just through everyday living, we are damaging the environment we depend on and wasting our resources.

Development (body paragraph)

For one thing, we pollute the land and our water supply with the by-products of modern life. We fill our garbage dumps and landfills with throwaway plastic products and "disposable" diapers that will not disintegrate for hundreds of years, if ever. Industries accidentally or willfully spill oil and chemicals into the ground or streams and pollute our water supply.

Development (body paragraph)

For another thing, we poison the air with exhaust from the cars and airplanes that have become such an important part of our lives. In some areas, the exhaust from cars creates smog that poisons our lungs and causes respiratory ailments. Air pollution also causes acid rain that, in turn, destroys rivers, lakes, woods, and farm crops.

Development (body paragraph)

Finally, we are wasting our resources shamefully. For example, we use far more water than we need to in brushing our teeth and taking showers. Even something as "harmless" as letting dripping faucets go unrepaired wastes a lot of valuable water. We water our lawns through automatic sprinkler systems that run even in rainstorms. We also waste oil by driving millions of cars hundreds of millions of needless miles each year and by keeping our houses warmer than we need to. We are even dangerously close to depleting our "renewable" resources. We cut down our forests with abandonment in order to eat from paper plates, drink from paper cups, and carry products home from the store.

Thesis and important points restated (concluding paragraph)

Yes, we have come to depend on technology to fulfill our needs, but we still need our natural environment. Unless we start developing technology to protect our natural world, it may soon pollute and poison us.

The essay has also been developed by using **classification, examples, cause and effect,** and **persuasion** as modes of development. The *classifications* are the *ways* we are damaging the environment: polluting, poisoning, wasting. *Examples* are plastics, diapers, and oil and chemical spills; exhaust fumes from cars and airplanes; using too much water to brush our teeth and water our lawns; driving needlessly, overheating our houses, and using paper products. In turn, the examples are *causes* of three *effects:* pollution, poisoning, and wasting. The smog created by car exhaust is also a *cause* of lung and respiratory ailments (*effects*). The essay also seeks to persuade readers to stop damaging the environment.

Notice, too, the use of the words *for one thing, for another thing,* and *finally* at the beginning of paragraphs 2, 3, and 4. These are called transitional words, and their purpose is to help the reader identify the connection among the ideas in a composition and to move the reader along from one idea to another.

Although the modes of development are often combined as they are in the students' collaborative essay, a single mode of development will often be dominant in a composition. For instance, if you are writing a **descriptive** essay, that does not mean you cannot use **examples** to illustrate your description, but it does mean that most of the paragraphs will be descriptive. Or you might write a **cause-and-effect** essay in which you **narrate** a series of events that constitute a cause and another event that is the effect. In general, however, you will learn to be comfortable with the modes of development if you first study them individually; and this text is organized so you can do that. You will see that chapters 2 through 10 each deal with a single mode of development and bring together paragraphs and essays in which that mode dominates. Chapter 11 contains essays that combine the modes, even though one mode may still dominate.

Before each paragraph or essay, you will find a note that tells you something about the reading, definitions of words that might be unfamiliar to you, and a question that either will help you think about the reading or will provide a writing idea. Following each reading selection are questions about the reading, questions about the writer's strategies, and suggestions for your own writing assignments.

The Glossary at the back of the book defines and explains the technical terms you will learn to use. These terms are boldfaced throughout the text. If you encounter a boldfaced term and cannot recall what it means, turn to the Glossary to refresh your memory.

The ability to state an idea and to develop it so that it is clear to your reader is essential to all forms of composition. The writing strategies covered in this text will help you develop those abilities. However, to produce an effective piece of writing you will generally need to follow this process:

- **Prewriting,** to get started and to define your idea
- **Drafting,** to learn what your idea is about
- **Rewriting,** to clarify your idea and to improve or add to the strategies used to develop it
- **Revising,** to improve the organization and content
- **Revising,** to polish the organization and content
- **Editing,** to improve word choices and sentences and to correct punctuation and spelling

Your instructor may also want you to keep a journal as a way to record your thoughts and experiences, to keep you writing, and perhaps to give you ideas for writing. Your instructor may also want you to compile a portfolio—a collection of all your drafts and revisions—as part of your course and to demonstrate your writing progress. Some instructors may want you to collaborate with your classmates on various writing assignments. Still other instructors may give you the option of submitting your drafts by computer and receiving their corrections and suggestions the same way. In any event, you should expect to draft, rewrite, revise, and edit all of your writing assignments until they are clear and convincing to your reader. You can then apply your skills to the many kinds of writing that will be required now, at school, and later, in your career.

2

Narration

HAVE YOU EVER seen a bad car accident, a fire, or a robbery? Have you had an especially sad or happy experience that made a lasting impression on you or made a difference in your life? If you later mention one of these **events** to friends, they will probably want to know more about it. What individual **incidents** made up the event? How did it happen? At what time? Where did it take place? On the spot, you become a narrator or storyteller and try to give a clear and lively account of the event. Thus you are already familiar with **narration,** one of the modes of development that writers frequently use to illustrate and explain their ideas. The purpose of narration is to interest the reader in a story that illustrates a particular idea clearly.

Narration is frequently used to tell about personal experiences. You have a variety of personal experiences every day. Your car won't start, you miss the bus, and then you are late for your class. Such experiences, although important to you, will not necessarily make for an effective narrative. For a narrative to be effective, the writer needs to describe an experience that has some unusual meaning or significance for both the writer and the reader. Usually, an experience is significant because it taught you—and may teach your reader—something new, something you never before realized about life. For example, in the following paragraph, the writer tells about a personal experience that taught him about being responsible, not only for making decisions but also for accepting the consequences of those decisions.

	As I was growing up, my father and I often disagreed about how I should spend my time. He began telling me, "If you get yourself into it, you'll have to get yourself out." But
Topic sentence	I learned what it meant to be responsible for the consequences of my decisions only after I went to a weekend party when I
Incident 1	should have studied for a math exam. I needed a good grade on the exam to stay eligible to play basketball. The conse-
Incident 2	quences of my decision to go to the party were clear when I got my exam back with a notice that I was on academic pro- bation. I spent two semesters of almost steady studying be-
Incident 3	fore I was back in good standing. Now, whenever I have a difficult decision to make, I remind myself, "If you get your-
Topic restated: significance of narrative	self into it, you'll have to get yourself out." It was a tough lesson, but I learned that making a decision means taking the responsibility for its consequences.

Effective narrative writing, like all good writing, is carefully organized. Since a narrative describes events, its organization must be governed by some form of time **order.** The writer often tells about events in the order in which they took place. This method of organization, called **chronological order,** ensures that the sequence of the incidents will be logical.

In the following sample paragraph, the writer uses narration to give a factual account of an event: the discovery of Wheaties. Notice that this writer has chosen to explain the different incidents in a simple chronological order.

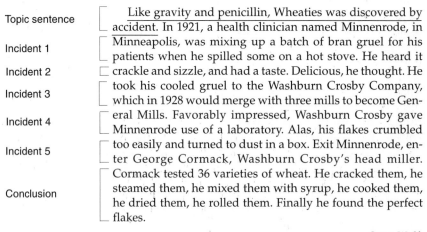

Topic sentence	Like gravity and penicillin, Wheaties was discovered by accident. In 1921, a health clinician named Minnenrode, in
Incident 1	Minneapolis, was mixing up a batch of bran gruel for his patients when he spilled some on a hot stove. He heard it
Incident 2	crackle and sizzle, and had a taste. Delicious, he thought. He
Incident 3	took his cooled gruel to the Washburn Crosby Company, which in 1928 would merge with three mills to become Gen-
Incident 4	eral Mills. Favorably impressed, Washburn Crosby gave Minnenrode use of a laboratory. Alas, his flakes crumbled
Incident 5	too easily and turned to dust in a box. Exit Minnenrode, en- ter George Cormack, Washburn Crosby's head miller.
Conclusion	Cormack tested 36 varieties of wheat. He cracked them, he steamed them, he mixed them with syrup, he cooked them, he dried them, he rolled them. Finally he found the perfect flakes.

Steve Wulf,
"The Breakfast of Champions"

Notice the **details** in this paragraph. In addition to re-creating the incidents that are significant to his topic, the writer uses descriptive words to tell what happened. Minnenrode "spilled" the gruel, heard it "crackle" and "sizzle," and found that the flakes "turned to dust in a box." By using words that provide descriptive detail, the writer adds variety and interest to his narrative. (**Description,** a mode of development in its own right, is the subject of the next chapter.)

Notice, too, that this paragraph contains only the incidents or details that contribute directly to the story. Avoiding irrelevant incidents and details is essential to effective narrative writing. Perhaps you have heard some long-winded person tell a story and found yourself wishing that the person would skip some of the trivial details. You should keep this in mind when you are writing and limit yourself to the details that are *essential* to the main idea of your narrative. In the following essay, for example, the writer does not include any incidents that happened before the robbery. He concentrates on those incidents and details that explain his actions and reactions only during key moments. As you read the essay, think about the details the writer provides and try to form an image of the scene in your mind.

Thesis statement	Recently I was unfortunate enough to be in a store when a robbery took place. I learned from that experience that a pointed gun makes people obey.	1
Incidents arranged as they occurred in time	I had stopped at the store on my way home from work to get a loaf of bread. I was at the check-out counter when a man standing nearby pulled out a gun and yelled, "Everyone on the floor and away from the cash register!"	2
Frozen in place	My first reaction was fear. Around me, people dropped to the floor. But I felt frozen where I stood.	3
Gun pointed	As I hesitated, the robber pointed his gun at me and yelled again, "On the floor!" Then I felt angry. I was bigger and stronger than he was. I was sure I could put *him* on the floor in a fair fight.	4
Sank to floor	But the gun, small enough to be cradled in the palm of my hand, was bigger and stronger than I was. I sank obediently to the floor.	5
Robbery took place	All of us watched silently as the robber scooped money out of the cash register into a paper bag. Then he ran out the door, jumped into a car that was waiting, and the car raced away.	6
After robbery	Everyone stood up and started talking. A clerk called the police, who asked if anyone could describe the robber or the car. No one could.	7
Dialogue Significance of narrative restated	Then one man, blustering defensively, told the clerk just what I was thinking. "Listen. Tell them when a gun is pointed at me, it's all I'm looking at. One look and I'm going to do whatever I'm told."	8

Look at each paragraph in this essay. The first paragraph is an introduction in which the main idea or thesis of the essay is stated. Each successive paragraph deals with an incident or a set of incidents in the narrative. Each incident contributes key information to the essay and moves the story forward in time. The final paragraph concludes the narrative by restating the main idea of the essay.

As you can see, the narrative mode is used for more than just retelling what happened. In addition to reporting the action, narrative writing often explains the *reactions*—emotions and thoughts—of the narrator and others involved. At other times, the writer may leave it to the reader to determine the narrator's feelings and reactions.

In this and other ways, the writer establishes a particular **point of view** for the essay. Point of view involves three elements: **person, time,** and **tone.** The essay may be written in the **first person** (*I/we*), **second person** (*you*), or **third person** (*he/she/it/they*). The time in which the essay is set may be the past, present, or future. The tone is the attitude (serious, humorous, angry, sad) that the writer adopts.

In a narrative essay, the point of view creates the context for the incidents described: that is, who saw or experienced the events, when the events occurred, and how the writer felt about the events. Narration is generally written from the first or third person point of view; that is, from the point of view of the person who observed or was a party to the event. Usually, too, the person—the narrator—is kept consistent throughout the narrative, though writers may sometimes use different narrators to express another view or opinion of an event.

Because narration deals with an event or personal experience that already has happened, it is usually written in the past tense. Experienced writers may change the verb tense from the present to the past in what is called a "flashback"—but in general the tense should be kept consistent.

In narration and the other modes of development, an important factor in point of view is whether the writer is being objective or subjective. An **objective** essay presents the **facts**—the basics of what occurred or what is being described—without including the writer's own interpretations or personal opinions of those facts. The writer tries to portray the subject of the essay as truly as possible and does not try to influence how the reader will react. A **subjective** essay, by contrast, expresses how the writer feels and may try to get the reader to feel a certain way. It may state an opinion or reveal the writer's emotions, or it may present facts in such a way that the reader will draw a conclusion favored by the writer. The Wheaties story is an example of objective writing; it presents the facts without interpreting them. The other two examples are written more subjectively, expressing the writers' own feelings about and interpretations of the events described.

Often, writers give clues that indicate that they are being subjective. Phrases like "in my opinion" or "I felt" or "I learned" signal a subjective interpretation. (Just because an essay is written in the first person does not mean it is entirely subjective, however.) As you will see in some of the selections in this text, writers may not always tell you when they are being subjective. Some writers may even take an objective tone when they are being quite subjective—perhaps, for instance, by presenting certain facts about a subject but not others. No matter what mode of development is used in an essay, you should try to make sure just how subjective or objective the writer is being.

Narrative writing is called **nonfiction** if the story or event is true and actually happened. All of the preceding examples are nonfictional accounts. This kind of factual narrative is found in biography, history, and newspaper writing. Narrative is also the predominant mode used in short stories and novels. If a story is not true or did not actually occur, it is called **fiction.**

In fiction and nonfiction narrative writing, writers use **dialogue** to recreate what characters or people in the narrative said. In the essay on the store robbery, notice that the writer often tells you exactly what was said and encloses the statement using quotation marks to let you know he is quoting word-for-word conversation. Quoted dialogue can help the writer accurately express the incidents in a narrative and can add variety and color. To practice working with dialogue, listen to your friends talking with one another and see if you can reproduce something like their conversation in dialogue in your own narratives.

Writers use narration to tell about personal experiences, about other people's lives and experiences, and about factual or historical events, such as the discovery of Wheaties. Narration adds interest, suspense, and clarity to writing, as you will find in the reading selections that follow. Consequently, it is a writing skill well worth mastering.

The questions and assignments at the ends of the readings in this chapter will help you to recognize and apply the principles of narration. They will give you practice with the concepts of chronological order, narrative detail, subjective and objective writing, and dialogue.

Stranger in the Village

James Baldwin

In this excerpt from his Notes of a Native Son, *James Baldwin (1924–1987) tells of his stay in a tiny village in Switzerland among people who apparently had never seen a black man. A novelist, playwright, and noted essayist, Baldwin is also known for his activism during the civil rights movement in the 1960s and 1970s.*

Words to Know

conceded   agreed
infernal   hateful, outrageous
jocularly   jokingly
phenomenon   unusual occurrence

Getting Started

Have you ever been to a small town where no one knew you?

It must be admitted that in the beginning I was far too shocked to have any real reaction. In so far as I reacted at all, I reacted by trying to be pleasant—it being a great part of the American Negro's education (long before he goes to school) that he must make people "like" him. This smile-and-the-world-smiles-with-you routine worked about as well in this situation as it had in the situation for which it was designed, which is to say that it did not work at all. No one, after all, can be liked whose human weight and complexity cannot be, or has not been, admitted. My smile was simply another unheard-of phenomenon which allowed them to see my teeth—they did not, really, see my smile and I began to think that, should I take to snarling, no one would notice any difference. All of the physical characteristics of the Negro which had caused me, in America, a very different and almost forgotten pain were nothing less than miraculous—or infernal—in the eyes of the village people. Some thought my hair was the color of tar, that it had the texture of wire, or the texture of cotton. It was jocularly suggested that I might let it all grow long and make myself a winter coat. If I sat in the sun for more than five minutes some daring creature was certain to come along and gingerly put his fingers on my hair, as though he were afraid of an electric shock, or put his hand on my hand, astonished that the color did not rub off. In all of this, in which it must be conceded there was the charm of genuine wonder and in which there was certainly no element of intentional unkindness, there was yet no suggestion that I was human: I was simply a living wonder.

————————————

Questions About the Reading

1. How did Baldwin react to the villagers' curiosity at the beginning of his visit?
2. What did the villagers think about Baldwin's hair?
3. What does Baldwin mean when he says, "No one, after all, can be liked whose human weight and complexity cannot be, or has not been, admitted"?
4. How did Baldwin finally feel about the villagers' reaction to him?

Questions About the Writer's Strategies

1. Does the writer state the main idea of the paragraph or is it implied?
2. What is the point of view (person, time, tone) of the paragraph?
3. Is the paragraph objective or subjective?
4. What details does the writer use to support his main idea?

Writing Assignments

1. Write a narrative paragraph telling how you felt on your first day in a new school.
2. Write a narrative paragraph describing the reactions of fellow students or employees to you the first day you met them.

I Like a Gershwin Tune

Joseph Epstein

In this paragraph, Joseph Epstein shares his childhood experience as a singer. Epstein is the author of several collections of personal essays— including With My Trousers Rolled *and* Once More Around the Block—*and a collection of short stories,* The Goldin Boys.

Words to Know

gloriously   spendidly, magnificently
modesty   moderation, humility

Getting Started

How did you feel the first time you were asked to read aloud to your class?

You may not have caught my act at the old Pratt-Lane Hotel. Brilliant stuff. A knockout, take my word for it. I came on and sang one number, and one number only: "Any Bonds Today?" Maybe you'll recall the song's most powerful line, which—modesty won't do here—I belted out gloriously: "Bonds of freedom, that's what I'm selling, any bonds today?" The crowd—my parents and their friends—went wild. The year was 1942, the war was on, and I was five. I retired as a singer later that same year, when I was told in nursery school not to sing so loudly, especially since I sang off-key. Knowing when to quit—that, I'd say, is the name of the game.

Questions About the Reading

1. What did the writer think of his performance at the hotel?
2. What did the audience think of his performance?
3. Do you think the audience was biased? Why or why not?
4. How old was the writer when he sang at the hotel?
5. When did the writer give up singing? Why?

Questions About the Writer's Strategies

1. What is the main idea of the paragraph?
2. Is the main idea stated or implied?

3. What is the point of view (person, time, tone) of the paragraph?
4. What order does the writer use in the paragraph?

Writing Assignments

1. Write a narrative paragraph about an experience you had performing in front of an audience.
2. Write a narrative paragraph about an experience playing on a sports team in front of a crowd.

The Discovery of Coca-Cola

E. J. Kahn, Jr.

E. J. Kahn, Jr. has written about the American scene for The New Yorker *for more than forty years. He has written about America at war, about Frank Sinatra, about Harvard, and about burlesque. He has also discussed that most American of drinks, Coca-Cola, in a book titled* The Big Drink. *In a paragraph from that book, he tells us of the invention of Coca-Cola as a medicine and the discovery that led to its becoming a soft drink.*

Words to Know

audit   analyze, figure out, verify
composition   contents, ingredients
concoction   a mixture of ingredients
dollop   a large portion or serving
factotum   an employee
testimonially   in honor of

Getting Started

Coca-Cola was first sold as a medicine. How do you imagine it became a popular soft drink?

Т he man who invented Coca-Cola was not a native Atlantan, but on the day of his funeral every drugstore in town testimonially shut up shop. He was John Styth Pemberton, born in 1833 in Knoxville, Georgia, eighty miles away. Sometimes known as Doctor, Pemberton was a pharmacist who, during the Civil War, led a cavalry troop under General Joe Wheeler. He settled in Atlanta in 1869, and soon began brewing such patent medicines as Triplex Liver Pills and Globe of Flower Cough Syrup. In 1885, he registered a trademark for something called French Wine Coca—Ideal Nerve and Tonic Stimulant; a few months later he formed the Pemberton Chemical Company, and recruited the services of a bookkeeper named Frank M. Robinson, who not only had a good head for figures but, attached to it, so exceptional a nose that he could audit the composition of a batch of syrup merely by sniffing it. In 1886—a year in which, as contemporary Coca-Cola officials like to point out, Conan Doyle unveiled Sherlock Holmes and France unveiled the Statue of Liberty—Pemberton unveiled a syrup that he called Coca-Cola. It was a modification of his French Wine Coca. He had taken out the wine and added a pinch of caffeine, and, when the end product tasted awful, had thrown in some extract of cola (or kola) nut and a few other oils, blending the mixture in a three-legged iron pot in his back yard and swishing it around with an oar. He distributed it to soda fountains in used beer bottles, and Robinson, with his flowing bookkeeper's script, presently devised a label, on which "Coca-Cola" was written in the fashion that is still employed. Pemberton looked upon his concoction less as a refreshment than as a headache cure, especially for people whose throbbing temples could be traced to overindulgence. On a morning late in 1886, one such victim of the night before dragged himself into an Atlanta drugstore and asked for a dollop of Coca-Cola. Druggists customarily stirred a teaspoonful of syrup into a glass of water, but in this instance the factotum on duty was too lazy to walk to the fresh-water tap, a couple of feet off. Instead, he mixed the syrup with some charged water, which was closer at hand. The suffering customer perked up almost at once, and word quickly spread that the best Coca-Cola was a fizzy one.

Questions About the Reading

1. Why did the drugstores in Atlanta honor John Pemberton by closing on the day of his funeral?
2. How is Frank M. Robinson significant to the story of Coca-Cola's origins?
3. Sherlock Holmes, the fictional detective in a series of short stories and books written by Arthur Conan Doyle, and the Statue of Liberty appeared in the same year as Coca-Cola. Why would Coca-Cola officials like to point out these facts?
4. The writer describes the way Pemberton mixed Coca-Cola and distributed it. What does the writer's explanation tell you about the standards that existed in 1886 for the production and sale of patent medicines? Which words and phrases help describe the standards?

Questions About the Writer's Strategies

1. Is the main idea of the paragraph directly stated? If so, in which sentence(s)? If not, state the idea in a sentence of your own.
2. What is the point of view in "The Discovery of Coca-Cola"? Could the writer have used another point of view, such as first person? Why or why not?
3. Does the writer include any details that are not essential to the idea of the narrative? If so, why did he include them?

4. What tone does the writer achieve by his description of how Robinson checked a batch of syrup? What is the effect of using the word *nose?* Why is the word *audit* appropriate?
5. The writer uses the words *dollop* and *factotum* in telling about the customer being served Coca-Cola in the drugstore in 1886. Why are these words more effective than *large serving* and *employee* would be?

Writing Assignments

1. Write a narrative paragraph in which you tell about an accidental discovery of your own.
2. **Working Together** Join with a classmate to write a narrative paragraph in which you describe the incidents that you imagine led to the discovery of fire or the wheel.
3. Write a narrative paragraph in the first person telling about something you did to help a friend, relative, or organization. Try to show how your action was significant to *you.*

Freedom

Iu-choi Chan (student)

Sometimes a single event can tell us a great deal about a person, culture, or way of life. In the following paragraph, a young Chinese man tells about his daring attempt to escape from a country where he felt oppressed to a place where he could feel free. Although this attempt failed, Iu-choi Chan has since managed to come to the United States. He wrote this paragraph while he was a student at California State University in Bakersfield.

Words to Know

Hong Kong   a former British colony on the coast of China
sentries   persons or soldiers posted to guard an area or position

Getting Started

What obstacles have you had to overcome to achieve a goal?

Two years ago, I attempted to escape from mainland China to Hong Kong. I planned and prepared well. I dressed up like a farmer and walked for two days from my village to the border between China and Hong Kong. That night, I was very excited and nervous, but I tried to keep calm. At the border there were a lot of sentries who tried to catch people like me, so I put some mud on myself to avoid being noticed. It was not easy for me to pass through the sentries, but I bit my tongue and climbed across the swampy area. Finally, I reached the river that runs across the border. I plunged into it. It was icy cold, and I used all my strength to swim as fast as I could. In about twenty minutes, I touched land. I had made it! My happiness was beyond description. But when I stood up, a Hong Kong policeman was immediately beside me. My dream was shattered. I was taken to a police station to wait for a truck that takes unsuccessful refugees back to China. The police put me in the truck with a great many other people, and we were driven like a herd of buffalo back to China. I had lost my freedom again.

Questions About the Reading

1. Which statement indicates the distance the young man lived from the Hong Kong border?
2. Describe the border area between China and Hong Kong.
3. Do many people try to leave mainland China and go to Hong Kong? Which details support your answer?
4. Why do you think the young man dressed like a farmer when he tried to escape?
5. The writer says, "I had lost my freedom again." What does the word *again* tell you about what happened to him before? Do you think the sentence reflects his opinion of life in mainland China?

Questions About the Writer's Strategies

1. Is the main idea of the paragraph directly stated? If so, in which sentence(s)? If not, state the main idea in a sentence of your own.
2. In what order are the major incidents of the story arranged? Could the order be changed? If so, in what way?
3. The writer compares the return of the refugees to China to being "driven like a herd of buffalo." Does this comparison help you see his situation?
4. What is the point of view in the narrative? Could another point of view be used? Using the first three sentences of the paragraph as an example, explain how you could change the point of view.

Writing Assignments

1. Think of a goal you have set for yourself but which you have not yet reached. Write a narrative paragraph in which you (a) state the goal; (b) explain what has happened to prevent you from reaching the goal; and (c) tell what you will do in the future to achieve the goal.
2. Write a narrative paragraph in which you tell what you or another person did to succeed in reaching a particular goal.
3. What career have you chosen for yourself? Write a narrative paragraph in which you tell what experiences made you choose the career.

The Jeaning of America—
and the World

Carin C. Quinn

*In "The Jeaning of America—and the World," Carin Quinn tells about
Levi Strauss's development of blue jeans, the sturdy and reliable American pants that are now famous worldwide. Quinn also explains some of
the reasons for the popularity and success of blue jeans.*

Words to Know

Alexis de Tocqueville (1805–1859)   French aristocrat, traveler,
and author; noted for his four-volume work, *Democracy in
America,* which was based on his travels in the United States
in 1831 to study the American penitentiary system and
democracy.

appropriated   took over

bureaucrats   government officials, particularly those who
rigidly follow rules and regulations

ensuing   following, subsequent

idiosyncratic   individual, unique

mother lode   rich, original vein of ore

proletarian   of the working class

rigors   hardships

ubiquitous   seeming to be everywhere at the same time

Getting Started

Do you believe that success in life comes from hard work, good
luck, or a combination of the two?

This is the story of a sturdy American symbol which has now spread   1
throughout most of the world. The symbol is not the dollar. It is not even
Coca-Cola. It is a simple pair of pants called blue jeans, and what the
pants symbolize is what Alexis de Tocqueville called "a manly and legitimate passion for equality." Blue jeans are favored equally by bureaucrats
and cowboys; bankers and deadbeats; fashion designers and beer drink-
ers. They draw no distinctions and recognize no classes; they are merely
American. Yet they are sought after almost everywhere in the world—
including Russia, where authorities recently broke up a teenaged gang
that was selling them on the black market for two hundred dollars a pair.

They have been around for a long time, and it seems likely that they will outlive even the necktie.

This ubiquitous American symbol was the invention of a Bavarian-born Jew. His name was Levi Strauss. 2

He was born in Bad Ocheim, Germany, in 1829, and during the European political turmoil of 1848 decided to take his chances in New York, to which his two brothers already had emigrated. Upon arrival, Levi soon found that his two brothers had exaggerated their tales of an easy life in the land of the main chance. They were landowners, they had told him; instead, he found them pushing needles, thread, pots, pans, ribbons, yarn, scissors, and buttons to housewives. For two years he was a lowly peddler, hauling some 180 pounds of sundries door-to-door to eke out a marginal living. When a married sister in San Francisco offered to pay his way West in 1850, he jumped at the opportunity, taking with him bolts of canvas he hoped to sell for tenting. 3

It was the wrong kind of canvas for that purpose, but while talking with a miner down from the mother lode, he learned that pants—sturdy pants that would stand up to the rigors of the diggings—were almost impossible to find. Opportunity beckoned. On the spot, Strauss measured the man's girth and inseam with a piece of string and, for six dollars in gold dust, had [the canvas] tailored into a pair of stiff but rugged pants. The miner was delighted with the result, word got around about "those pants of Levi's," and Strauss was in business. The company has been in business ever since. 4

When Strauss ran out of canvas, he wrote his two brothers to send more. He received instead a rough, brown cotton cloth made in Nîmes, France—called *serge de Nîmes* and swiftly shortened to "denim" (the word "jeans" derives from *Gênes*, the French word for Genoa, where a similar cloth was produced). Almost from the first, Strauss had his cloth dyed the distinctive indigo that gave blue jeans their name, but it was not until the 1870s that he added the copper rivets which have long since become a company trademark. The rivets were the idea of a Virginia City, Nevada, tailor, Jacob W. Davis, who added them to pacify a mean-tempered miner called Alkali Ike. Alkali, the story goes, complained that the pockets of his jeans always tore when he stuffed them with ore samples and demanded that Davis do something about it. As a kind of joke, Davis took the pants to a blacksmith and had the pockets riveted; once again, the idea worked so well that word got around; in 1873 Strauss appropriated and patented the gimmick—and hired Davis as a regional manager. 5

By this time, Strauss had taken both his brothers and two brothers-in-law into the company and was ready for his third San Francisco store. Over the ensuing years the company prospered locally and by the time of 6 his death in 1902, Strauss had become a man of prominence in California. For three decades thereafter the business remained profitable though small, with sales largely confined to the working people of the West— cowboys, lumberjacks, railroad workers, and the like. Levi's jeans were first introduced to the East, apparently, during the dude-ranch craze of the 1930s, when vacationing Easterners returned and spread the word about the wonderful pants with rivets. Another boost came in World War II, when blue jeans were declared an essential commodity and were sold only to people engaged in defense work. From a company with fifteen salespeople, two plants, and almost no business east of the Mississippi in 1946, the organization grew in thirty years to include a sales force of more than twenty-two thousand, with fifty plants and offices in thirty-five countries. Each year, more than 250,000,000 items of Levi's clothing are sold— including more than 83,000,000 pairs of riveted blue jeans. They have become, through marketing, word of mouth, and demonstrable reliability, the common pants of America. They can be purchased pre-washed, pre-faded, and pre-shrunk for the suitably proletarian look. They adapt themselves to any sort of idiosyncratic use; women slit them at the inseams and convert them into long skirts, men chop them off above the knees and turn them into something to be worn while challenging the surf. Decorations and ornamentations abound.

The pants have become a tradition, and along the way have acquired a   7 history of their own—so much so that the company has opened a museum in San Francisco. There was, for example, the turn-of-the-century trainman who replaced a faulty coupling with a pair of jeans; the Wyoming man who used his jeans as a tow-rope to haul his car out of a ditch; the Californian who found several pairs in an abandoned mine, wore them, then discovered they were sixty-three years old and still as good as new and turned them over to the Smithsonian as a tribute to their toughness. And then there is the particularly terrifying story of the careless construction worker who dangled fifty-two stories above the street until rescued, his sole support the Levi's belt loop through which his rope was hooked.

Questions About the Reading

1. What reasons does Quinn give for the success of blue jeans? Identify the sentences that support your answer.
2. What are the main incidents in the development of blue jeans?
3. Speculate about why Levi's brothers lied to him about their status in America. Why do you think the writer included this detail?

4. What conclusions can you draw about Strauss's character?
5. How do you think Quinn feels about Levi's jeans and their popularity?

Questions About the Writer's Strategies

1. What order does the writer use for paragraphs 3 through 6? What is the purpose of the first paragraph of the essay? What is the purpose of the last paragraph?
2. Is the thesis of the essay stated? If so, in which sentence(s)? If not, state the thesis in a sentence of your own.
3. What are the main ideas in paragraphs 3, 4, 5, and 6? Are the main ideas directly stated?
4. What is the point of view in person, time, and tone in the essay?
5. Could the first sentence in paragraph 5 be made into more than one sentence? Why or why not? Could the third sentence in paragraph 5 be made into more than one sentence? If so, how? If not, why not?

Writing Assignments

1. *Working Together*   Join with some classmates to write a narrative essay explaining how your classmates achieved success by working hard, being lucky, taking a risk, or being innovative. Describe the series of events that led to the successes.
2. Write a narrative essay about an important opportunity that you once had. Explain how the opportunity arose, how you took or did not take advantage of it, and what the results of your action were.

When We Were Colored

Clifton L. Taulbert

In his story of growing up in segregated Glen Allan, Mississippi, Clifton Taulbert remembers his "colored" childhood for the love and strength given him by his extended family of relatives and friends.

Words to Know

agrarian   agricultural or rural

antiquated   old, out-of-date, obsolete

delta   the area at the mouth of a river or inlet created by sediment

gentry   people of an upper class or group

pilgrimage   a journey to a special or sacred place

solace   comfort, consolation

verified   proved to be true

Getting Started

How do you feel when you return to a familiar, childhood place?

————————

It was a beautiful October day in the 1970s. It was not quite like those   1
other October days when I was a child growing up in this southern cotton community, but it was beautiful nonetheless. I had come home for my yearly pilgrimage to see Glen Allan, Mississippi, to remember the life I once knew and visit my older relatives. Somehow I always felt better after visiting those tired people who had given me strength when I was a child. So many changes had taken place in Glen Allan. "Colored" people were now "black," soap operas had replaced quilting bees in their homes, and the schools their children attended were now integrated. But the land was the same; the rich delta land had not changed. And the cotton smelled as it did in the early '50s when I picked it as a way of life. Now, however, the quarter of a mile long cotton rows seemed shorter and instead of the bent backs and scratched hands of hundreds of coloreds picking cotton, there were scores of big red machines harvesting the white fields. As always, the land was giving life, being faithful, fruitful and productive, providing stability and a sense of worth.

I made it a point to visit my old aunt, Mozella Alexander. She insisted   2
I sit and listen as she vividly recalled the times when her grandparents

owned a plantation five miles from Glen Allan—a plantation they called Freemount. As we sat in her shotgun house that was falling on one end and propped up on the other, she rocked, swatted flies and told me all about old man Sidney Williams, Miss Phoebe, Rosa Morgan, Tom Williams and the rest that were known at the turn of the century as "the big colored landowners."

As she talked, her smooth black face shone with a pride that I don't 3 know if I'll ever possess. "Son, my pa and your great-great grandpa were somebody. Oh chile, they had plenty land, mules, hogs and chickens and jest 'bout eberthang."

She talked with increasing excitement. Even though she was renting a 4 run-down house, she knew that she was descended from the colored landed gentry. I guess that's why she was labelled "uppity." Even at her age she walked straight as an arrow.

"All out dar in de colony was colored when I wuz a chile. Yez sir my 5 ole grandpa worked dat land like it was no t'morrow."

I knew the land she spoke of, although Freemount no longer existed. It 6 was near the colored colony, a large parcel of land which I'd also heard was once in my family. I remember some of the older people saying, "Chile y'all folks shore had some land out dar in de colony." But for some reason those sayings never reached my belly. Land ownership and the sense of worth it brings seemed to have died out during my parents' time. I responded to this story as if it might be colored folklore. All my life most of the land owners had been white. When I'd go to the colony, it was their stately homes I'd see first. It never dawned on me that these houses, so seemingly permanent on their sites, were not the beginning. Little did I know they were built upon the sweat and blood of a different set of land owners, black men and women who tamed the land and gave it such an appropriate name, "Freemount."

Aunt Mozella talked for hours and I listened politely. At last I attempted 7 to take my leave, but she stopped me.

"Set down, son. Lemme give ya something. And you hold onto it. It's 8 valuable. No matter what happened to me, I'se always held onto these."

She got up and walked over to a trunk that was probably twice her 9 age. She was old, colored and proud, with not a wrinkle in her cinnamon face. As she bent over her trunk and undid the double locks, I looked around at her tattered home, wall papered with pages from the Sears catalog. I wondered what of value she could possibly give me, her educated grand nephew.

Turning from the trunk she stood in front of me holding in her black 10 hands a bundle of papers tied securely with old rags. Her cinnamon face shone as she pressed the papers to my hands.

"Here son, take 'em. Hold 'em. Yessir, here's de proof. It's all here. All dat my grandaddy worked for is right here."

I would later learn that in that moment, she had released to my generation the legal proof of our family's land ownership. All I had heard as a child was true.

I stood there at the foot of her iron bed holding the ancient papers. I'd been led to believe that coloreds never kept their papers. Nervously I untied the bundle and unfolded the fragile deeds. I was holding not the copies but the actual documents signed in ink by my great-great-grandfathers Sidney Williams and Ben Morgan, and the land commissioner for the State of Mississippi. Almost a century later these deeds spoke to me from their faded pages and verified for all time to come that Freemount had once really existed.

My discovery of these deeds affected me oddly. All my life, growing up in the colored section of the little Mississippi town of Glen Allan, I had been taught to respect the owners of the large plantations. In the agrarian South, land ownership more than any other factor decided who had status; the more land a person owned, the more he was worth. The realization that I was the descendant of black plantation owners gave me a sudden sense of pride. At the same time I felt cheated. The land which should have been my birthright had been lost, taken from my family during the Depression, sold without my great grandparents' knowledge at a tax auction for money they'd never known they owed. I'd grown up in the '50s, under a system of segregation which enforced on all people of my race an inferior status—a sense of worthlessness which was wholly illegitimate, but which I had striven all my life to overcome.

On further reflection, I realized that many of the values of the Southern culture had been illegitimate, even, perhaps, the value placed on land ownership. For the truth is, man cannot really own the land; we are only trustees for a time. Eventually the land will claim us and we'll return to our mother earth. Knowing this gives me some solace as I look at antiquated deeds dated in the late 1800s and signed over to my great-great-grandparents by the vice-president of the Yazoo and Mississippi Valley Railroad Company and its land commissioners. This land, once called Freemount, has probably had more trustees and names than we'll ever know.

If land ownership is not a legitimate measure of a people's worth, I wondered, what is? I began to think about my childhood and other values I'd learned as I grew up in an environment much like that experienced by thousands of other colored Americans. Even though segregation was a painful reality for us, there were some very good things that happened. Today I enjoy the broader society in which I live and I would never want to return to forced segregation, but I also have a deeply-felt sense that important values were conveyed to me in my colored childhood, values we're in danger of losing in our integrated world. As a child, I was not only protected, but also nourished, encouraged, taught, and loved by people who, with no land, little money and few other resources, displayed the strength of a love which knew no measure. I have come to believe that this love is the true value, the legitimate measure of a people's worth.

I was barely seventeen when I left my childhood home in Glen Allan 17 and boarded the Illinois Central north to Saint Louis and into the 1960s, which would forever change the fabric of our society. Today my children are growing up in a world where "color" is something that comes in a box of crayons—a world of Bill Cosby and Yves St. Laurent. I have written *Once Upon A Time When We Were Colored* because I want my children to know of the life-style that gave them their father and their mother. It is very difficult to master the present and make a meaningful contribution to the future unless you understand and appreciate the past. In our desire as black Americans to put segregation behind us, we have put ourselves in danger of forgetting our past—the good with the bad. I believe that to forget our colored past is to forget ourselves, who we are and what we've come from.

This book is not the story of Freemount and the years when blacks 18 owned the land. It is the story of a mostly landless people, the coloreds, who lived in Glen Allan and other small Southern towns during the last years of segregation. I have written it to recall a treasure more valuable and enduring than land ownership. It is the treasure that stood out in my colored childhood when there was so little else, and it has been a source of strength to me in all the years since then. That treasure is the nourishing love that came to me from my extended family of aunts, uncles, parents, grandparents, great-grandparents, cousins, neighbors and friends. Rich in love, this congregation of black maids, field hands and tenant farmers worked the cotton fields, fished Lake Washington, gathered at St. Mark's Missionary Baptist Church to sing and pray, and gathered at the Greenville train station to bid farewell to loved ones moving north. In ordinary daily living through very difficult times, they showed themselves to be a great people. They are the reason I want today's world to remember an era that in our haste we might mistakenly forget—that era when we were called colored.

———————————

Questions About the Reading

1. Why does Taulbert make his yearly pilgrimage to Glen Allan?
2. What changes have taken place in Glen Allan since Taulbert's childhood? What things have remained the same?
3. Who did the writer visit in Glen Allan and what did the person value highly?
4. Does the writer share the person's opinion of what is highly valuable?
5. Why does the writer think it is important to his children for him to go back to Glen Allan?
6. What does the writer feel is the most valuable "treasure" he gained from his childhood in Glen Allan?

Questions About the Writer's Strategies

1. What is the thesis of the essay? Is the thesis stated? If so, in which sentences? If not, state the thesis in a sentence of your own.
2. What is the point of view of the essay in person, time, and tone?
3. What is the main idea of paragraph 15? Is the main idea directly stated or is it implied? If directly stated, in which sentence(s)?
4. What order does the writer use in paragraphs 2 through 13?
5. Identify the descriptive details in paragraphs 2, 9, and 10.

Writing Assignments

1. Write a narrative essay in which you explain the influence of relatives or friends on your thinking about or attitude toward life.
2. Write a narrative essay in which you imagine you are visiting a place that you lived in as a child. Explain the significance the place had in shaping your personal values or your attitude toward life.

Daughter's Doll Teaches Mom Lesson on Race

Connie Schultz

Mothers may usually know best, but Connie Schultz, a reporter for the Cleveland (Ohio) Plain Dealer, *learned that when it came to choosing a doll, her daughter had a perfectly logical reason for the one she wanted. (© 2000* The Plain Dealer. *All rights reserved. Reprinted with permission.)*

Words to Know

balked   refused

furrowed   wrinkled, rutted

nuzzling   caressing with the nose

venue   location, site

Getting Started

What was your favorite plaything as a child, and why did you like it?

Sometimes our kids teach us lessons we thought we were teaching them.   1

That's how Addy made her way into our family's life five years ago.   2

Addy is an American Girl doll. She is based on the main character in a   3
series of books about a slave girl whose family escaped to freedom in the
1800s.

Addy is black. My daughter is white. But from the moment Cait read   4
her first sentence about Addy, she was convinced she and that slave girl
were practically twins. And since her father and I had recently separated,
it didn't take much lobbying on Cait's part to get exactly what she wanted
from this mother steeped up to her furrowed brow in guilt: An Addy
doll. An almost-$100 Addy doll, to be precise.

That Christmas morning, my then 8-year-old daughter greeted her new   5
friend with squeals of delight. Not only did she get Addy, she and Addy
got matching nightgowns, which Cait quickly snatched up before running off to her bedroom.

A few minutes later, there they were: Addy and Cait, cheek to cheek   6
and dressed in matching white, ruffly nightgowns. "Don't we look alike,
Mommy?" Cait said, her face beaming as she wrapped her arms around
her doll.

I looked at my blue-eyed daughter, as pale as a calla lily, squeezing her　7
doll with the creamy brown skin and big dark eyes, and wondered what
she could be thinking. Tread gently here, I told myself.

"How do you and Addy look alike?" I asked.　　　　　　　　　　　8

Cait just smiled as she brushed back Addy's hair. "Oh, you know," she　9
said, nuzzling the doll's cheek. But I didn't know, and I felt left out, blinded
to the bigger picture only my daughter seemed to see.

For the next two months, Cait took Addy everywhere she went. You　10
can learn a lot about strangers by their reaction to a pretty black doll in a
white girl's arms. One woman, who was white, glared at me as we stood
in line at a McDonald's. "You *made* her buy that, didn't you?" she hissed,
shaking her head as she looked at Cait clutching Addy to her chest. "There
is no way she would have asked for a doll like that."

A young black woman working at a local drugstore stared at Cait and　11
Addy and then politely leaned in to whisper to me. "Did she want that
doll?" When I nodded my head, she winced. "Why?"

"We're a lot alike," piped up Cait. I looked at the bewildered woman,　12
shrugged my shoulders and smiled.

I thought of Addy recently after talking to a mother with two adopted　13
sons from Korea. For years, Linda has sent her boys to a camp for Korean
children adopted by Americans. "I thought it was a good idea," she said.
"All year long they are with kids who don't look like them, who didn't
come from Korea, and everything I had heard and read said this is a good
thing to do."

One of her sons, however, balked last year, announcing he did not want　14
to go to that camp again. Her 10-year-old did this in what is all children's
venue of choice for serious conversations: In the car, while his mother
was driving.

Linda was surprised, but undeterred. "Don't you like to be some place　15
where everyone is like you?" Her son's response so startled her she nearly
ended up on a tree lawn: "Isn't the important thing supposed to be liking
who you are and not being like everyone else?"

Linda smacked her forehead in recounting this conversation. "You　16
know, you raise them to believe certain things, to get beyond the issues of
race and gender and all that, but then you're blown away when you realize they're there, all your lessons took, and *you're* the one who isn't getting it."

At that point I was required to welcome Linda into the Clueless Moth-　17
ers Club, of which I am president. Then I told her about Addy, and how
I finally found out why Cait wanted the doll in the first place.

"Addy and I are so alike," Cait said yet again as I tucked them into bed　18
one night. "How so?" I asked. Cait reached up and touched my face.
"Addy had to leave with her mom, just like you and me."

I froze. For eight years I had been teaching my daughter that it's what's 19 on the inside that counts. Obviously, only one of us had been listening.

And you know what? Cait was right. She and Addy, they're so alike. 20 They're practically twins.

Questions About the Reading

1. When did Cait get Addy, the black doll?
2. Why did Cait want Addy?
3. How did people react to Cait having Addy?
4. What did Linda's Korean son tell her when she asked why he didn't want to go back to camp?
5. What is the lesson the writer learned?

Questions About the Writer's Strategies

1. Where is the main idea (thesis) of the essay? Is it stated more than once? If so, where?
2. What is the order the writer uses in the essay?
3. What technique does the writer use to re-create what Addy, Linda, and the writer said?
4. Is the essay objective or subjective?

Writing Assignments

1. Write a narrative essay telling about your favorite plaything as a child and explaining why it was your favorite.
2. Write a narrative essay telling about why you wanted to learn to drive a car and the first time you drove someplace by yourself.

Learning to Write

Russell Baker

Russell Baker is a Pulitzer Prize winner noted for his humorous writing. Although this passage from his autobiographical book Growing Up *is lighthearted, we learn in the end that Baker is earnestly describing an event of serious, almost touching, personal importance.*

Words to Know

antecedent   the word to which a pronoun refers

listless   without energy, boring

prim   formal and neat, lacking humor

reminiscence   memory of a past experience

Getting Started

Describe an experience that changed the way you thought about yourself.

When our class was assigned to Mr. Fleagle for third-year English I 1 anticipated another grim year in that dreariest of subjects. Mr. Fleagle was notorious among City students for dullness and inability to inspire. He was said to be stuffy, dull, and hopelessly out of date. To me he looked to be sixty or seventy and prim to a fault. He wore primly severe eyeglasses, his wavy hair was primly cut and primly combed. He wore prim vested suits with neckties blocked primly against the collar buttons of his primly starched white shirts. He had a primly pointed jaw, a primly straight nose, and a prim manner of speaking that was so correct, so gentlemanly, that he seemed a comic antique.

I anticipated a listless, unfruitful year with Mr. Fleagle and for a long 2 time was not disappointed. We read *Macbeth*. Mr. Fleagle loved *Macbeth* and wanted us to love it too, but he lacked the gift of infecting others with his own passion. He tried to convey the murderous ferocity of Lady Macbeth one day by reading aloud the passage that concludes

> . . . I have given suck, and know
> How tender 'tis to love the babe that milks me.
> I would, while it was smiling in my face,
> Have plucked my nipple from his boneless gums. . . .

The idea of prim Mr. Fleagle plucking his nipple from boneless gums was too much for the class. We burst into gasps of irrepressible snickering. Mr. Fleagle stopped.

"There is nothing funny, boys, about giving suck to a babe. It is the— 3 the very essence of motherhood, don't you see."

He constantly sprinkled his sentences with "don't you see." It wasn't a 4 question but an exclamation of mild surprise at our ignorance. "Your pronoun needs an antecedent, don't you see," he would say, very primly. "The purpose of the Porter's scene, boys, is to provide comic relief from the horror, don't you see."

Late in the year we tackled the informal essay. "The essay, don't you 5 see, is the . . ." My mind went numb. Of all forms of writing, none seemed so boring as the essay. Naturally we would have to write informal essays. Mr. Fleagle distributed a homework sheet offering us a choice of topics. None was quite so simpleminded as "What I Did on My Summer Vacation," but most seemed to be almost as dull. I took the list home and dawdled until the night before the essay was due. Sprawled on the sofa, I finally faced up to the grim task, took the list out of my notebook, and scanned it. The topic on which my eye stopped was "The Art of Eating Spaghetti."

This title produced an extraordinary sequence of mental images. Surg- 6 ing up out of the depths of memory came a vivid recollection of a night in Belleville when all of us were seated around the supper table—Uncle Allen, my mother, Uncle Charlie, Doris, Uncle Hal—and Aunt Pat served spaghetti for supper. Spaghetti was an exotic treat in those days. Neither Doris nor I had ever eaten spaghetti, and none of the adults had enough experience to be good at it. All the good humor of Uncle Allen's house reawoke in my mind as I recalled the laughing arguments we had that night about the socially respectable method for moving spaghetti from plate to mouth.

Suddenly I wanted to write about that, about the warmth and good 7 feeling of it, but I wanted to put it down simply for my own joy, not for Mr. Fleagle. It was a moment I wanted to recapture and hold for myself. I wanted to relive the pleasure of an evening at New Street. To write it as I wanted, however, would violate all the rules of formal composition I'd learned in school, and Mr. Fleagle would surely give it a failing grade. Never mind. I would write something else for Mr. Fleagle after I had written this thing for myself.

When I finished it the night was half gone and there was no time left to 8 compose a proper, respectable essay for Mr. Fleagle. There was no choice next morning but to turn in my private reminiscence of Belleville. Two days passed before Mr. Fleagle returned the graded papers, and he re-

turned everyone's but mine. I was bracing myself for a command to report to Mr. Fleagle immediately after school for discipline when I saw
him lift my paper from his desk and rap for the class's attention.

"Now, boys," he said, "I want to read you an essay. This is titled 'The 9
Art of Eating Spaghetti.'"

And he started to read. My words! He was reading *my words* out loud 10
to the entire class. What's more, the entire class was listening. Listening
attentively. Then somebody laughed, then the entire class was laughing,
and not in contempt and ridicule, but with openhearted enjoyment. Even
Mr. Fleagle stopped two or three times to repress a small prim smile.

I did my best to avoid showing pleasure, but what I was feeling was 11
pure ecstasy at this startling demonstration that my words had the power
to make people laugh. In the eleventh grade, at the eleventh hour as it
were, I had discovered a calling. It was the happiest moment of my entire
school career. When Mr. Fleagle finished he put the final seal on my happiness by saying, "Now that, boys, is an essay, don't you see. It's—don't
you see—it's of the very essence of the essay, don't you see. Congratula-
tions, Mr. Baker."

Questions About the Reading

1. Why did the writer not want to write an essay? What discovery changed
   his mind?
2. Why did eating spaghetti so delight the people at the supper table?
   What does this imply about the time and place of the event?
3. What comment does the writer make on the role of formal rules in
   writing?
4. What is your opinion of Mr. Fleagle? How did it change during the
   course of reading the essay?
5. What was the significance of the essay's main event for the writer?

Questions About the Writer's Strategies

1. What is the main idea in this essay?
2. At what point in the essay did you begin to figure out what the main
   idea would be?
3. What order does the writer use in describing the incidents in his narrative?
4. Is this essay written objectively or subjectively? Cite examples to help
   explain your answer.

Writing Assignments

1. *Working Together*   Join with some classmates to write a narrative essay about the most important experience each of you had in school. Use chronological order to describe each experience and the incidents leading up to it.
2. Write a narrative essay on one of the following events in your life: leaving high school, learning to read a novel, using a computer for the first time, learning to have confidence, learning not to jump to conclusions, or controlling your temper. Try to indicate the significance that the event has had for you since it took place.

The Deli

Carmen Machin (student)

Carmen Machin was a student at East Los Angeles College when she wrote this account of running a small food store in New York. She is especially effective at letting us see what happened exactly as she saw it at the time. Her account gives us a good idea of her own refreshing character: a bit wide-eyed and innocent but ready to discover things, to learn, and to take the world as it comes.

Words to Know

albeit   although, even though
brogue   accent
fortitude   strength
naiveté   innocence
purloined   stolen
sorties   entries, invasions
syndrome   symptoms, feelings

Getting Started

In what ways are people and situations not always as they first appear?

My husband and I were about a year into wedded bliss, when we were   1
made an offer we couldn't refuse. There was a delicatessen whose owner
was anxious to sell. He was moving to another state. We could have the
store at payments we could afford. We accepted. There was an apartment
behind and connected to it which was included in the deal. We had no
idea what the neighborhood was like, but with youthful energy and opti-
mism, we moved in.

The first week was tragic. As the days passed and the end of the month   2
approached, we realized that if things continued as they were, we would
not only be unable to make the payments, but would probably have to
close the doors. In the midst of this anxiety was the surly attitude of the
customers. One lady in particular seemed to relish my discomfort and
attempts at self-control while she, on each of her sorties into the estab-
lishment, accused us, now of underweighing the cold cuts and salads, or
then, of miscounting her change. For weeks I remained courteous and

patient before her onslaught. I did not want to alienate the very few customers that we had.

Then suddenly, we began to see new faces. Our business started a defi-   3
nite upward swing. Even our first customers seemed more pleasant. All,
that is, except HER. The day came when I felt I could no longer tolerate
her attacks, and still smiling, I suggested that since we did not seem to be
able to satisfy her, that it might be a good idea if she went elsewhere. She
burst out laughing and in her thick Irish brogue, proclaimed to the other
customers who were there at the time, that at last she had made me show
some "backbone." Then she turned to me and said: "I wondered how
long you'd be taking it." She went on to marvel at the intestinal fortitude
or innocence of two "spics" moving into an Irish neighborhood. I stood
there in complete awe, as the other customers assured me that they had,
at first, abandoned the store when they heard that "spics was buying,"
but that, thanks to Madeline Hannon, for that was our tormentor's name,
they had, one by one, come back.

New York is a great big city; most folks call it unfriendly, and yet, I   4
never found it so. This area, from 96th Street to 100th Street, between
Amsterdam and Columbus avenues, was absolutely small townish.
Everyone knew everybody else and most were related in some way. Outsiders who moved in had to prove themselves worthy of acceptance or
remain forever strangers. We were fortunate. Even the local gang, called
"The Dukes," on whose turf our place was located, accepted us whole-
heartedly.

The "Dukes," unknown to us, had terrorized all the shopkeepers in   5
the area. In order to be able to stay in business without being harassed by
vandalism, shoplifting, out and out robberies, and, in certain cases, beatings, the Dukes were paid whatever they felt the traffic could bear. In
their opinion, we were to be no exception.

One day three of the young men swaggered into the store. At the time,   6
my husband was in the cellar arranging a shipment of merchandise that
had just arrived, and I, expecting him momentarily, was preparing a sandwich which was to be my lunch. As I glanced up, I saw one of them quickly
grab some Hostess Cupcakes and put them in his pocket; another leaned
against the fruit bin which was immediately minus an apple. Such was
my naiveté that I firmly believed the only reason anyone stole food was
hunger. My heart broke and at the same time opened and embraced them
in the mother syndrome. They asked to speak to my husband. "He's not
here at the moment, but if you don't mind waiting, he should be back in
a jiffy." They nodded.

As they started to turn to walk around the customer area, I proceeded   7
to introduce myself and, at the same time, commenced making three more

sandwiches. While I made small talk (actually, it was a monologue), they stood silent, looking fiercely, albeit hungrily at the masterpieces I was concocting: Italian rolls, piled high with juicy roast pork and, on top, my husband's wonderful homemade cole slaw. I placed them on paper plates along with pickles and plenty of potato chips, then I said, "Come on, you'll have to eat in the kitchen, because we're not licensed to serve in the store. Do you want milk or soda?" "Don't you know who we are?" "I've seen you around, but I don't know your names," I replied. They looked at me in disbelief, then shrugging their shoulders, marched as one into the kitchen which was the first room behind the store. They ate to their hearts' content and, before they left, emptied their pockets, depositing each purloined article in its appointed place. No apologies were given, none were expected. But from that day on, we were protected, and the only payment we ever made was that which we also received: friendship, trust, and acceptance.

Questions About the Reading

1. Explain how the writer proved she was "worthy of acceptance." Did she use the same method in each of the two incidents she tells about in the narrative?
2. What final conclusion can you draw about Madeline Hannon's character? Was she prejudiced? Were her friends prejudiced?
3. Why do you think Madeline and her neighbors behaved as they did?

Questions About the Writer's Strategies

1. In paragraph 4, the writer says, "Outsiders who moved in had to prove themselves worthy of acceptance." What purpose does this statement serve in the essay?
2. What order does the writer use in explaining the incidents that took place? Are there any paragraphs in which the writer seems to change that order?
3. What is the point of view of the narrative? If the writer had known at the time of the incidents what she knew when she was writing, do you think the events would have proceeded in the same way and with the same outcomes?
4. The writer does not use very much dialogue in her narrative. Rewrite paragraphs 6 and 7, changing some of the descriptive statements into quoted dialogue.

Writing Assignments

1. Write a narrative essay about an experience in which you did not fully understand what was happening until after the event—perhaps, for instance, when you were the target of a practical joke, or when you misinterpreted a friendly gesture as a romantic overture.
2. Write a narrative essay in which you tell about a person who achieves a goal only after standing up to another person.
3. Write a narrative essay about a situation in which you were at a serious disadvantage. Tell how you were able to work around that disadvantage.

——————————— Connections ———————————

1. Some of the selections in this chapter deal with an important lesson or skill taught to the narrator by an older person. Find connections between the Russell Baker and Carmen Machin readings in terms of the positive impact adults can have on young people.
2. Iu-choi Chan and Carmen Machin both write about personal experiences that involved risk taking. How did their risk-taking experiences differ? How were they alike?
3. What does Levi Strauss have in common with the factotum who mixed John Pemberton's Coca-Cola syrup with charged water?

3

Description

DESCRIPTION PROVIDES THE reader with a "word picture" of a specific person, the flavor of a special place, or the look of a particular object. To help the reader visualize the object, the writer chooses key details to develop the description: a certain liveliness in a person's eyes, the movement of ocean waves, the design of a favorite chair.

We saw in chapter 2 that writers use descriptive words to add color and vividness to the details they describe. The specific descriptive words the writer chooses depend on the particular **impression,** or image, the writer wants to create. For example, the writer can create the impression of a person who is likable by describing the person's face as "friendly" and "good natured." The writer can create the opposite impression by using such descriptive words as "shifty" or "scowling." In the following paragraph, the writer develops an effective impression of a chair by the buildup of details and descriptive words that re-create the object for the reader.

Detail:
location

Detail:
appearance

Detail:
appearance

The chair was the one piece of furniture I wanted to take with me when I closed up my parents' house for the final time. To look at it, sitting in the same kitchen corner where it had been for fifty years, you'd wonder how it could be my favorite chair. It was nothing but a straight-backed wooden chair, its seat scratched here and there from the soles of a small boy's shoes. The only thing unusual about it was the intricate design carved into its back. But the carving was what made the chair meaningful to me. I had sat in that chair many times as punishment for errors in my ways. I suppose my mother thought it was defiance that led me to sit cross-legged on the seat with my back to her in the kitchen. But it was not

Details:
decoration of
chair

> defiance. Rather, in that position my eyes and then my fin-
> gers could trace the <u>intertwining leaves and flowers</u> of the
> design carved in the back of the chair. Each time <u>I sat</u> there
> I seemed to see lines and shapes I hadn't seen before:
> <u>a heart-shaped leaf, a budding rose, a blade of grass.</u> Per-
> haps that chair had something to do with my lasting interest
> in well-made antique furniture. Who knows? I do know that
> when I drove away on that last day, the chair, carefully
> wrapped in several old quilts, lay tenderly cradled on the
> back seat of my car.

Notice that the chair is described only as being a straight-backed wooden chair with a scratched seat and a design carved into its back. However, the writer creates the dominant impression that the chair—in spite of being associated with childhood punishment—remained beautiful to him and probably influenced his lifelong interest in fine woods and antiques. The words *intricate, trace, intertwining, heart-shaped,* and *budding* describe and help the reader picture the design in the back of the chair. And in the last sentence, the phrases *carefully wrapped* and *tenderly cradled* convey indirectly the writer's feelings about the chair. The reader must be given enough detail not only to picture an object but also to understand what touched or moved the writer to single it out.

In descriptive writing you will often find stylistic devices that help convey both the essential qualities of the subject and its significance to the writer. Consider the following paragraph.

Details:
simile

> *Erethizon dorsatus,* an antisocial character of the northern
> U.S. and Canadian forest, commonly called a porcupine,
> looks like an uncombed head, has a grumpy personality,
> fights with his tail, hides his head when he's in trouble, floats
> like a cork, attacks backing up, retreats going ahead, and eats
> toilet seats as if they were Post Toasties. It's a sad commen-
> tary on his personality that people are always trying to do
> him in.

> R. T. Allen,
> "The Porcupine"

In this paragraph, the writer uses a **figure of speech** called a **simile** to help enhance the description of the porcupine. A simile takes items that are considered unlike and then compares them in a way that shows an unexpected similarity. Usually, a simile uses *like* or *as* to establish the connection between the items. Two similes in this paragraph, for example, are "looks like an uncombed head" and "floats like a cork." (Can you find another?)

A figure of speech related to the simile is the **metaphor,** which also compares unlike items, but does so without directly stating the connection with *like* or *as*. Metaphors may be used to express an idea that is rather abstract, as in "the *scales* of justice." But they can be used for other effects, too, and they may only be **implied** by the use of a certain verb—"The swimmer *waddled* across the sand."

Read the paragraph that follows. What is the metaphor for the matron and for the electric car? Is there another metaphor?

> In 1900, electric cars were a common sight on city streets. They were high, boxy, and heavy—those early electric cars—and they couldn't get up much speed. Nor could they be driven very far before the battery had to be recharged. So by the 1930s, the electric car was a curiosity piece that now and then sailed out of a carriage house, usually with a stern-faced matron at the steering tiller. Car and driver were somehow suited to each other: heavily built, elegantly appointed, and quietly majestic. They were quality products. They didn't guzzle fuel, raise their voices above a murmur, or create a public problem as they floated across the streets. But they both disappeared in favor of slim-lined, stripped-down models that drink high-powered fuels, make noise in the streets, and create a public nuisance. Now maybe only a few people would like to see that old-style matron come back. But these days, most of us would like to have a car that didn't use gas, was really quiet, and didn't pollute the environment. That's why, as soon as our engineers can solve the battery problem, we'll probably have electric cars again.

Personification, another figure of speech, attributes human qualities or abilities to animals or objects. For example, after Red Riding Hood observes that the wolf has big teeth, the wolf answers, "The better to eat you with, my dear!"

Exaggeration, which is called **hyperbole,** is also used. "I could have danced all night" might be possible for a few people, but for most of us, it would be hyperbole.

The organization of a description also contributes to its effectiveness. The writer may arrange the details in **order of importance,** usually moving from the less important to the more important details. The details in the paragraph on pages 47–48 are arranged so that they build to the most significant point—the deeper meaning of the chair to the writer. The writer may choose to arrange the details according to space, called **spatial order.** When a description is organized according to space, the writer takes a physical position in a room or at a scene and then describes what can be seen from that position, using some consistent order such as moving from left to right, from foreground to background, or from top to bottom.

In creating a description, the writer must identify the important characteristics of the object or scene being described and then find the words—nouns and verbs, as well as adjectives and adverbs—that best express these characteristics. In the essay that follows, the student describes the house in which she is living. Notice that she describes the house in **spatial order**—first from the outside and then as she walks through its rooms.

Notice, too, that the descriptive details provide the reader with an image
of both the house and its owner.

<table>
<tr><td>

View of the outside
of the house

Details:
preciseness of
the landscaping

Thesis statement

Entering the house

Details:
cleanliness and
coldness of
kitchen

Moving to dining
room

Details:
formality and
whiteness of room

Entering the
living room

</td><td>

It's really not a striking house, nor is it an old charming
house. It is, in fact, very plain—just like the houses on each
side of it. As I climb up the hilly driveway, its whiteness
stares blankly back at me, reminding me that I am not the
owner but just a temporary, unwanted trespasser. There are
flowers lining the driveway, which push their faces toward
the sun as they lie in their bed perfectly spaced, not too close
and not too far apart, perfectly coordinated to reflect all the
colors of the spectrum. Through the windows of the house
nothing but my reflection can be seen. They are like the house,
clean and tinted, allowing no one a look in, keeping life in
the house shut off from the rest of the world, uninviting of
intrusion, only interested in cleanliness, only leading the
people inside to a feeling of loneliness.

   Upon entering the house the smell of Pinesol and disin-
fectant engulfs my nostrils and shoots directly to my brain,
anesthetizing any emotions that might surface. Like the win-
dows, the kitchen floor reflects the cleanliness of the house
with its spotless white surface, scrubbed and shined, casting
off reflections from the bright lights overhead. There is wall-
paper on the walls of the kitchen, but it is void of any pattern
and lends very little color to the whiteness of the room. Only
items of importance for the duties of the kitchen are dis-
played, all in their properly appointed places, with the ap-
propriate covers placed over them to hide them from prying
eyes. The only personality the kitchen portrays is a cold, cal-
culating, suspicious one, wary of intruders who may cause
unnecessary filth to enter.

   Around the corner from the kitchen lies the dining room.
An elegant, dark, formal table sits in the center of the room,
the surface of which is smooth as glass under my fingertips.
A white centerpiece is carefully placed at the table's center,
with two white candles that have never been lit standing erect
at the centerpiece's ends. The chairs around the table are hard,
providing support for the back but lending the body no com-
fort. Above hangs a crystal chandelier—expensive, elegant,
giving the room an artificial brightness. It is made up of many
dangling, teardrop-shaped crystals, all cleaned and polished,
and is the only object in the dining room that speaks clearly
of conspicuous consumption. The drapes covering the tinted
windows are a dark color and keep out the sun of the day.
This room is often cleaned, often walked through, but never
used.

   Having walked through the dining room, I enter the living
room. Although this is the only room in the house where the
family can all converge to spend time together, it is not a
cheerful place. The walls are white, like the rest of the house,

</td></tr>
</table>

Details:
impersonality of
living room

with the same drapery as the dining room, and the couch and loveseat are velvet, <u>stiff, uncomfortable, and well main-tained</u>. A television set is placed in the corner but <u>lies blank with disuse</u>. The <u>air of coldness</u> here seems to hold tension though at the same time it gives the impression of ossification.

I have heard it said that a person's home is a reflection of that person, a sentiment that, with few exceptions, is true of this home. <u>Cleanliness</u> is a priority of the owner, and social-izing with people in this house is considered a nuisance that only causes more work because of the dirt that people carry in with them. The walls are kept white because it looks clean and repainting is made easy. And the smell of disinfectant pleases the owner, as it proves to the few who do enter that the house is clean. This house, the place I am calling home for this period of my life, offers me no comfort but does pro-vide shelter and quiet. And with the <u>dark stillness</u> in its rooms, I can think, read, and plan my escape.

Thesis restated
and conclusion

Carol Adams (student),
"An Intruder in the House"

In the introduction to chapter 2, you learned about the difference be-tween writing **objectively** and **subjectively.** Notice, in the previous es-say, that although the writer's style is objective, her choice of specific descriptive details and words supports her subjective, negative opinion of the house and its owner.

When brainstorming for a description, it may help to begin by listing all the features of the subject that come to mind and all the details that seem related to those features.

Descriptive details often are combined with other modes of develop-ment. The following paragraphs, for example, are from a narrative essay about a young man's visit to the Mexican town that he had left soon after he was born. Notice his descriptions of the people and the Spanish archi-tecture of the town.

Description:
Spanish
architecture

On my arrival at Morelia airport, I was greeted by the most attractive architecture I had ever seen. All the build-ings had a very strong Spanish influence. Was it possible I had taken the wrong plane and landed somewhere in Spain?

1

People and their
clothing

No, indeed; it was Morelia, and what a town! Its people were very plain and small-townlike. I was amused by some very oddly dressed people who wore white cotton clothing. On their heads the men wore straw hats, and the women wore large Spanish scarves called mantillas. I asked a ticket agent about the oddly dressed people. He explained that they were the native people, known as Tarascos. They were the founders of the land, and even today they are very tradi-tional in their beliefs and ways.

2

I took a taxi to El Hotel Virrey de Mendoza, located in the   3
middle of the town square. The hotel was made of hewn
stone that was cut and shaped into the most captivating three-
story building I had ever seen. It was built in the traditional

Architectural features

Spanish style, with a central open patio completely surrounded
by the building. My room had a spacious view of the town
square and its cathedral. The cathedral was built in the seven-
teenth century in a baroque style that was popular in Europe.
Beside the cathedral was the municipal palace and other government buildings, all in Colonial Spanish style. The feeling
I had from the view was that I was back in the days when
Spanish viceroys ruled the land, and the Catholic priests
taught religion to the native inhabitants.

Arturo E. Ramirez (student),
"Back to Where the Seed Was Planted"

Descriptive words and phrases are essential to effective writing. They
can make an object concrete for the reader by describing how it looks,
sounds, tastes, smells, or feels. Such sensory details can create a distinct
impression or **image** of that which is described and thus help the reader
visualize the writer's ideas. You will find specific descriptive words and
details in all the paragraphs and essays that follow. As you read, notice
that experienced writers select revealing details because, as with the incidents in narrative writing, these details produce the most effective description. In your own writing, select—as the writers of the reading selections do—the most essential qualities of whatever you describe.

The Hiroshima Museum

Barbara Kingsolver

In this selection from her book High Tide in Tucson, *Barbara Kingsolver describes her visit to the Peace Memorial Museum in Hiroshima and the items displayed there that speak silently of the impact of an atomic bomb.*

Words to Know

artifacts   objects of historical importance
histrionic   emotional, theatrical, dramatic
hypocenter   surface beneath the center of a nuclear explosion
ideological   reflective of an idea, belief, or culture
saki   wine made from rice

Getting Started

How do you feel when you look at paintings and exhibits in a museum?

Since that day, I've had the chance to visit another bomb museum of a different kind: the one that stands in Hiroshima. A serene building set in a garden, it is strangely quiet inside, with hushed viewers and hushed exhibits. Neither ideological nor histrionic, the displays stand entirely without editorial comment. They are simply artifacts, labeled: china saki cups melted together in a stack. A brass Buddha with his hands relaxed into molten pools and a hole where his face used to be. Dozens of melted watches, all stopped at exactly eight-fifteen. A white eyelet petticoat with great, brown-rimmed holes burned in the left side, stained with black rain, worn by a schoolgirl named Oshita-chan. She was half a mile from the hypocenter of the nuclear blast, wearing also a blue short-sleeved blouse, which was incinerated except for its collar, and a blue metal pin with a small white heart, which melted. Oshita-chan lived for approximately twelve hours after the bomb.

Questions About the Reading

1. Why do you think the displays in the museum "stand entirely without editorial comment"?
2. What do the exhibits tell you about the effect of an atomic bomb?
3. Why do you think the museum visitors are "hushed"?
4. What is the significance of all the watches being "stopped at exactly eight-fifteen"?

Questions About the Writer's Strategies

1. What is the main idea of the paragraph? Is it stated or implied? State the main idea in your own words.
2. What order does the writer use to describe the artifacts in the museum? Why do you think she chose that order?
3. Is the paragraph objective or subjective or both? Support your answer with examples.
4. What descriptive details does the writer give about Oshita-chan and her clothing? Do the details provide an image of what happened to Oshita-chan?

Writing Assignments

1. Write a narrative paragraph in which you describe your feelings during a visit to a museum.
2. Write a narrative paragraph in which you describe a visit to a city you had never been to before.
3. Visit an elder-care center, a church other than your own, or a day-care center for preschoolers, and write a narrative paragraph describing the place.

The Marion

Richard Ford

Sometimes an author uses a long list of objective details to help the reader visualize a specific place. Richard Ford's paragraph about the Marion Hotel, his grandfather's place of business, is full of factual details. However, when you read carefully about the fanciest hotel in Little Rock, Arkansas, you will also find some subtle judgments being made.

Words to Know

assignation   an appointment or meeting

blowsy   unkempt, rundown

escritoires   writing tables or desks

mezzanine   a middle or partial story between two main stories of a building

porte-cochère   a porch roof extending over the driveway at the entrance to a building

Getting Started

What do you suppose happens behind the closed doors of a grand, ornate movie theater, restaurant, or hotel?

The hotel was named the Marion, and it was not a small place. Little Rock was a mealy, low-rise town on a slow river, and the hotel was the toniest, plushest place in it. And still it was blowsy, a hotel for conventioneers and pols, salesmen and late-night party givers. There was a curving marble fish pond in the lobby; a tranquil, banistered mezzanine with escritoires and soft lights; a jet marble front desk; long, green leather couches, green carpets, bellboys with green twill uniforms and short memories. It was a columned brownstone with a porte-cochère, built in the twenties, with seven stories, three hundred rooms. Ladies from the Delta stayed in it on shopping trips. The Optimists and the Rotarians met. Assignations between state officials went on upstairs. Senator McClellan kept a room. Visiting famous people stayed, and my grandfather kept their pictures on his office wall—Rex Allen the cowboy, Jack Dempsey the boxing champion, June Allyson and Dick Powell, Harry Truman (whose photograph I have, still), Ricky Nelson, Chill Wills. Salesmen rented sample rooms, suicides took singles. There were hospitality suites, honeymoon suites, a Presidential, a Miss America, Murphy beds,

silver service, Irish napkins. There was a bakery, a print shop, an uphol-
sterer, two rooms (the Rendezvous, the Continental) for intimate parties,
six more for large, and a ballroom with a Hammond organ for banquets.
There was a beer bar in the lower lobby, a two-chair barbershop, a cigar
stand, a florist, a travel agent, a news agent, a garage where you parked
for nothing while you stayed. There was a drummer's rate, a serviceman's
rate, a monthly rate, a day rate, even an hourly rate if you knew my grandfather. Everything happened there, at all hours. Privacy had a high value.
To live in a hotel as a boy knowing nothing was to see what adults did to
each other and themselves when only adults were present.

Questions About the Reading

1. Why is Ford so knowledgeable about the Marion Hotel?
2. What does the author think of Little Rock?
3. Why had the Marion become such a popular gathering place?
4. Why do you think it was important for the bellboys to have short
   memories?

Questions About the Writer's Strategies

1. In his description of the hotel, the author gives you the insider's point
   of view. Which details would not be obvious to a first-time visitor to
   the Marion?
2. Many of the sentences in this paragraph consist of a list of places or
   things. What overall impression is the author trying to achieve with
   these lists?
3. In what ways is this paragraph subjective? In what ways is it objective?

Writing Assignments

1. Write a descriptive paragraph about a public building you know well.
   To create a picture of the place for the reader, include as many specific
   details as you can.
2. Think of the grandest place in your own town and imagine what it
   would be like to work there. Write a paragraph describing what happens behind the scenes.
3. Do you know someone who isn't as wonderful as he or she appears to
   be? Write a paragraph that describes the person both as he or she appears and as the person really is.

Maycomb

Harper Lee

In this paragraph from her novel To Kill a Mockingbird, *Harper Lee describes a place called Maycomb. In this small Southern town, Atticus Finch, a lawyer, defends a black man, Tom Robinson, against a rape charge in spite of the opposition of many white people.*

Words to Know

flicked   snapped, whipped
sweltering   extremely hot
talcum   bath powder

Getting Started

How would you describe the town in which you live?

Maycomb was an old town, but it was a tired old town when I first knew it. In rainy weather the streets turned to red slop; grass grew on the sidewalks, the courthouse sagged in the square. Somehow, it was hotter then: a black dog suffered on a summer's day; bony mules hitched to Hoover carts flicked flies in the sweltering shade of the live oaks on the square. Men's stiff collars wilted by nine in the morning. Ladies bathed before noon, after their three-o'clock naps, and by nightfall were like soft teacakes with frostings of sweat and sweet talcum.

Questions About the Reading

1. What was Maycomb like when the narrator first knew it?
2. What happened to Maycomb when it rained?
3. What happened when it was hot in Maycomb?

Questions About the Writer's Strategies

1. What is the impression of Maycomb that the writer creates?
2. What details does the writer use to create that impression?
3. What simile does the writer use in the paragraph?

Writing Assignments

1. Write a paragraph describing the town in which you live.
2. Write a paragraph describing your neighborhood.

Overindulgence

Heidi Hall (student)

In the following paragraph, Heidi Hall, a student at George Fox College, uses descriptive language to make her Aunt Helen's chicken and dumplings seem larger than life. Through language alone, the reader can almost taste what she describes—and feel the aftereffects of too much of a good thing.

Words to Know

celestial   heavenly
primordial   having to do with the beginning of time
resolve   determination
sentry   guard; a soldier standing guard

Getting Started

What would make you want to overindulge in a favorite food?

One of my weaknesses is my Aunt Helen's famous chicken and dumplings. If anything could break my resolve to only have one helping it'd be this celestial dish: Chicken pieces lightly seasoned with herbs and cooked till fork-tender—dumplings floating in the flavorful broth like sentry icebergs in a thick, primordial sea. Never could I stop at just one helping; too many delicious tastes scream, "More! More! This next bite will be even better!" Alas, too often I have staggered from her gracious table a few too many bites past "comfortable," Alka-Seltzer in hand, waistband begging for relief, and my resolve all the firmer to "NEXT time only have one serving."

Questions About the Reading

1. What are some of the sensory details the writer uses to bring her aunt's chicken and dumplings to life? Do you think the dish Hall describes sounds appetizing? Why or why not?
2. What do you learn about the writer from reading this paragraph?
3. Think about the images Hall uses in this paragraph. Is there anything other than the appearance, taste, and smell of the chicken and dumplings that makes her enjoy them so much?

4. Is there anything that can never be "too much of a good thing"—for instance, a hobby, work, a creative endeavor? If you think there is, why do you think that? If you don't think there is, describe some of the possible negative effects of even the most productive activities.

Questions About the Writer's Strategies

1. Does the writer state the main idea of the paragraph? If so, in which sentence does she state it?
2. The writer uses unusual vocabulary in the second sentence. Why do you think Hall chose to use the words *sentry* and *primordial?*
3. What is the tone of this paragraph? Identify words and expressions that support your answer.
4. Why do you think the writer quotes the food talking to her and then her talking to herself?

Writing Assignments

1. Write a paragraph in which you describe your own favorite—or least favorite—food. Try to use as many unusual but appropriate descriptive words as possible to make the reader imagine vividly what you describe.
2. Write a paragraph describing a family tradition other than a meal. Describe as vividly as possible some of the things that you find comforting about this tradition.

Hush, Timmy—
This Is Like a Church

Kurt Anderson

In this essay, Kurt Anderson, a writer for Time *magazine, describes the
Viet Nam Veterans Memorial in Washington, D.C., and the behavior of
the people who visit it.*

Words to Know

catharsis   relief, purification
contemplative   thoughtful
liturgical   public worship
mandarins   officials, authorities
rambunctious   boisterous, noisy, unruly
sanctum   holy place
stigmatized   branded, disgraced
vertex   highest point

Getting Started

Is there a place that makes you feel sad or happy?

The veteran and his wife had already stared hard at four particular 1
names. Now the couple walked slowly down the incline in front of the
wall, looking at rows of hundreds, thousands more, amazed at the roster
of the dead. "All the names," she said quietly, sniffling in the early-spring
chill. "It's unreal, how many names." He said nothing. "You have to see it
to believe it," she said.

Just so. In person, close up, the Viet Nam Veterans Memorial—two 2
skinny black granite triangles wedged onto a mount of Washington sod—
is some kind of sanctum, beautiful and terrible. "We didn't plan that,"
says John Wheeler, chairman of the veterans' group that raised the money
and built it. "I had a picture of seven-year-olds throwing a Frisbee around
on the grass in front. But it's treated as a spiritual place." When Wheeler's
colleague Jan Scruggs decided there ought to be a monument, he had
only vague notions of what it might be like. "You don't set out and *build*
a national shrine," Scruggs says. "It *becomes* one."

Washington is thick with monuments, several of them quite affecting. 3
But as the Viet Nam War was singular and strange, the dark, dreamy,

redemptive memorial to its American veterans is like no other. "It's more solemn," says National Park Service Ranger Sarah Page, who has also worked at the memorials honoring Lincoln, Washington and Jefferson. "People give it more respect." Lately it has been the most visited monument in the capital: 2.3 million saw it in 1984, about 45,000 a week, but it is currently drawing 100,000 a week. Where does it get its power—to console, and also to make people sob?

The men who set up the Viet Nam Veterans Memorial Fund wanted 4 something that would include the name of every American killed in Viet Nam, and would be contemplative and apolitical. They conducted an open design competition that drew 1,421 entries, all submitted anonymously. The winner, Maya Ying Lin, was a Chinese-American undergraduate at Yale: to memorialize men killed in a war in Asia, an Asian female studying at an old antiwar hotbed.

Opposition to Lin's design was intense. The opponents wanted some- 5 thing gleaming and grand. To them, the low-slung black wall would send the same old defeatist, elitist messages that had lost the war in the '60s and then stigmatized the veterans in the '70s. "Creating the memorial triggered a lot of old angers and rage among vets about the war," recalls Wheeler, a captain in Viet Nam and now a Yale-trained government lawyer. "It got white hot."

In the end, Lin's sublime and stirring wall was built, 58,022 names 6 inscribed. As a compromise with opponents, however, a more conventional figurative sculpture was added to the site last fall (at a cost of $400,000). It does not spoil the memorial, as the art mandarins had warned. The three U.S. soldiers, cast in bronze, stand a bit larger than life, carry automatic weapons and wear fatigues, but the pose is not John Wayne-heroic: these American boys are spectral and wary, even slightly bewildered as they gaze southeast toward the wall. While he was planning the figures, sculptor Frederick Hart spent time watching vets at the memorial. Hart now grants that "no modernist monument of its kind has been as successful as that wall. The sculpture and the wall interact beautifully. Everybody won." Nor does Lin, his erstwhile artistic antagonist, still feel that Hart's statue is so awfully trite. "It captures the mood," says Lin. "Their faces have a lost look." Out at the memorial last week, one veteran looked at the new addition and nodded: "That's us."

But it is the wall that vets approach as if it were a force field. It is at the 7 wall that families of the dead cry and leave flowers and mementos and messages, much as Jews leave notes for God in the cracks of Jerusalem's Western Wall. Around the statue, people talk louder and breathe easier, snap vacation photos unselfconsciously, eat Eskimo Pies and Fritos. But near the wall, a young Boston father tells his rambunctious son, "Hush, Timmy—this is like a church." The visitors' processionals do seem to have a ritual, even liturgical quality. Going slowly down toward the vertex, looking at the names, they chat less and less, then fall silent where the names of the first men killed (July 1959) and the last (May 1975) appear. The talk begins again, softly, as they follow the path up out of the little valley of the shadow of death.

For veterans, the memorial was a touchstone from the beginning, and the 1982 dedication ceremony a delayed national embrace. "The actual act of being at the memorial is healing for the guy or woman who went to Viet Nam," says Wheeler, who visits at least monthly. "It has to do with the felt presence of comrades." He pauses. "I always look at Tommy Hayes' name. Tommy's up on panel 50 east, line 29." Hayes, Wheeler's West Point pal, was killed 17 years ago this month. "I know guys," Wheeler says, "who are still waiting to go, whose wives have told me, 'He hasn't been able to do it yet.'" For those who go, catharsis is common. As Lin says of the names, chronologically ordered, "Veterans can look at the wall, find a name, and in a sense put themselves back in time." The war has left some residual pathologies that the memorial cannot leach away. One veteran killed himself on the amphitheatrical green near the wall. A second, ex-Marine Randolph Taylor, tried and failed in January. "I regret what I did," he said. "I feel like I desecrated a holy place."

The memorial has become a totem, so much so that its tiniest imperfec- 9
tions make news. Last fall somebody noticed a few minute cracks at the seams between several of the granite panels. The cause of the hairlines is still unknown, and the builders are a little worried.

Probably no one is more determined than Wheeler to see the memorial's 10
face made perfect, for he savors the startlingly faithful reflections the walls give off: he loves seeing the crowds of visitors looking simultaneously at the names and themselves. "Look!" he said the other day, gesturing at panel 4 east. "You see that plane taking off? You see the blue sky? No one expected that."

Questions About the Reading

1. About how many people a week visited the Viet Nam Veterans Memorial in 1984?
2. How many people a week were visiting the memorial at the time the essay was written (1985)?
3. What did the men who set up the Viet Nam Veterans Memorial Fund want the memorial to include?
4. Who won the contest for the design of the memorial? Why was her design controversial?

5. How many names were inscribed on the wall?
6. What differences are there between people's behavior at the wall and their behavior at the sculpture?

Questions About the Writer's Strategies

1. What is the main idea (thesis) of the essay?
2. Is the main idea directly stated or implied?
3. What is the point of view (person, time, tone) of the essay?
4. What is the impression of the memorial that the writer creates?
5. Is the essay objective, subjective, or both?

Writing Assignments

1. Write a descriptive essay about a place you visited that made you feel particularly sad.
2. Write a descriptive essay about a place you visited that made you feel particularly happy.

3. Use the Internet to research the following historical monuments: the Statue of Liberty in New York City; the Lincoln Memorial in Washington, D.C.; and Mount Rushmore in Keystone, South Dakota. Write an essay describing each monument, who or what it represents, and when and by whom it was built or created. Include a list of the web addresses you use.

    To find helpful web sites, use a search engine—such as AltaVista (**http://www.altavista.com/**), Yahoo! (**http://www.yahoo.com/**), or Excite (**http://www.excite.com/**)—and type in keywords, such as "Statue of Liberty" or "national monuments."

On Literature

Karel Čapek

Karel Čapek (1890–1938) is considered one of the greatest Eastern European writers of the first half of the twentieth century. His plays often appeared on Broadway as well as in Prague, and his books were translated into English. In the following essay, published originally in 1935, Čapek writes eloquently about the wonder and magic of village life as seen through the eyes of a child.

Words to Know

bellows   apparatus for producing a strong current of air

celestial   heavenly

consecrated   made sacred

contempt   bitter scorn

cordovan   a fine leather

Cyclops   one-eyed mythological creature who forged thunderbolts

dominion   rule

Homer   Greek epic poet believed to be the author of the *Iliad* and the *Odyssey*

hurdy-gurdy man   a street musician who played an instrument such as a barrel organ

miller   one who works in a mill for grinding grain

revelation   something revealed

skeptic   one who doubts, questions, or disagrees with assertions

stoker   one who tends a furnace

Getting Started

Who are the people in your neighborhood and what are their professions?

Forgive me if I start off with something quite other than literature, something from the days when I was a small boy. Your city boy is a kind of super-boy, a born skeptic, lord of the streets; and it is quite natural that he have a huge contempt for hayseeds, nincompoops, bumpkins, and clodhoppers, as he calls country boys. Your country boy looks down with immense and justified contempt on city boys, for he is lord of the fields

and forests; he knows all about horses and is on friendly terms with the
beasts of the field; he can crack a whip and he has under his dominion all
the treasures of the earth, from willowswitches to ripe poppy-heads. And
even your boy from a small country town is by no means the least among
worldly princes, for he includes in his circle more than any other mortal
creature: he can watch all human activities at close quarters.

When I was a boy in a small country town I saw at home how a doctor's 2
business is run, and at my grandfather's I could inspect the business of a
miller and baker, which is especially fine and amusing. And at my uncle's
I saw what a farmer has to do; but if I started on that I would never stop
telling you all the things I learned. Our nearest neighbor was the painter
who stenciled designs on walls, and that is a tremendously interesting
job. Sometimes he used to let me mix the colors in their pots, and once,
almost bursting with pride, I was allowed to smear a stencil pattern with
his brush; it came out crooked, but otherwise most successfully. I'll never
forget how that painter used to stride up and down the planks whistling,
gloriously splashed with all the colors of the rainbow; and he stenciled in
such miraculously straight lines, sometimes even painting something free-
hand—perhaps an amazingly well-nourished rose the color of stale liver,
on the ceiling. It was my first revelation of the painter's art, and I lost my
heart to it then and have been in love with it ever since. And then I used
to go every day and have a look at how the innkeeper does his job, to see
how they roll casks down into the cellar and how they draw beer and
blow off the froth, and hear the wise tales the old gossips tell as they wipe
froth from their whiskers with the backs of their hands. Every day I would
look in on neighbor cobbler and watch in silence how he cut leather and
hammered it on his last and then put on the heel, and all manner of other
things, for shoemaking is intricate and delicate work, and if you haven't
seen leather in a cobbler's hands you know nothing about it at all, even if
you do wear shoes of cordovan or even of celestial leather. Then there
was neighbor hurdy-gurdy man, and I went to see him too, when he was
at home, and was so surprised that he didn't play his hurdy-gurdy at
home, but sat and stared at one corner of the room till I felt quite uncomfortable. There was the mournful stone-mason who carved crosses and
strange, short, dumpy angels on gravestones; he'd tap away all day and
never say a single word, and I'd stand watching for perhaps an hour
while he chipped away at the unseeing eye of a weeping angel. And then,
ha ha! yes! there was the wheelwright with his beautiful wood throwing
off sparks and his yard full of hastening wheels, as Homer says; and a
wheel, you know, is a wonder in itself. Then there was the smith in his
black smithy: I burst with pride when I was allowed sometimes to work
the bellows for him while, looking like a black Cyclops, he heated an iron
bar red-hot and hammered it till it sent out a shower of sparks; and when

he put a shoe on a horse it smelled of burnt horn, and the horse would turn his wise eyes on the smith as much as to say, "All right, go on, I won't make a fuss."

A little farther on lived Tonca, the prostitute; I didn't understand her   3 business very well, and I used to pass her little house with an odd, dry feeling in my throat. Once I looked in through the window, but it was all empty—just striped feather-beds, and some consecrated pussy willows above the bed. I had a look at the mill owners' businesses, and watched them hurrying through their counting-houses, and collected foreign stamps out of their wastepaper baskets; and I watched the mill hands at the vats full of tow, and the weavers at the mysterious mechanical looms. I went into the red-hot hell of the jute-drying kilns and scorched myself beside the stokers at the boilers, wondering at their long shovels, which I could hardly lift. I would visit the butcher, eyeing him with interest to see if he would cut off a finger. I would have a look in at the shopkeeper as he weighed and measured; stop at the tinsmith's, and go into the carpenter's yard where everything was a-whirr and a-clatter. I went to the poorhouse to see what the poor do with themselves, and went with them to the fair in the city one Friday to learn how the business of begging was carried on.

Now I have a profession of my own, and I work at it the livelong day.   4 But even if I were to sit on the porch with my work I don't think a single boy would come—standing on one bare foot and rubbing his calf with the other—and watch my fingers to see how a writer's business is done. I don't say that it is a bad or useless profession: but it isn't one of the superlatively fine and striking ones, and the material used is of a strange sort—you don't even see it. But I'd like all the things I used to see to be in it: the ringing hammer-strokes of the smith and the colors of the whistling house painter, the patience of the tailor and the careful chipping of the stone-mason, the bustling of the baker, the humility of the poor, and all the lusty strength and skill which men of towering stature put into their work before the astonished and fascinated eyes of a child.

Questions About the Reading

1. Why does Čapek begin the essay by describing different types of childhood experiences? Pick out images he uses to describe each kind of life. Based on the writer's descriptions, which childhood would you prefer? Why?
2. Pick out some of the colorful images that Čapek uses to describe each kind of work.

3. How does the writer compare his profession to the many he observed as a child? What does Čapek mean when he says, "the material used is of a strange sort—you don't even see it"?
4. What does the final sentence of the essay mean?

Questions About the Writer's Strategies

1. What is the main idea of the essay? Is there a thesis statement? If so, what is it and where is it?
2. Identify the sensory details the writer uses to create images that bring each profession to life through the "astonished and fascinated eyes of a child."
3. Why do you think the writer saved the description of the profession of writing until the end of the essay? What purpose does it serve there?
4. In what deliberate order does the writer present the descriptions of the various professions he observed as a child?
5. What effect do the details about professions have on the reader's understanding of the main idea of this essay?
6. Čapek uses colorful words and images to enliven his descriptions. Identify five particularly effective words or images, and explain why you think each works well in its sentence.
7. This essay is subjective but also has objective elements. What details add objectivity to the descriptions of the different kinds of work?

Writing Assignments

1. *Working Together*   Join with one or two classmates to write an essay in which you describe several different professions you admire. Use specific examples to help your readers understand what you especially like about each kind of work.
2. Imagine you are a child observing the life of a student. Write an essay describing student life as observed by a child. Which parts of the student's life would seem special? Which would seem boring? Use colorful words to describe how a child might witness your life.
3. Imagine you are taking a walk through your neighborhood or the town in which you live. In an essay, describe the people you would see and what they would be doing.

Angela's Ashes

Frank McCourt

Born in Brooklyn, New York, Frank McCourt moved with his family to Limerick, Ireland, when he was four years old. In his Pulitzer Prize–winning book, Angela's Ashes, *he describes his difficult childhood in Ireland. He became a writing teacher at Stuyvesant High School in Manhattan and recently appeared at the school as a guest lecturer in a writing class taught by one of his former students.*

Words to Know

cacophony   harsh, discordant sounds
loquacious   talkative
piety   devoutness, reverence

Getting Started

Have you ever experienced rain, heat, or cold that seemed to never end?

My father and mother should have stayed in New York where they 1
met and married and where I was born. Instead, they returned to Ireland
when I was four, my brother, Malachy, three, the twins, Oliver and Eugene, barely one, and my sister Margaret, dead and gone.

When I look back on my childhood I wonder how I survived at all. It 2
was, of course, a miserable childhood: the happy childhood is hardly
worth your while. Worse than the ordinary miserable childhood is the
miserable Irish childhood, and worse yet is the miserable Irish Catholic
childhood.

People everywhere brag and whimper about the woes of their early 3
years, but nothing can compare with the Irish version: the poverty; the
shiftless loquacious alcoholic father; the pious defeated mother moaning
by the fire; pompous priests; bullying schoolmasters; the English and the
terrible things they did to us for eight hundred long years.

Above all—we were wet. 4

Out in the Atlantic Ocean great sheets of rain gathered to drift slowly 5
up the River Shannon and settle forever in Limerick. The rain dampened
the city from the Feast of the Circumcision to New Year's Eve. It created
a cacophony of hacking coughs, bronchial rattles, asthmatic wheezes, consumptive croaks. It turned noses into fountains, lungs into bacterial

sponges. It provoked cures galore; to ease the catarrh you boiled onions in milk blackened with pepper; for the congested passages you made a paste of boiled flour and nettles, wrapped it in a rag, and slapped it, sizzling, on the chest.

From October to April the walls of Limerick glistened with the damp. 6 Clothes never dried: tweed and woolen coats housed living things, sometimes sprouted mysterious vegetations. In pubs, steam rose from damp bodies and garments to be inhaled with cigarette and pipe smoke laced with the stale fumes of spilled stout and whiskey and tinged with the odor of piss wafting in from the outdoor jakes where many a man puked up his week's wages.

The rain drove us into the church—our refuge, our strength, our only 7 dry place. At Mass, Benediction, novenas, we huddled in great damp clumps, dozing through priest drone, while steam rose again from our clothes to mingle with the sweetness of incense, flowers and candles.

Limerick gained a reputation for piety, but we knew it was only the rain. 8

Questions About the Reading

1. How old was the writer when he went to Ireland?
2. Where was the writer born?
3. What is the writer's attitude toward the English?
4. What does the writer think is the most miserable childhood?
5. What does the writer think gave Limerick its reputation for piety?

Questions About the Writer's Strategies

1. What is the main idea of the essay? Is it stated? State the main idea in your own words.
2. What image does the writer create in paragraph 5?
3. Identify the details the writer uses to describe the cures for illnesses.
4. Is the essay objective, subjective, or both? Use examples from the essay to support your answer.

Writing Assignments

1. Write an essay about a period in your childhood when it seemed always to rain or be extremely hot or extremely cold, and describe how the weather affected you.
2. Write an essay about a time in your childhood when you were sick, and describe the cures your parents and doctors used to help you get well.

The Sounds of the City

James Tuite

A sports writer and former sports editor for the New York Times, *James
Tuite here describes the sounds of New York City and maintains that
visitors hear the sounds but the people who live there do not.*

Words to Know

aviary   enclosure for birds
cacophony   harsh, discordant sounds
converging   coming together
Doppler effect   drop in the pitch of a sound
masticate   chew
surcease   relief, cessation

Getting Started

Have you ever listened to the sounds of your neighborhood or of
the town in which you live?

New York is a city of sounds: muted sounds and shrill sounds; shatter- 1
ing sounds and soothing sounds; urgent sounds and aimless sounds. The
cliff dwellers of Manhattan—who would be racked by the silence of the
lonely woods—do not hear these sounds because they are constant and
eternally urban.

The visitor to the city can hear them, though, just as some animals can 2
hear a high-pitched whistle inaudible to humans. To the casual caller to
Manhattan, lying restive and sleepless in a hotel twenty or thirty floors
above the street, they tell a story as fascinating as life itself. And back of
the sounds broods the silence.

Night in midtown is the noise of tinseled honky-tonk and violence. 3
Thin strains of music, usually the firm beat of rock'n'roll or the frenzied
outbursts of the discotheque, rise from ground level. This is the cacophony,
the discordance of youth, and it comes on strongest when nights are hot
and young blood restless.

Somewhere in the canyons below there is shrill laughter or raucous 4
shouting. A bottle shatters against concrete. The whine of a police siren
slices through the night, moving ever closer, until an eerie Doppler effect
brings it to a guttural halt.

There are few sounds so exciting in Manhattan as those of fire appara- 5
tus dashing through the night. At the outset there is the tentative hint of
the first-due company bullying his way through midtown traffic. Now a
fire whistle from the opposite direction affirms that trouble is, indeed,
afoot. In seconds, other sirens converging from other streets help the
skytop listener focus on the scene of excitement.

But he can only hear and not see, and imagination takes flight. Are the 6
flames and smoke gushing from windows not far away? Are victims
trapped there, crying out for help? Is it a conflagration, or only a trash-
basket fire? Or, perhaps, it is merely a false alarm.

The questions go unanswered and the urgency of the moment dissolves. 7
Now the mind and the ear detect the snarling, arrogant bickering of automobile horns. People in a hurry. Taxicabs blaring, insisting on their check-
ered priority.

Even the taxi horns dwindle down to a precocious few in the gray and 8
pink moments of dawn. Suddenly there is another sound, a morning
sound that taunts the memory for recognition. The growl of a predatory
monster? No, just garbage trucks that have begun a day of scavenging.

Trash cans rattle outside restaurants. Metallic jaws on sanitation trucks 9
gulp and masticate the residue of daily living, then digest it with a satisfied groan of gears. The sounds of the new day are businesslike. The growl
of buses, so scattered and distant at night, becomes a demanding part of
the traffic bedlam. An occasional jet or helicopter injects an exclamation
point from an unexpected quarter. When the wind is right, the vibrant
bellow of an ocean liner can be heard.

The sounds of the day are as jarring as the glare of a sun that outlines 10
the canyons of midtown in drab relief. A pneumatic drill frays countless
nerves with its rat-a-tat-tat, for dig they must to perpetuate the city's dizzy
motion. After each screech of brakes there is a moment of suspension, of
waiting for the thud or crash that never seems to follow.

The whistles of traffic policemen and hotel doormen chirp from all 11
sides, like birds calling for their mates across a frenzied aviary. And all of
these sounds are adult sounds, for childish laughter has no place in these
canyons.

Night falls again, the cycle is complete, but there is no surcease from 12
sound. For the beautiful dreamers, perhaps, the "sounds of the rude world
heard in the day, lulled by the moonlight have all passed away," but this
is not so in the city.

Too many New Yorkers accept the sounds about them as bland parts 13
of everyday existence. They seldom stop to listen to the sounds, to think
about them, to be appalled or enchanted by them. In the big city, sounds
are life.

Questions About the Reading

1. Why do the people who live in Manhattan not hear the sounds of the city?
2. Why does the writer think the sounds tell a "fascinating" story (paragraph 2)?
3. Where is the writer when he is listening to the sounds?
4. What period of time is covered by the writer's description of the sounds of the city?

Questions About the Writer's Strategies

1. What order does the writer use to describe the sounds of the city? Why do you think he chose to use that order?
2. What is the metaphor in paragraph 9?
3. What is the thesis of the essay? Is it stated? State the thesis in your own words.

Writing Assignments

1. Sit outside your house for a while in the morning, afternoon, evening, and night and listen for the sounds of your neighborhood. Write an essay in which you describe the sounds of your neighborhood.
2. Write an essay describing the sounds of your school or of a classroom.
3. In an essay, describe the sounds of your home as everyone gets up in the morning and gets ready to go to school or work.

Limbo

Rhonda S. Lucas (student)

A new experience, a change in our lives, can make us see familiar objects in a new light. And a new location can make an old possession—a piece of furniture, an article of clothing—look strange. Rhonda S. Lucas, a student at East Los Angeles College, discovered both these things one day as she sat in a garage full of packing boxes and old furniture. In this essay, she describes what she saw.

Words to Know

cryptic   secret, mystifying

dilapidated   fallen into a state of disrepair

elegy   a mournful poem or song, often lamenting the dead

futility   uselessness

irony   the use of words to convey the opposite of their literal meaning

limbo   an intermediate place or state; a region or condition of oblivion or neglect

tubular   having the form of a tube

Getting Started

If you had to leave your house tomorrow, what would you miss most about it?

My parents' divorce was final. The house had been sold and the day 1
had come to move. Thirty years of the family's life were now crammed into the garage. The two-by-fours that ran the length of the walls were the only uniformity among the clutter of boxes, furniture, and memories. All was frozen in limbo between the life just passed and the one to come.

The sunlight pushing its way through the window splattered against a 2
barricade of boxes. Like a fluorescent river, it streamed down the sides and flooded the cracks of the cold, cement floor. I stood in the doorway between the house and garage and wondered if the sunlight would ever again penetrate the memories packed inside those boxes. For an instant, the cardboard boxes appeared as tombstones, monuments to those memories.

The furnace in the corner, with its huge tubular fingers reaching out 3
and disappearing into the wall, was unaware of the futility of trying to

74

warm the empty house. The rhythmical whir of its effort hummed the elegy for the memories boxed in front of me. I closed the door, sat down on the step, and listened reverently. The feeling of loss transformed the bad memories into not-so-bad, the not-so-bad memories into good, and committed the good ones to my mind. Still, I felt as vacant as the house inside.

A workbench to my right stood disgustingly empty. Not so much as a 4 nail had been left behind. I noticed, for the first time, what a dull, lifeless green it was. Lacking the disarray of tools that used to cover it, now it seemed as out of place as a bathtub in the kitchen. In fact, as I scanned the room, the only things that did seem to belong were the cobwebs in the corners.

A group of boxes had been set aside from the others and stacked in 5 front of the workbench. Scrawled like graffiti on the walls of dilapidated buildings were the words "Salvation Army." Those words caught my eyes as effectively as a flashing neon sign. They reeked of irony. "Salvation— was a bit too late for this family," I mumbled sarcastically to myself.

The houseful of furniture that had once been so carefully chosen to 6 complement and blend with the color schemes of the various rooms was indiscriminately crammed together against a single wall. The uncoordinated colors combined in turmoil and lashed out in the greyness of the room.

I suddenly became aware of the coldness of the garage, but I didn't 7 want to go back inside the house, so I made my way through the boxes to the couch. I cleared a space to lie down and curled up, covering myself with my jacket. I hoped my father would return soon with the truck so we could empty the garage and leave the cryptic silence of parting lives behind.

Questions About the Reading

1. Why is the title of this essay "Limbo"? Between which two stages of life is the writer?
2. How does the writer feel about moving out of the house?
3. Why does the writer view the empty workbench as disgusting (paragraph 4)?
4. Why didn't she want to go back inside the house?
5. What does Lucas mean in the last line by the "cryptic silence" of the house?

Questions About the Writer's Strategies

1. Although she never says it, the writer is saddened by her parents' divorce and the subsequent need to move. What details does she use to convey this feeling?
2. In what ways is this an extremely subjective essay?
3. Give your impression of the writer's life before her parents' divorce. What methods does she use to suggest this impression?
4. What is the thesis statement in the essay? Which paragraphs are used to develop the thesis statement? Is there a concluding paragraph?
5. What is the purpose of the metaphor in the last sentence of paragraph 2? In which sentence of paragraph 3 is the metaphor repeated?

Writing Assignments

1. Write an essay describing your favorite room in the house where you live now or the one where you grew up. Try to use examples from your life to give meaning to the objects you describe.
2. Write an essay describing a walk through your neighborhood or another one with which you are familiar. Describe the things that most interest you or that you think you will remember best in the future.

Connections

1. Many of the writers in this chapter describe their innermost feelings on a wide range of topics, from childhood memories of food to the sights and sounds of a city. Which descriptions deal mostly with feelings? How are the emotions of the different writers revealed in these selections? Choose two or more of the descriptions and describe what each writer reveals about his or her own emotions.
2. Several richly varied and fascinating places are described in this chapter. Which descriptions capture your imagination, allowing you perfectly to visualize the places the writers are describing? Choose two of your favorite place descriptions in this chapter. What connections can you make between these two descriptions? How are they alike? How are they different? Explain why and how these descriptions "speak" to your inner self.
3. Although many of these descriptions are different in tone and content, several deal with the connection between the writer and his or her past. Describe some of the connections these writers make to their personal or cultural inheritances. In what ways are these descriptions similar? In what ways are they different?

4. Most of the writers in this chapter have used colorful details and images to help their readers visualize their subjects. Barbara Kingsolver and Karel Čapek, for example, have chosen detailed images to portray people, whereas Frank McCourt and Rhonda Lucas have used imagery to describe emotional responses to painful experiences. Choose at least two of the descriptions and describe how the use of detail and imagery helped you visualize the writers' subjects.

4

Examples

AN EXAMPLE IS a specific instance or fact that is used to support an idea or a general statement. As you learned in chapter 1, the topic sentence states the main idea of a paragraph, and the thesis statement states the main idea of an essay. Both must be supported through a mode of development, which the writer selects. Writers frequently use **examples** to explain or illustrate a main idea, as in the following paragraph.

Topic sentence	Today, the president is more protected from contact with the people than in earlier times. Ordinary citizens, for example,
Example	could get to see Abraham Lincoln directly in the White House and make their requests to him in person. Now, all people must be cleared by the Secret Service before they can be in
Example	contact with the president. Even when a president visits people in their own homes, as Jimmy Carter sometimes did, the people and their homes are cleared by the Secret Service
Example	in advance. Citizens are even subjected to a search of their packages and clearance through metal detectors before they can be admitted to an event the president is attending. In fact, it requires a ticket and clearance through security devices to even enter the White House, and visitors can be sure the president will be nowhere in sight.

Some writers announce their strategy by the transitional words *for instance, to illustrate,* or *for example,* as in the sentence about Lincoln. Other times, as in the sentences about Jimmy Carter and visiting the White House, the writer expects the reader to notice that these are examples and that they support the topic of the paragraph.

To make a clear case, the writer usually needs to give several examples. The order in which the examples are presented may be chronological—that is, in sequence according to time—as in the paragraph on the previous page. In other cases, **order of importance** may be more effective, with the most important or convincing example presented last. In still other cases, the writer may use an example at the beginning of the essay to capture the reader's interest and to illustrate the **thesis,** which is stated later. The selection that follows illustrates the use of an introductory example.

Example used to introduce essay

1   The red-and-white pickup bounced along a gravel road in north-central Washington State. It was just past midnight on a summer Saturday last year. Two boys and two girls, recent graduates of Tonasket High School, had been "cruising" for a couple of hours, talking and laughing. At a sharp curve, the pickup somehow went off the road, rolled down the steep, rocky mountainside and twisted around a pine tree. All four occupants—none wearing a seat belt—were tossed out of the cab.

2   Driver Joe McDaniel escaped with cuts on his face and arms. Josh Wheeler suffered bruises but was able to cradle Amy Burdick in his arms until help arrived. She died the next day. Katy Watson, a former cheerleader who had won a scholarship to college, was dead at the scene, with massive chest and back injuries.

Thesis statement

3   Motor-vehicle injury is the greatest threat to the lives of adolescents in America. During the 1980s, over 74,000 teenagers were killed in such accidents, more than died from all diseases combined. On average, every two or three weeks the equivalent of a senior class at a typical high school is wiped out on our streets and highways. The National Safety Council (NSC) estimates that the financial toll is at least $10 billion annually for medical and insurance costs, property damage and lost wages resulting from accidents involving teen drivers.

Reader's Digest, June 1991

Examples in an essay can both illustrate and **support** the thesis. That is, if a writer makes a claim or a point in the **thesis statement** and then provides evidence in the form of actual situations that illustrate the thesis, it will help convince the reader that the thesis is valid. When you write, you should also search for examples as a way to test your thesis. For example, if you cannot think of a single specific example that supports your main idea, you will need to rethink your main idea. Or if you think of several examples that support your thesis, but also of several that work against it, you might want to revise your thesis and develop an **objective** essay presenting both sides of the issue.

In addition to providing concrete support for the thesis, examples can be used to enliven and clarify writing. In a description, for instance, examples can supply concrete details that add variety and interest. A single example may also be **extended** throughout an essay to illustrate the thesis, as in the following essay about the Kickapoo Indian Medicine Company. Notice, too, that minor examples are also used within the essay, as in paragraphs 2 and 3, to support the topic sentences of some paragraphs.

Thesis	By 1880 several hundred medicine shows were traveling in the United States, giving performances varying from 1
Major extended example—from here to end of essay	simple magic acts to elaborate "med-presentations." Among the largest of such operations from 1880 to 1910 was the Kickapoo Indian Medicine Company, "The King of Road Shows." Founded by two veteran troupers, John E. "Doc" Healy and Charles H. "Texas Charlie" Bigelow, the Kickapoo Company maintained a large headquarters building, "The Principal Wigwam," in New Haven, Connecticut, and from there sent out shows, as many as twenty-five at a time, to cities and villages throughout the country.
Minor examples of *performers* who were hired	Doc Healy hired performers, both Indian and white— dancers, singers, jugglers, fire-eaters, acrobats, comedians, fiddlers—and Texas Charlie managed the medicine business and trained the "Doctors" and "Professors" who gave "Medical Lectures." 2
Minor examples of *distinctively garbed* troupe members	All troupe members were distinctively garbed. The Indians—including Mohawks, Iroquois, Crees, Sioux, and Blackfeet—billed as "all pure-blooded Kickapoos, the most noted of all Indian Medical People," were adorned with colored beads and feathers and loaded down with primitive weapons; they trailed great strings of unidentified hairy objects. Some lecturers wore western-style leather clothes and boots with silver-capped toes, others fancy silk shirts, frock coats, and high silk hats. One of the most colorful Kickapoo figures was smooth-talking Ned T. Oliver—"Nevada Ned, the King of Gold"—who wore an enormous sombrero from the brim of which dangled 100 gold coins, and a fancy suit loaded with buttons made of gold pieces. 3

The Kickapoo shows were presented under canvas at "Kickapoo Camps" during the summer and in opera houses and town halls in winter. On many nights the show was free to all, on others each adult was charged 10¢. The money poured in from medicine sales. 4

The wonder-working Kickapoo concoctions were "compounded according to secret ancient Kickapoo Indian tribal formulas" from "blood root, feverwort, spirit gum, wild poke berries, sassafras, slippery elm, wintergreen, white oak bark, yellow birch bark, dock root, sarsaparilla, and other Natural Products." The medicines were made in the Connecticut 5 factory in vats so huge the "mixers" had to perch on ladders and wield long paddles. The leader of the Kickapoo line was Sagwa, which sold at 50¢ and $1 per bottle—"Sagwa, the wonderful remedy for catarrh, pulmonary consumption, and all ills that afflict the human body. It is made from roots, barks, gums, leaves, oils, and berries gathered by little Kickapoo children from God's great laboratory, the fertile fields and vast forests. Sagwa, Nature's own great secret cure, now available to all mankind!"

Long after the Kickapoo Company was dissolved, a woman who had worked in the medicine factory recalled that one of the ingredients of Kickapoo Cough Syrup was Jamaica rum. Could this "cure" have been the inspiration for the "Kickapoo Joy Juice" Al Capp featured in his popular comic strip?   6

Peggy Robbins,
"The Kickapoo Indian Medicine Company"

In this essay, the writer's use of concrete examples gives us a clear picture of the Kickapoo medicine show. In addition, the great number and the variety of minor examples give us a good idea of the crazy-quilt nature of medicine shows in general.

When using examples in your own writing, **brainstorm** for possibilities (as described in chapter 1) and select those that illustrate your idea most accurately. In choosing among possibilities, select those that you sense your reader will respond to as convincing and colorful. Several well-chosen examples will hold your reader's interest and add credibility to your main idea.

The Pencil Rack

John Ciardi

*In this paragraph, by poet John Ciardi, we see how an experienced writer
can push himself to begin writing. This inventory of Ciardi's pencil rack,
the little trough at the front of his desk drawer, gives the reader a colorful
and amusing portrait of the ordinary litter of day-to-day living.*

Words to Know

obscure   not easily seen or understood
unsubstantiated   unproven

Getting Started

What would you find in the glove compartment of your car?

Moved by what might be called an obscure impulse (to obscure my
average reluctance to get to work), I recently fell to taking inventory of
my average pencil rack and came up with the following itemization: two
red pencils (unsharpened), one black grease pencil, one ball point and
one fountain pen (both broken), one mailing sticker that had curled up
into a small tube and which I unrolled to find that I had once printed on
it with some care my social security number (032-10-1225), one purchaser's
receipt for a money order in the amount of $7.15, one theater ticket stub
(R 108) for the opening night of *The Rise of Arturo Ui*, one second-best
(and therefore unused) letter opener, one spool of J. & P. Coats black thread
(15¢, 125 yards, number 60, origin and purpose unknown), one dentist's
tool (broken, but obviously useful for picking things out of things if I had
anything of that sort to pick related things out of), two nail files, one pair
of cuff links, one metal pill box (empty, origin and purpose unknown),
one glass marble (probably a souvenir of a visit from Benn), one four-for-
a-quarter-while-you-wait-press-the-button photo taken, as I recall, at, then,
Idlewild Airport and showing Jonnel and me looking at one another in
some sort of fond but unsubstantiated pride, one twenty-cent stamp (1938
Presidential issue, James A. Garfield), two rubber bands, one pocket comb,
a litter of paper clips, one 1889 quarter (to give to the kids for their collection as soon as I am sure that they will not spend it on candy), one Canadian dime and one British halfpenny (to be given to them any time), one
air-mail sticker, two six-penny nails, three thumb tacks, two match

folders, one broken tie clip (probably repairable), one small screw driver (in case any small screws show up to be driven?), one pocket pack of Kleenex, one pair of paper scissors, one staple remover, assorted grit.

Questions About the Reading

1. Why do you think the writer saved all of these things? Is a reason implied?
2. Who do you think Benn and Jonnel are? Give reasons for your answer.
3. Does the writer ever use the dentist's tool? How do you know?
4. What thoughts did you have when you finished reading this paragraph? What do you think the writer wants you to conclude about the contents of his pencil rack?

Questions About the Writer's Strategies

1. Examine the arrangement of examples in this paragraph. See if you can detect any obvious or implied order in their arrangement.
2. Besides being a paragraph of examples, in what sense is this a descriptive paragraph?
3. One could say that this paragraph is just a list of junk. How does the writer hold your interest and keep you reading?

Writing Assignments

1. We all save some things we do not need or use, sometimes without even knowing why. Write a paragraph giving examples of such things— your own possessions or those of your friends—and try to describe some of the reasons for keeping them.
2. In a paragraph, use examples to describe the contents of the average refrigerator, garage, attic, or some other place where things tend to collect and be forgotten. Try to include examples that will interest or amuse your reader.

Folk Art in the Barrios

Eric Kroll

In this paragraph, Eric Kroll describes the wall paintings in Santa Fe, New Mexico, that depict a bold and colorful Chicano history and that defy stereotypes.

Words to Know

Aztec   early people of Mexico

disproportionate   not in proportion, not actual size

Father Hidalgo   Miguel Hidalgo y Costilla (1753–1811), a Catholic priest who launched the revolution to free Mexico from Spanish rule

Pancho Villa   Mexican revolutionary leader

Getting Started

Have you ever looked at a painting of a famous person and thought that it wasn't accurate?

———————

On ten Santa Fe walls, the history of the Chicanos, both mythical and actual, is depicted in brilliant colors and disproportionate figures. Aztec medicine figures dance and gods protect peasants, all for the glory of the Chicano in the present. On some walls, the chains of bondage are being broken and the Lady of Justice, depicted as an Indian Maiden, watches over both Indians and Chicanos. On others, Pancho Villa and Father Hidalgo lead the Mexican peasants to freedom. But the clenched fist at the end of the grotesquely muscled arms is the most predominant image. It symbolizes unity, determination, ambition, and pride, all traits that Los Artes believe should be a part of Chicano psychology. The figures they paint are bold, upright, strong, and grasping, far from the stereotype of the Mexican-American with drooping moustache and floppy sombrero lying in the shade of a stucco building.

———————

Questions About the Reading

1. On how many walls in Santa Fe are there paintings of Chicano history?
2. What is the purpose of the paintings?

3. What does the clenched fist in the paintings symbolize?
4. How do the figures in the paintings differ from the stereotype the author describes at the end of the paragraph?

Questions About the Writer's Strategies

1. What is the main idea (topic) of the paragraph?
2. What examples depict the freedom of Mexican peasants?
3. What is the metaphor for the traits that the artists believe the Chicanos should have?
4. What descriptive words are used for the figures in the paintings?
5. What descriptive words are used for the Mexican-American stereotype?

Writing Assignments

1. Write a paragraph in which you use examples to describe the behavior of a television personality.
2. Write a paragraph using examples to illustrate the traditions of different ethnic groups in your city.

Sports Stuff

Scott Russell Sanders

*How much sports equipment can a person need or want? Scott Russell
Sanders provides enough examples of the equipment he and his son have
acquired to make us think that, for them, there may not be any limit.*

Words to Know

festooned   draped
hieroglyphs   symbols, emblems
paraphernalia   equipment, articles

Getting Started

Do you collect something? If so, do you think your collection will
ever be complete?

My daughter has never allowed me to buy her a single item of sports
paraphernalia. My son, on the other hand, has never declined such an
offer. Day and night, visions of athletic gear dance on his head. With religious zeal, he pores over magazine ads for sneakers, examining the stripes
and insignia as if they were hieroglyphs of ultimate truth. Between us,
Jesse and I are responsible for the hoard of equipment on our back porch,
which contains at present the following items: one bicycle helmet and
two bicycles; a volleyball set, badminton set, and a bag of golf clubs; three
racquets for tennis, two for squash, one for paddle ball; roller skates and
ice skates, together with a pair of hockey sticks; goalie gloves, batting
gloves, three baseball gloves and one catcher's mitt; numerous yo-yos;
ten pairs of cleated or waffle-soled shoes; a drying rack festooned with
shorts and socks and shirts and sweatsuits; and a cardboard box heaped
with (I counted) forty-nine balls, including those for all the sports impli-
cated above, as well as for ping-pong, lacrosse, juggling, and jacks.

Questions About the Reading

1. How does the writer's daughter feel about having him buy her sports
   equipment?

2. How does the writer's son feel about having his father buy him sports equipment?
3. How many bicycles are on the porch?
4. How many different kinds of gloves are on the porch?

Questions About the Writer's Strategies

1. What is the point of view (person, time, tone) of the paragraph?
2. What is the main idea (topic) of the paragraph?
3. Is the main idea stated or implied?
4. What can you infer from the examples of sports equipment that the writer provides?

Writing Assignments

1. Write a paragraph in which you provide examples of a collection you have or would like to have.
2. Write a paragraph in which you provide examples of a collection you have seen in a museum.
3. Write a paragraph in which you provide examples of a collection belonging to a family member or a friend.

My Suit

Ricardo Galvez (student)

Ricardo Galvez, a student at Los Angeles Harbor College in California, shows us with examples that the way people dress influences the way they are treated by others.

Words to Know

drenching   soaking, saturating
merit   value, worth

Getting Started

Have you ever felt you were treated better or worse because of the clothes you were wearing?

I had once been told that people are treated primarily according to the way they dress. With this in mind, I gathered all of my suits and selected the best one. I wore it to church that Sunday. To my surprise, I found this statement to have some merit. After mass I went to lunch with the singles' group from church. Wearing a tie made my neck feel as if I had been hanging at the end of a rope. I was beginning to perspire quite heavily under the miserably hot sun and drenching humid air. The dress shoes were also uncomfortable and I almost fell as I slipped on a slice of banana near the buffet table. Nevertheless, it was well worth the sacrifice. Usually I had to wait fifteen minutes for a table for two. That day I was tended to immediately, and I even reserved a large table for all of the singles while they found parking spaces outside. More important, I met a sweet, attractive young lady who asked me to accompany her to a dance. The next fourteen months of courtship that followed made me aware of the fact that to feel miserable didn't have to mean that I had to be miserable. Being with her made me forget all discomfort.

Questions About the Reading

1. Did the writer have several suits? If so, which of his suits did the writer select to wear?
2. Whom did the writer go to lunch with after church?

3. How did wearing a tie make the writer feel?
4. Did the writer feel it was worthwhile to be uncomfortable in his suit and shoes? Why?

Questions About the Writer's Strategies

1. What is the main idea of the paragraph? Does the writer state the main idea directly? If so, in which sentence?
2. What are the examples the writer uses to prove his main idea?
3. What is the order in which the writer tells us about his experience?
4. What is the point of view of the paragraph in person, time, and tone?

Writing Assignments

1. Write a paragraph in which you use examples to tell about an experience you had that was related to the clothes you were wearing.
2. Assume you have had an interview for a job you want. Write a paragraph in which you give examples of what you wore and how you think your clothes influenced the success or failure of the interview.

The Internet Instills Family Values—Really

Alcestis "Cooky" Oberg

Alcestis "Cooky" Oberg, a science and technology writer and member of the contributing board of USA Today, *counters the claim that people spend too much time on the Internet.*

Words to Know

cosmic   vast, grandiose
guttural   rasping, throaty
intergalactic   between the galaxies
monosyllables   single-syllable words
primal   primitive
sanctuary   safe place
virtual   not actual

Getting Started

What do you use the Internet for and how much time do you spend each day on the Internet?

When the study came out last month claiming that some people are 1
spending too much time on the Internet and not enough time living real life, I laughed.

Not 10 minutes before, I had rounded up my herd for dinner with the 2
usual cattle call: "Join the land of the living!" Out from behind their computers, they emerged—answering the primal call of hunger and of Mom.

I have noticed that family life takes on a zombie-esque quality when 3
the computers are on. I dislike television for the same reason. I always wondered whether family life would be richer if we just shut everything off. A poet-friend of mine actually tried it with his young family: no television, no computers, just books.

Unfortunately, after a while, the adults exhibited that out-of-touch aura 4
bookish people get—and the kids would sneak out to watch *Sesame Street* at the neighbor's house almost as soon as they could walk.

Let's face it: Real life is hard work. There are all of those disagreeable 5
chores such as earning a living, paying taxes, cleaning windows and toilets, not to mention puzzling out what your significant other, your spouse,

your kids and your parents want from you—all of these things that put the *real* into real life. Tuning all of that out and going to that "better place" on the Internet is like dying and going to heaven, only you're still alive. Sort of.

In the right hands, though, that computer mouse can actually take you over the rougher bumps on real life's road. Take adolescence. When kids hit that uncommunicative, "I don't know those people who call themselves my parents" stage, you can reach your kids by e-mail. For instance, even though we lived under the same roof, I found I could get a good, long, sometimes funny e-mail response from my teenager during "the surly years." I never would have gotten beyond monosyllables and guttural utterances in face-to-face real life. 6

And the Internet has turned out to be a new, fairly wholesome vehicle for socializing teens—safer than fast cars and seedy hangouts. One shy boy I know set up a virtual drama club on the Net, with 150 kids across the nation. 7

They took on the roles of various science-fiction characters and played out cosmic dramas they wrote themselves. One night, they simulated an incredibly detailed and clever intergalactic battle—one the Pentagon would envy. In high school, these gentle kids didn't particularly fit in with the body-piercing gang or the fast-car crowd. The Internet provided them with a social sanctuary where they met their real peers and made very real friends. 8

Then there's our own Virtual Granny. When my husband's mom visited us last year, he introduced her to the joys of e-mail, file-attach photos, eBay, Amazon and the virtual portfolio. She took to it all like a born nerd. She found old pals, communicated with nieces and grandchildren, bought stuff to be delivered to her doorstep at the click of a mouse. It was midnight before I got past her and sent out my business e-mail. "You created a monster," I confided to my husband, "and it's your mother!" 9

Let's face it: Anyone who accuses the Internet of taking too much time away from "real life" must first consider what that real life is. The elderly, for instance, are often shut in and isolated by their health. Sometimes, they are "retired" to a different city, uprooted from their old hometowns where they spent most of their lives and raised their families. These seniors are a fast-growing population of Internet users, not because they're fleeing attachments, but because they are seeking them. They can connect with old friends and feel a part of the lives of their far-flung children and grandchildren, which they couldn't possibly do without physically living in the same town or under the same roof. 10

In our family, the Internet didn't isolate Granny further, didn't stop her from doing charity work, going to church or seeing her nearby friends. It didn't stop my kids from taking out the garbage, doing their chores or 11 having real-life friends. The Internet just became one more social avenue in our lives.

Indeed, we're not far from the day when whole intellectual and cul- 12 tural communities are established on the Net, like that teenage virtual-drama club: People who are separated by accident of geography but have common interests and circumstances can finally meet and form a circle of their own—beyond the circle of the family they were born into, the jobs they go to and the cities where they live.

And it doesn't mean that at some point our Net life and our "real" life 13 can't meet face to face. My Net life and my real life meet every month—on my Visa bill. And I still have to pay for my virtual merchandise with very, very real money.

Questions About the Reading

1. How does the writer call her family to dinner?
2. What happened to the family that turned off its televisions and computers?
3. How did the writer reach her teenagers during their "surly years"?
4. What club did the shy boy set up through the Internet?
5. What advantages does the Internet provide for elderly people?

Questions About the Writer's Strategies

1. What is the main idea of the essay? Is there a thesis statement? If so, where is it located?
2. What specific examples does the writer use?
3. What order does the writer use in presenting the examples? Why do you think she chose that order?
4. Besides examples, what modes of development does the writer use?
5. Is the essay objective or subjective?

Writing Assignments

1. *Working Together*   Join with some classmates to write an essay that illustrates your different uses of the Internet with examples.
2. *Working Together*   Join with some classmates to write an essay about the advantages and disadvantages of using the Internet. Use examples to support each position.

3. Write an essay about three web sites that provide career information. Include the address for each site, describe the kind of information each site provides, and use examples to show which site is the most useful.

Homeless

Anna Quindlen

In this essay, New York Times *columnist Anna Quindlen makes a distinction between "the homeless" and people who have no "homes."*

Words to Know

anonymous   nameless, unidentified
compassionate   sympathetic
crux   crucial or main point
global   wide, big

Getting Started

What is the different between a house and a home?

Her name was Ann, and we met in the Port Authority Bus Terminal 1
several Januarys ago. I was doing a story on homeless people. She said I
was wasting my time talking to her; she was just passing through, although she'd been passing through for more than two weeks. To prove to
me that this was true, she rummaged through a tote bag and a manila
envelope and finally unfolded a sheet of typing paper and brought out
her photographs.

They were not pictures of family, or friends, or even a dog or cat, its 2
eyes brown-red in the flashbulb's light. They were pictures of a house. It
was like a thousand houses in a hundred towns, not suburb, not city, but
somewhere in between, with aluminum siding and a chain-link fence, a
narrow driveway running up to a one-car garage and a patch of backyard. The house was yellow. I looked on the back for a date or a name,
but neither was there. There was no need for discussion. I knew what she
was trying to tell me, for it was something I had often felt. She was not
adrift, alone, anonymous, although her bags and her raincoat with the
grime shadowing its creases had made me believe she was. She had a
house, or at least once upon a time had had one. Inside were curtains, a
couch, a stove, potholders. You are where you live. She was somebody.

I've never been very good at looking at the big picture, taking the glo- 3
bal view, and I've always been a person with an overactive sense of place,
the legacy of an Irish grandfather. So it is natural that the thing that seems
most wrong with the world to me right now is that there are so many

people with no homes. I'm not simply talking about shelter from the elements, or three square meals a day or a mailing address to which the welfare people can send the check—although I know that all these are important for survival. I'm talking about a home, about precisely those kinds of feelings that have wound up in cross-stitch and French knots on samplers over the years.

Home is where the heart is. There's no place like it. I love my home 4 with a ferocity totally out of proportion to its appearance or location. I love dumb things about it: the hot-water heater, the plastic rack you drain dishes in, the roof over my head, which occasionally leaks. And yet it is precisely those dumb things that make it what it is—a place of certainty, stability, predictability, privacy, for me and for my family. It is where I live. What more can you say about a place than that? That is everything.

Yet it is something that we have been edging away from gradually 5 during my lifetime and the lifetimes of my parents and grandparents. There was a time when where you lived often was where you worked and where you grew the food you ate and even where you were buried. When that era passed, where you lived at least was where your parents had lived and where you would live with your children when you became enfeebled. Then, suddenly where you lived was where you lived for three years, until you could move on to something else and something else again.

And so we have come to something else again, to children who do not 6 understand what it means to go to their rooms because they have never had a room, to men and women whose fantasy is a wall they can paint a color of their own choosing, to old people reduced to sitting on molded plastic chairs, their skin blue-white in the lights of a bus station, who pull pictures of houses out of their bags. Homes have stopped being homes. Now they are real estate.

People find it curious that those without homes would rather sleep 7 sitting up on benches or huddled in doorways than go to shelters. Certainly some prefer to do so because they are emotionally ill, because they have been locked in before and they are damned if they will be locked in again. Others are afraid of the violence and trouble they may find there. But some seem to want something that is not available in shelters, and they will not compromise, not for a cot, or oatmeal, or a shower with special soap that kills the bugs. "One room," a woman with a baby who was sleeping on her sister's floor, once told me, "painted blue." That was the crux of it; not size or location, but pride of ownership. Painted blue.

This is a difficult problem, and some wise and compassionate people 8 are working hard at it. But in the main I think we work around it, just as we walk around it when it is lying on the sidewalk or sitting in the bus terminal—the problem, that is. It has been customary to take people's pain and lessen our own participation in it by turning it into an issue, not a collection of human beings. We turn an adjective into a noun: the poor, not poor people; the homeless, not Ann or the man who lives in the box or the woman who sleeps on the subway grate.

Sometimes I think we would be better off if we forgot about the broad 9 strokes and concentrated on the details. Here is a woman without a bureau. There is a man with no mirror, no wall to hang it on. They are not the homeless. They are people who have no homes. No drawer that holds the spoons. No window to look out upon the world. My God. That is everything.

Questions About the Reading

1. Where did the writer meet the woman named Ann?
2. What does the writer mean by "You are where you live"?
3. Does the writer think people regard where they live the same way they used to?
4. According to the writer, why do some homeless people refuse to go to shelters?
5. What does the writer mean by "We turn an adjective into a noun: the poor, not poor people; the homeless, not Ann or the man who lives in the box or the woman who sleeps on the subway grate"?

Questions About the Writer's Strategies

1. Why do you think the writer described Ann and her photographs at the beginning of the essay?
2. What metaphor does the writer use in the third paragraph?
3. What is the thesis of the essay? Is it stated or implied?
4. Is the essay objective or subjective?

Writing Assignments

1. Write an essay, using examples, about the organizations in your city that provide shelters for homeless people.
2. *Working Together*   Join with some classmates to write, using examples, an essay about organizations in your city that help homeless people.

Each Game
Was a Crusade

Mark Harris

Jackie Robinson broke the color line in baseball in 1947 when he joined the Brooklyn Dodgers. He was the first black player to wear the uniform of a major league team. By the time he died a quarter-century later, all of baseball and much of American life were integrated.

Words to Know

anguish   pain, extreme discomfort

feint   pretend, fake

fortitude   courage, strength

incalculable   more than can be counted

innovators   inventors

manifestation   demonstration, showing, form

nurtured   cultivated

shrewdest   most clever, most cunning

sustained   kept up

Getting Started

What influence has Tiger Woods had on golf, its players, and its fans?

Sometimes on summer television when I watch a black fellow come to bat during somebody's Game of the Day or Night or Week, I wonder how much he knows about a recent fellow named Jackie Robinson.

Who was Jackie Robinson? I wondered if my students at the University of Pittsburgh knew, so I asked them to scribble me a little answer to the question, "What does the name 'Jackie Robinson' mean to you?" For fun, try it on your own resident student. My students were born, on the average, in 1957. Some of their answers were these. "A very beautiful blonde woman I met in my dental office." "Jackie Robinson—female or male, related possibly to Mrs. Robinson in the movie *The Graduate* & in the song 'Mrs. Robinson' by Simon & Garfunkel. Or is it a baseball player? A musician? I'm guessing."

Yes, baseball player, getting warm. Who was Jackie Robinson? "I thought of a boxer," one student wrote. Another: "He might be a baseball player or a numbers runner." My one black student wrote: "Jackie Robinson is a baseball player. This is a real person, in fact, he played on a baseball team. Not sure what the team was."

The most nearly correct answer was this: "All I know (think) is he's the first black man to play major-league baseball—broke the color barrier." ... 4

In ancient 1947, Robinson, male, a baseball player, a real person, became the first black man to play big-league baseball, and a lonesome figure he was. In 1947 we had sixteen major-league baseball teams, and every player on every team was white and *that was that.* Except for Robinson, who played first base for the (then) Brooklyn Dodgers of the National League. 5

If some people had had their way he would have been not only the first but the last. The fact that those people did not have their way is due in large part to Robinson's interior fortitude. But he could also hit and run and field with superior skill at several positions. He had played in four sports at UCLA. He soon became not only an outstanding player but the spiritual leader of his own group (the Dodgers) and a dreaded opponent of all the other groups (the other teams of the National League), whose spirits he often destroyed with his daring and his surprises. 6

Robinson had been specially selected by Branch Rickey for the pioneer work he did. Rickey, the Dodgers' president, was one of baseball's shrewdest innovators. He had invented the minor-league "farm system" by which big-league organizations developed and nurtured talented young players. Now he was to embark upon a second major innovation: the introduction of black players into organized baseball. The first black player would need to be an extraordinary human being. He would suffer anguish and abuse throughout the cities of the league. The shock of Robinson's presence would not be cushioned in a day. 7

In 1946, when Robinson was signed to a contract by the Brooklyn organization, a sportswriter in St. Louis assured me that neither Robinson nor any other Negro (that was the proper word then) would ever play ball against the Cardinals. But after an extremely productive season in Montreal, which was (then) in the International League, Robinson *did* play baseball—for the Dodgers, against the Cardinals, who at first refused to take the field. When at length the St. Louis players obeyed the order of (then) National League president Ford Frick to play or be punished, baseball and America had arrived at a new moment. 8

In his first game for Montreal, Robinson hit one home run and three singles, stole two bases, scored four runs. It was only the beginning. He was to be remembered finally, however, not for statistics alone but for incalculable moments when he won baseball games in ways that never enter the box score. He played several positions afield, and he was sev- 9 eral persons at the bat; he could hit long balls and he could bunt. He could hit to left or right. He could run very fast and stop very short. He could feint, and he could feint feinting.

He took long, careless leads off base, forcing opposition pitchers into 10 foolish errors. Since he was not only powerful but frequently enraged, he often inflicted injury upon other players in skirmishes along the base paths. His power was sustained by a mission not only personal but historic. Every game, every event, was in the interest of Robinson, of the Dodgers, and of Robinson's equalitarian interpretation of the United States Constitution. During warm-up for an exhibition game in New Orleans he once took time to condemn the black fans when they cheered because a new section of grandstand was opened to them: in Robinson's view, their expanded location was not a gift but a *right*. . . .

What if the Robinson experiment had failed? Nobody will ever know 11 whether the thing that succeeded was good old-fashioned liberal tradition in its most happy manifestation, or whether the thing that succeeded was old-fashioned dollar pragmatism. Robinson was a winner, and Brooklyn loved a winner, even if he was black. One winner drew a second, and so forth, and their names were Campanella, Black, Newcombe, Gilliam, and they were black, and they all played for Brooklyn during the decade 1947–1956, when the Dodgers won six pennants.

In the American League the Cleveland Indians with a black outfielder 12 named Larry Doby won the pennant in 1948. Doby was the first black American League player at a time when I could count on my fingers all the black players. As time passed, my fingers were unable to keep up.

It began with Robinson, Brooklyn, 1947—and radio. In those days— 13 my diary always tells it this way—I "listened to the ball game." In 1950 I more and more "watched the ball game," and anyone could see that the hitter's head or the pitcher's head was the size of the screen itself, and sometimes black. It was color television.

Thus the generation of my students, born in 1957 and propped at an 14 early age in front of the tube for the Game of the Day or Night or Year, must have believed from infancy that baseball players had always come in two colors. One never imagined that any such person existed who could be described as "the first black player" any more than anyone could name the first white player. . . .

The appearance of Robinson and the consciousness he raised among 15 athletes quickened thinking and hastened expectations upon many topics apart from race. He broke more than the color barrier. Robinson meant not only to play the game equally with all Americans but to sleep equally in hotels, and he rallied other black players, often to their discomfort, for they sometimes said to him, "Jackie, we like it here, don't rock the boat."

But he had already rocked it climbing in, and the spirit of reform was contagious. White players joined black players to demand unprecedented rights through union organization and other forms of professional representation.

Their ultimate achievement was freedom from the "reserve clause" in 16 players' contracts. In the past, this clause gave the baseball organization or "club" exclusive rights to the players' services. Simply stated, a player was deprived of the opportunity to seek another employer, and therefore he was effectively denied the opportunity to bargain for his own wage. Players now won the right to be "free agents," to own themselves. The odd resemblance of the "reserve clause" to features of black slavery was remote in quality but similar in outline. . . .

A good deal of my own perception of Robinson's character and his- 17 toric uniqueness I gleaned from Roger Kahn's wonderful book, *The Boys of Summer.* When Robinson died, October 24, 1972, Kahn was quoted in the papers. Someone asked him what Jackie Robinson had done for his race. Kahn, a white man, beautifully replied, "His race was humanity, and he did a great deal for us."

Questions About the Reading

1. What is the most important reason for Jackie Robinson's fame?
2. Who was responsible for giving Robinson his start in baseball? Did this person pick Robinson for his skill in baseball or for another reason? If so, what was the reason?
3. What happened when Robinson played baseball for the Dodgers against the Cardinals?
4. Explain why Robinson condemned black baseball fans in New Orleans.

Questions About the Writer's Strategies

1. What is the point of view—in regard to time—at the beginning of the essay? What words does the writer use to indicate a change in time?
2. What is the dominant mode that the writer uses in the essay? What other modes does he use?
3. In paragraphs 13 and 14, how does the writer indicate the time frame of events? What is the purpose of the two paragraphs?
4. Does the writer develop the essay by primarily using one extended example or by using several examples?

Writing Assignments

1. Write an essay in which you tell about a person who changed the attitudes of another person or group. Use specific examples.
2. Write an essay in which you use two or more examples of individuals who have made a particular contribution to one of the following: sports, art, music, literature, science, or business.

Dear Dr. Seuss

Jim Sollisch

Jim Sollisch, a free-lance writer who lives in Ohio, shows us how Dr. Seuss's famous children's book The Cat in the Hat *would need to be censored to meet the standards for diversity, which he calls "practically an academic discipline." (Reprinted with permission from* The Plain Dealer, *September 19, 1997, © 1997. All rights reserved.)*

Words to Know

insidious   stealthy, sneaky
litigation   legal action or process
sadistic   deliberately cruel
spectrum   broad range of ideas or qualities

Getting Started

Have you ever read a book, watched a talk show, or seen a movie that you think should have been censored in some way?

———————

E‌very year, it seems, another group of parents, educators or school board 1 members—who understand too well the power of literature to shape the human heart—attempt to ban more of my family's favorite books.

In an effort to expose their censorship, the American Library Associa- 2 tion, the American Booksellers Association, the Library of Congress and others sponsor National Banned Books Week, which begins this weekend.

The list of authors whose books were banned or challenged this year 3 looks like a required reading list for any educated American: Toni Morrison, Mark Twain, Alice Walker, Shakespeare, Harper Lee, J. D. Salinger, Maya Angelou, Chaucer, Henry James. Even children's favorites like Maurice Sendak's *In the Night Kitchen,* Roald Dahl's *Matilda* and R. L. Stine's *Goosebumps* series were taken off shelves and put somewhere where children would be safe from the nudity, disobedience and destructive ideas they promote.

While this brand of censorship, which stems mostly from the conser- 4 vative social agenda of the religious right, is frightening, at least it's out in the open. You can see it and respond to it at your local school board meeting. And most of it is so foolish and pigheaded that it has the opposite-than-intended effect.

There's another kind of censorship I worry about. It comes from the 5
liberal side of the spectrum, from our attempts at making diversity practically an academic discipline, from our fear of offending any group or
person, of promoting any idea that possibly could be misconstrued and
result in litigation.

We have no way to measure the damage this insidious kind of censor- 6
ship might be doing to children's literature. For example, how many
children's books are censored at their source—either by a wary author or
by editors and publishers who have to market to educators living in fear
that anything they say, do or teach might be used against them?

The other day as I read to my daughter "The Cat in the Hat"—which 7
has not yet been banned—I imagined the way an editor might respond to
this manuscript had it come across his desk today rather than in 1957.
Here is the rejection letter Ted Geisel, aka Dr. Seuss, might receive.

Dear Mr. Geisel: 8

Beyond the need to authenticate your credentials as a doctor— 9
necessary to avoid potential litigation—I have a few minor problems with
this otherwise witty and amusing manuscript.

First, you tread on dangerous ground right from the start of your story: 10
A young boy and his sister allow a stranger into their house. It's small
consolation that this stranger is a cat in a hat, for today's social climate
dictates that we teach our children to avoid all strangers, even one in
sheep's (or cat's) clothing, for that matter.

Even more troubling, we soon learn that the children's mother is out 11
for the day. While we applaud your effort to deal with a possible single-
parent family situation, we cannot publish a book that shows small children being left home alone. That story line is best left to Hollywood, not
to publishers of children's literature.

My last problem concerns the Cat in the Hat's treatment of the fish in 12
the pot, who incidentally, is the only moral voice in the story, warning the
children that the cat should not be about when their mother is out. The
cat's little game of "Up Up with a Fish" borders on the sadistic as the fish
lands in a pot with no water where he spends the remainder of the story.
Animal rights groups would have a field day with this book.

In conclusion, if you were to revise your story, incorporating these re- 13
vision suggestions and provide authentication of your doctorate—is it in
child psychology, perhaps?—we would be happy to reconsider your
manuscript, "The Cat in the Hat."

Sincerely,   14

P. C. Litmus, Editor-in-Chief, Child Safe Books   15

Back in 1937, 43 publishers rejected Dr. Seuss's first book, *And to Think* 16
that I Saw It on Mulberry Street. But the 44th gave him a shot, and Seuss

went on to change children's literature forever, selling more than 200 million books. What a sad thought that in 1997, that 44th publisher no longer might be willing to take the chance.

Questions About the Reading

1. What reasons does the writer give for conservatives to ban the authors he lists in paragraph 3?
2. What is the writer's view of the conservative brand of censorship? Does he think it is successful? Why or why not?
3. What is the writer's view of the censorship that "comes from the liberal side of the spectrum"? Does he think it is successful? Why or why not?

Questions About the Writer's Strategies

1. What is the tone of the essay? How is it expressed?
2. What order does the writer use in presenting his examples of conservative and liberal censorship? Why do you think he used that order?
3. What is the thesis of the essay? State it in your own words.

Writing Assignments

1. Write an essay in which you explain why you think there should or should not be censorship of books, talk shows, or movies. Support your explanation with examples.
2. *Working Together* Join with some classmates to write an essay in which you explain whether or not some restrictions or controls over television programming are needed. If restrictions are needed, give examples of what you think they should be.
3. Write an essay in which you give examples of good and bad children's television programs. Explain why you consider each program to be good or bad.

My Mother Never Worked

Bonnie Smith-Yackel

Bonnie Smith-Yackel's family survived on a farm during the Great Depression, a time when both the weather and the economy made the hardships of farm life nearly overwhelming. In this personal essay, Smith-Yackel uses the example of her mother's life to illustrate the unfairness in American attitudes toward women and the work they do to keep their families intact.

Words to Know

cholera   a contagious, often fatal disease, usually restricted to farm animals in this country

reciprocated   returned

sustenance   nourishment, support for life

widow's pension   the Social Security payments made to a widow, based on her deceased husband's eligibility

Getting Started

What do you think about our government's policy that homemakers are not legally workers?

"Social Security Office." (The voice answering the telephone sounds very 1
self-assured.)

"I'm calling about . . . I . . . my mother just died . . . I was told to call you 2
and see about a . . . death-benefit check, I think they call it . . ."

"I see. Was your mother on Social Security? How old was she?"   3

"Yes . . . she was seventy-eight . . ."   4

"Do you know her number?"   5

"No . . . I, ah . . . don't you have a record?"   6

"Certainly. I'll look it up. Her name?"   7

"Smith. Martha Smith. Or maybe she used Martha Ruth Smith . . . Some- 8
times she used her maiden name . . . Martha Jerabek Smith."

"If you'd care to hold on, I'll check our records—it'll be a few 9
minutes."

"Yes . . ."   10

Her love letters—to and from Daddy—were in an old box, tied with 11
ribbons and stiff, rigid-with-age leather thongs: 1918 through 1920; hers

written on stationery from the general store she had worked in full-time
and managed, single-handed, after her graduation from high school in
1913; and his, at first, on YMCA or Soldiers and Sailors Club stationery
dispensed to the fighting men of World War I. He wooed her thoroughly
and persistently by mail, and though she reciprocated all his feelings for
her, she dreaded marriage . . .

"It's so hard for me to decide when to have my wedding day—that's 12
all I've thought about these last two days. I have told you dozens of times
that I won't be afraid of married life, but when it comes down to setting
the date and then picturing myself a married woman with half a dozen
or more kids to look after, it just makes me sick . . . I am weeping right
now—I hope that some day I can look back and say how foolish I was to
dread it all."

They married in February, 1921, and began farming. Their first baby, a 13
daughter, was born in January, 1922, when my mother was 26 years old.
The second baby, a son, was born in March, 1923. They were renting farms;
my father, besides working his own fields, also was a hired man for two
other farmers. They had no capital initially, and had to gain it slowly,
working from dawn until midnight every day. My town-bred mother
learned to set hens and raise chickens, feed pigs, milk cows, plant and
harvest a garden, and can every fruit and vegetable she could scrounge.
She carried water nearly a quarter of a mile from the well to fill her wash
boilers in order to do her laundry on a scrub board. She learned to shuck
grain, feed threshers, shuck and husk corn, feed corn pickers. In September, 1925, the third baby came, and in June, 1927, the fourth child—both
daughters. In 1930, my parents had enough money to buy their own farm,
and that March they moved all their livestock and belongings themselves,
55 miles over rutted, muddy roads.

In the summer of 1930 my mother and her two eldest children reclaimed 14
a 40-acre field from Canadian thistles, by chopping them all out with a
hoe. In the other fields, when the oats and flax began to head out, the
green and blue of the crops were hidden by the bright yellow of wild
mustard. My mother walked the fields day after day, pulling each mustard plant. She raised a new flock of baby chicks—500—and she spaded
up, planted, hoed, and harvested a half-acre garden.

During the next spring their hogs caught cholera and died. No cash 15
that fall.

And in the next year the drought hit. My mother and father trudged 16
from the well to the chickens, the well to the calf pasture, the well to the
barn, and from the well to the garden. The sun came out hot and bright,
endlessly, day after day. The crops shriveled and died. They harvested
half the corn, and ground the other half, stalks and all, and fed it to the

cattle as fodder. With the price at four cents a bushel for the harvested crop, they couldn't afford to haul it into town. They burned it in the furnace for fuel that winter.

In 1934, in February, when the dust was still so thick in the Minnesota 17 air that my parents couldn't always see from the house to the barn, their fifth child—a fourth daughter—was born. My father hunted rabbits daily, and my mother stewed them, fried them, canned them, and wished out loud that she could taste hamburger once more. In the fall the shotgun brought prairie chickens, ducks, pheasant, and grouse. My mother plucked each bird, carefully reserving the breast feathers for pillows.

In the winter she sewed night after night, endlessly, begging cast-off 18 clothing from relatives, ripping apart coats, dresses, blouses, and trousers to remake them to fit her four daughters and son. Every morning and every evening she milked cows, fed pigs and calves, cared for chickens, picked eggs, cooked meals, washed dishes, scrubbed floors, and tended and loved her children. In the spring she planted a garden once more, dragging pails of water to nourish and sustain the vegetables for the family. In 1936 she lost a baby in her sixth month.

In 1937 her fifth daughter was born. She was 42 years old. In 1939 a 19 second son, and in 1941 her eighth child—and third son.

But the war had come, and prosperity of a sort. The herd of cattle had 20 grown to 30 head; she still milked morning and evening. Her garden was more than a half acre—the rains had come, and by now the Rural Electricity Administration and indoor plumbing. Still she sewed—dresses and jackets for the children, house dresses and aprons for herself, weekly patching of jeans, overalls, and denim shirts. Still she made pillows, using the feathers she had plucked, and quilts every year—intricate patterns as well as patchwork, stitched as well as tied—all necessary bedding for her family. Every scrap of cloth too small to be used in quilts was carefully saved and painstakingly sewed together in strips to make rugs. She still went out in the fields to help with the haying whenever there was a threat of rain.

In 1959 my mother's last child graduated from high school. A year 21 later the cows were sold. She still raised chickens and ducks, plucked feathers, made pillows, baked her own bread, and every year made a new quilt—now for a married child or for a grandchild. And her garden, that huge, undying symbol of sustenance, was as large and cared for as in all the years before. The canning, and now freezing, continued.

In 1969, on a June afternoon, mother and father started out for town so 22 that she could buy sugar to make rhubarb jam for a daughter who lived in Texas. The car crashed into a ditch. She was paralyzed from the waist down.

In 1970 her husband, my father, died. My mother struggled to regain 23
some competence and dignity and order in her life. At the rehabilitation
institute, where they gave her physical therapy and trained her to live
usefully in a wheelchair, the therapist told me: "She did fifteen pushups
today—fifteen! She's almost seventy-five years old! I've never known a
woman so strong!"

From her wheelchair she canned pickles, baked bread, ironed clothes, 24
wrote dozens of letters weekly to her friends and her "half dozen or more
kids," and made three patchwork housecoats and one quilt. She made
balls and balls of carpet rags—enough for five rugs. And kept all her love
letters.

"I think I've found your mother's records—Martha Ruth Smith; mar- 25
ried to Ben F. Smith?"

"Yes, that's right."   26

"Well, I see that she was getting a widow's pension . . ."   27

"Yes, that's right."   28

"Well, your mother isn't entitled to our $255 death benefit."   29

"Not entitled! But why?"   30

The voice on the telephone explains patiently: 31

"Well, you see—your mother never worked."   32

Questions About the Reading

1. Why didn't the writer's mother want to get married?
2. How old was the writer's mother when she had her eighth child? How
   old was she when she was paralyzed?
3. In her later years, how do you think Mrs. Smith's attitude had changed
   from the one she expressed in the letter quoted in paragraph 12? What
   had become of her fears of marriage?
4. Why did Mrs. Smith do the pushups, and why did she continue to
   work in her final years, when she really didn't have to?
5. Speculate about why Mrs. Smith kept her love letters. Why do you
   think the writer mentions the fact in paragraph 24?

Questions About the Writer's Strategies

1. What is the thesis in this essay? Where is it expressed?
2. How well do the writer's examples support her thesis?
3. Aside from the extended example of her mother's life, what other mode
   of development does the writer use in the essay?

4. Describe the writer's point of view in the essay. How does she use time? Does her tone change during the essay?
5. Why does the writer provide so few details about her father and the family's children?

Writing Assignments

1. Write an essay giving examples of the obstacles women have to overcome in today's society.
2. Think of an extraordinary person you know, and write an essay using examples to show what makes that person extraordinary and why he or she is important to others.
3. Write an essay using examples, or one extended example, to show what the word *sacrifice* means.

———— Connections ————

1. What connections can you make between "The Pencil Rack" and "Sports Stuff" paragraphs and their writers?
2. What connection can you make between the main idea of "My Suit" and the women described by Anna Quindlen in "Homeless"?
3. What connection can you make between the points made by the writers of "Dear Dr. Seuss" and "My Mother Never Worked"?

5

Classification
and Division

SUPPOSE YOU ARE looking over the clothing in your closet, trying to sort out the confusion. You decide to classify your clothing into several categories: good clothes for looking your best on the job; older clothes for weekends and informal occasions; and very old clothes that have some stains and holes (but that you can still use when you wash the car or the dog). You have now classified all your clothes into three orderly categories, according to their various uses. You may even want to expand your classification by adding a fourth category: clothes that are no longer useful and should be thrown away. You may have washed the dog in them once too often.

The purpose of **classification** is to take many of the same type of thing—for example, clothing, school papers, presidents, recipes, or music—and organize this large, unsorted group into categories. You may decide to classify your group of similar things, such as music, into the categories of classical, jazz, and rock and roll. Or you might classify recipes into main dishes, salads, and desserts.

You should determine your categories by a quality or characteristic that the items have in common. In each case, you will have to search for the categories that will help you classify an unsorted group of items.

In the following example, the writer classifies mothers of handicapped children in three categories of attitudes.

Classification

> Researchers note three frequent attitudes among mothers of   1
> handicapped children. The first attitude is reflected by those

Category 1: rejection

mothers who reject their child or are unable to accept the child as a handicapped person. Complex love-hate and acceptance-rejection relationships are found within this group. Rejected children not only have problems in adjusting to themselves and their disabilities, but they also have to contend with disturbed family relationships and emotional insecurity. Unfortunately, such children receive even less encouragement than the normal child and have to absorb more criticism of their behavior.

Category 2: overcompensation

A second relationship involves mothers who overcompensate in their reactions to their child and the disorder. They tend to be unrealistic, rigid, and overprotective. Often, such parents try to compensate by being overzealous and giving continuous instruction and training in the hope of establishing superior ability.

2

Category 3: acceptance

The third group consists of mothers who accept their children along with their disorders. These mothers have gained the ability to provide for the special needs of their handicapped children while continuing to live a normal life and tending to family and home as well as civic and social obligations. The child's chances are best with parents who have accepted both their child and the defects.

3

Janet W. Lerner,
Learning Disabilities, Fifth Edition

A **division** paper requires taking one thing—a man's suit, for example—and dividing it into its component parts or characteristics: jacket, pants, and vest (maybe).

Classification and division are often used together. For example, you might want to *divide* your neighborhood into sections (north, south, east, west). You might then *classify* the sections by how much noise and traffic are present in each—noisy, relatively quiet, and quiet. The purpose of classification and division is to categorize a complex whole into simple, useful categories or subdivisions.

In the following example, the writer classifies wood-sill construction into platform and balloon and then divides each class into its components.

Classification

The two general types of wood-sill construction used over the foundation wall conform either to platform or balloon framing. The box sill is commonly used in platform construction.

Category 1: components

It consists of a 2-inch or thicker wooden board, called a plate, anchored to the top of the foundation wall over a sill sealer. The plate provides support and fastening for the joists, the large boards that support the floor, and the header at the ends of the joists into which they are nailed. . . .

Category 2: components

Balloon-frame construction uses a 2-inch or thicker wood sill upon which the joists rest. The studs, which form the interior of the walls, also rest on this sill and are nailed both into the floor joists and the sill. The subfloor is laid diagonally or at right angles to the joists, and a firestop, a wood block that restricts air flow within the wall, is added between the studs at the floorline. When diagonal subfloor is used, an extra board for nailing is normally required between joists and studs at the wall lines.

Adapted from L. O. Anderson,
Wood-Frame House Construction

Whether using classification or division, you should be sure the categories are logical and appropriate, with as little overlap between categories as possible. If you are classifying chocolate desserts, you should not add vanilla custard to your list. You should also make your categories reasonably complete. You would not want to leave out chocolate cake in your classification of chocolate desserts.

If you are groping for a method of classification, you may want to try *several* ways of categorizing the same information. If you are classifying your clothes based on how attractive they look in your closet, you might sort them by color. But if you want to make the best use of the space in your closet, you might sort your clothes by type of garment—jackets, pants, shirts, and so forth. In short, you should choose your method of classifying any group of items based on the idea or point you want to support.

In the following paragraph, the writer uses classification to discuss the different kinds (categories) of book owners and clearly signals the reader to expect to read about three kinds.

Topic sentence: classification

Category 1: nonreaders

Category 2: occasional readers

Category 3: devoted readers

There are three kinds of book owners. The first has all the standard sets and best-sellers—unread, untouched. (This deluded individual owns woodpulp and ink, not books.) The second has a great many books—a few of them read through, most of them dipped into, but all of them as clean and shiny as the day they were bought. (This person would probably like to make books his own, but is restrained by a false respect for their physical appearance.) The third has a few books or many—every one of them dog-eared and dilapidated, shaken and loosened by continual use, marked and scribbled in from front to back. (This man owns books.)

Mortimer J. Adler,
"How to Mark a Book"

Notice, too, that the transitional words *first, second,* and *third* are used to identify the book owner according to how much each owner reads books. The words *first, second,* and *third* also help move the reader from one point to another. Some other transitional words and phrases that often are used in classification and division are *one, two, three;* and *for one thing, for another thing, finally.* As you write and revise your paragraphs and essays, you will want to think about using transitions to help maintain the **unity** and logical flow, or **coherence,** of your writing.

Like Adler, author of the paragraph on book owners, writers often use topic sentences such as "A safe city street has three main qualities" or "The treatment prescribed for the disease was aspirin, bed rest, and fluids" to indicate the categories that will follow in the body of a paragraph or essay. Following "A safe city street has three main qualities," the writer would explain the three specific qualities that make a city street safe. Following "The treatment prescribed for the disease was aspirin, bed rest, and fluids," the writer would probably explain the reasons for prescribing aspirin, bed rest, and fluids.

Usually, too, writers will *follow the same order* in discussing the divisions (or categories) that they used in first introducing them. For instance, suppose the topic is "Four methods can be used to cook fish: broiling, baking, poaching, and frying." Ordinarily the writer would explain (1) broiling, then (2) baking, (3) poaching, and (4) frying. Listing the categories and explaining them in order can make the composition easier for the reader to follow. In the revised student essay that follows, the three students who collaborated in writing it initially classified students as "unconcerned," "ambitious," and "inconsistent." Although they did not follow this order in their first draft, in **revising** the essay, the students changed the order to unconcerned, inconsistent, and ambitious. This order—which followed an undesirable-to-desirable pattern—was then used as the basis for the order of the paragraphs.

Thesis statement: classification	Students come in all ages, races, and genders. You can find the unconcerned, inconsistent, and ambitious in any group of students.
Category 1: unconcerned students	First, Ralph, a student in my English class, is an example of a student who has an unconcerned attitude. He has a negative outlook on life, and at times his attitude is downright hostile. He enters the classroom late and disrupts the class by slamming the door or by talking to other students while the teacher is giving a lecture. He does not care at all about the importance of an education. Ralph is more interested in watching sports, enjoying some form of entertainment, or going to parties.
	Second, an inconsistent student can be described as a person whose attitude toward education changes or varies. For example, a first grader's grades have gone up and down.

Category 2: inconsistent students

She has been in school for only two semesters, but she has shown a big change in her grades. The first semester she received an E (Excellent) in reading and an S (Satisfactory) in math. The second semester she received an N (Not satisfactory) in reading and an E in math. When asked why her reading grade dropped, she said because she no longer liked reading. After her teacher taught her how to have fun doing her math, she no longer concentrated on reading. As a result, she would only take her math homework out of her book bag when it came time to do her homework.

Category 3: ambitious students

Last, there are many ambitious students who are eager to do well in their studies and to achieve degrees. Their priorities have been set, and they have made plans for reaching their goals. Their sole ambition is to excel and succeed. Many students can be classified as ambitious. Valerie, who is pursuing a degree in nursing, is a classic example. She attends class eagerly and regularly, even though she has two children and a home to care for. Recently, she had an illness that caused her to be absent for two weeks and to fall behind in her assignments. She returned and, with her usual ambition, soon caught up with her overdue assignments and achieved Bs or better grades in her courses.

Conclusion: restatement of thesis

In conclusion, the attitudes exemplified above can be found in students of any age, race, or gender. Whether they are attending grade school, high school, or college, students can be found who are unconcerned, inconsistent, or ambitious.

As with any piece of writing, a useful practice is to jot down many ideas and make rough lists as part of your **brainstorming** and prewriting. Do not skimp on your planning, and do expect to revise—perhaps several times—to produce a clear, understandable, and effective paragraph or essay.

The Three New Yorks

E. B. White

*There is, of course, only one New York. But our largest city presents a
different face to each person who experiences it. E. B. White was a student of the city. In this paragraph, he describes three ways of looking at
New York and suggests these are also three ways of using New York—to
live, to work, and to dream.*

Words to Know

Consolidated Edison Company　the electric power company
　　serving most of New York City
continuity　uninterrupted existence over a long period
deportment　behavior, conduct
solidarity　wholeness, unity
turbulence　agitation, disturbance

Getting Started

What are your thoughts about the different groups of people who
inhabit your hometown?

There are roughly three New Yorks. There is, first, the New York of the
man or woman who was born here, who takes the city for granted and
accepts its size and its turbulence as natural and inevitable. Second, there
is the New York of the commuter—the city that is devoured by locusts
each day and spat out each night. Third, there is the New York of the
person who was born somewhere else and came to New York in quest of
something. Of these three trembling cities the greatest is the last—the
city of final destination, the city that is a goal. It is this third city that
accounts for New York's high-strung disposition, its poetical deportment,
its dedication to the arts, and its incomparable achievements. Commut-
ers give the city its tidal restlessness, natives give it solidarity and continuity, but the settlers give it passion. And whether it is a farmer arriving
from Italy to set up a small grocery store in a slum, or a young girl arriving from a small town in Mississippi to escape the indignity of being
observed by her neighbors, or a boy arriving from the Corn Belt with a
manuscript in his suitcase and a pain in his heart, it makes no difference:
each embraces New York with the intense excitement of first love, each

absorbs New York with the fresh eyes of an adventurer, each generates heat and light to dwarf the Consolidated Edison Company.

Questions About the Reading

1. Which of the New Yorks does White think is the greatest? Why? Support your answer with statements from the paragraph.
2. What do the people who make up the first New York contribute to it? Which statements tell you?
3. What is the meaning of the essay's final clause ("each generates heat")?
4. Do you think all cities and towns have different groups of people who view them differently? Why or why not?
5. White is writing about the city of New York, but what about your town or city? According to White's classification, how would you describe your feelings about the place?

Questions About the Writer's Strategies

1. Does the paragraph have a topic sentence? If so, identify it. If not, state the topic in a sentence of your own.
2. What transitions does White use to help the reader identify the relation of ideas?
3. Identify the metaphor in the essay's third sentence and interpret what it means.
4. Is the paragraph developed by classification, division, or both?

Writing Assignments

1. Write a paragraph in which you classify the different groups of people in the town where you grew up.
2. Write a paragraph in which you identify and classify at least three groups of people in your school or workplace.
3. Suppose you are getting ready to do your laundry. Write a paragraph in which you explain how you sort the clothes for washing.

Fans

Paul Gallico

Paul Gallico is known for his sports writing and for his books, including Mrs. 'Arris Goes to New York *and* The Snow Goose. *In the following paragraph he classifies sports fans.*

Words to Know

aristocratic   upper-class
commiseration   sympathy
incandescents   very bright, shining lights
lurks   lies in wait

Getting Started

How would you classify the people who attend a rock concert, a musical play, a symphony, and an opera performance?

The fight crowd is a beast that lurks in the darkness behind the fringe of white light shed over the first six rows by the incandescents atop the ring, and is not to be trusted with pop bottles or other hardware. The tennis crowd is always preening and shushing itself. The golf crowd is the most unwieldy and most sympathetic, and is the only horde given to mass production of that absurd noise written generally as "tsk tsk tsk tsk," and made between tongue and teeth with head-waggings to denote extreme commiseration. The baseball crowd is the most hysterical, the football crowd the best-natured and the polo crowd the most aristocratic. Racing crowds are the most restless, wrestling crowds the most tolerant, and soccer crowds the most easily incitable to riot and disorder. Every sports crowd takes on the characteristics of the individuals who compose it. Each has its particular note of hysteria, its own little cruelties, mannerisms, and bad mannerisms, its own code of sportsmanship and its own method of expressing its emotions.

Questions About the Reading

1. What are the classifications of sports fans that the writer discusses?
2. Which crowd is the most likely to be disorderly?

3. What determines the characteristics of each sports crowd?
4. What do you think happens to make a golf crowd go "tsk tsk tsk tsk" to show "extreme commiseration"?
5. Which crowd is the most hysterical?

Questions About the Writer's Strategies

1. What is the main idea (topic) of the paragraph?
2. Which sentence(s) state the topic of the paragraph?
3. Where are the topic sentence(s) located in the paragraph?
4. What is the metaphor the writer uses for the fight crowd?
5. What appears to determine the order in which the writer discusses the different crowds? If you were writing the paragraph, would you use a different order? If so, explain how you might change the order.

Writing Assignments

1. Write a paragraph in which you classify the crowds at three different musical events.
2. Write a paragraph in which you classify the cars in a parking lot.

Wordstruck

Robert MacNeil

Have you ever considered how language is like clothing? The noted writer and television journalist Robert MacNeil has done just that. In this paragraph from his memoir, Wordstruck, *MacNeil compares language to clothing, from the dark-suited formal to the barest of informalities.*

Getting Started

Why do you speak differently in different circumstances?

It fascinates me how differently we all speak in different circumstances. We have levels of formality, as in our clothing. There are very formal occasions, often requiring written English: the job application or the letter to the editor—the darksuit, serious-tie language, with everything pressed and the lint brushed off. There is our less formal out-in-the-world language—a more comfortable suit, but still respectable. There is language for close friends in the evenings, on weekends—bluejeans-and-sweat-shirt language, when it's good to get the tie off. There is family language, even more relaxed, full of grammatical short cuts, family slang, echoes of old jokes that have become intimate shorthand—the language of pyjamas and uncombed hair. Finally, there is the language with no clothes on; the talk of couples—murmurs, sighs, grunts—language at its least self-conscious, open, vulnerable, and primitive.

Questions About the Reading

1. What are the various levels of formality MacNeil describes?
2. What are some of the colorful images and examples MacNeil uses to help his reader visualize the different levels?
3. Do you agree or disagree with the writer's main idea in this paragraph?
4. What are some concrete examples for each level of formality the writer describes?

Questions About the Writer's Strategies

1. Is there a topic sentence in this paragraph? If so, where is it? If not, state the main idea in a sentence of your own.
2. Is this a paragraph of classification, division, or both? Support your answer with examples from the paragraph.
3. Does the writer use any other modes of development in this paragraph? If so, what are they and where in the paragraph are they used?
4. MacNeil uses an extended metaphor to help his readers understand the levels of formality he is describing. What is the metaphor and how does it help you understand his distinctions?

Writing Assignments

1. Imagine you are writing about yourself for a job interview, writing to exchange news with an old friend, and writing your sister to ask for a favor. Using three different levels of formality, write three separate paragraphs.
2. Write a paragraph in which you classify the different books you read or movies you enjoy. Be sure to include examples, details, or images that help your reader understand exactly what you mean.

From Cakewalks to Concert Halls

Thomas L. Morgan and William Barlow

Ragtime has been enormously popular since it appeared on the American music scene near the end of the nineteenth century. Excerpted from the book From Cakewalks to Concert Halls, *a chronicle of the triumphant African-American voice in the history of American music, the following paragraph focuses on the reasons for the widespread appeal of ragtime.*

Words to Know

affirmation a positive statement

cakewalk a strutting dance or the music for the dance

parody an artistic work that mimics a characteristic style, holding it up to ridicule

transposed transferred from one place to another

trope the use of an expression in a different sense from that which properly belongs to it

Getting Started

Why do you think music appeals to a broad range of people?

Ragtime's complex historical legacy was perhaps a major reason for its widespread appeal among both blacks and whites. First and foremost, it was a dance music which drew on both European and African traditions. Second, ragtime was a style grounded in an ongoing, cross-cultural, racial parody: the slaves' parody of their masters, blackface minstrels' trope of the slaves' parody, black minstrels' trope of the blackface parody, and so on. In addition, ragtime was a rural folk music transposed to an urban and industrial context, where its machine-like rhythms became an expression of the lost innocence of bygone days and ways. And finally, as a novel popular music created by the first generation of African Americans born after slavery, ragtime represented an affirmation of their newly experienced freedoms and an optimistic vision of the future.

Questions About the Reading

1. According to the writers, what was the foremost reason for the widespread appeal of ragtime?

2. According to the writers, what is an "ongoing, cross-cultural, racial parody"?
3. How was ragtime an expression of the "lost innocence of bygone days"? What other kinds of music do you think express a sense of lost innocence? How do they do that?
4. What did ragtime represent to the first generation of African-Americans born after slavery?

Questions About the Writers' Strategies

1. Is there a topic sentence in this paragraph? If so, where is it? If not, state the main idea in a sentence of your own.
2. Is this a paragraph of classification, division, or both? Support your answer with examples from the paragraph.
3. Do the writers use any other modes of development in this paragraph? If so, what are they and where in the paragraph are they used?
4. What transitions do the writers use to help the reader understand the relationship between the ideas in this paragraph?

Writing Assignments

1. Write a paragraph in which you classify the different reasons you think a certain kind of music is popular. Support your reasons with examples and details.
2. Choose an activity or hobby you enjoy. For example, you might choose playing a sport or practicing a musical instrument. Write a paragraph in which you classify the different reasons you enjoy that activity.

The ABCs of the U.S.A.

Michael Dobbs

*Michael Dobbs, a Briton, finds America a strange experience and classi-
fies American characteristics—from the open display of "Ambition" to
the invention of "Zillion." ("The ABCs of the U.S.A." by Michael Dobbs,
The Washington Post, June 21, 1987. © 1987, The Washington Post.
Reprinted with permission.)*

Words to Know

arteriosclerosis hardening or thickening of the arteries
bemused confused, puzzled
Hechinger garden superstore company located in the
   Washington, D.C., area
injunction directive or order
la linea Italiana literally, the Italian line
la queue Française literally, the French line
queue line of people
visa authorization to visit and travel within a country

Getting Started

Do you think there are characteristics that are unique to the American people?

America can be a strange experience for a foreigner. My wife and I ar- 1
rived in the United States in January after seven years overseas—four in
France, three in Poland. From the jumble of first impressions, we com-
piled an A-to-Z explanation of why America can be such a foreign country to those who arrive here from Europe.

I should explain at the outset that I am from Britain, but my Florida- 2
born wife, Lisa, is as American as apple pie. In this alphabet, however, A
does not stand for apple pie. It stands for:

Ambition. In the Old World, people are taught to hide it. An exception 3
was Macbeth who (Shakespeare tells us) nurtured "an ambition that o'er-
leaps itself and falls on the other side"—and look what happened to him.
Here, it seems quite proper to announce that you are after the boss's job
or want to make a million dollars by the age of 30.

Breakfast. The American habit of conducting business at breakfast has 4
reached Europe, but I doubt that it will ever really catch on. In France
and Britain, breakfast is too much a family affair. Here, it has become part
of the power game.

Credit cards. You really can't leave home without them. It is interesting, 5
and somewhat infuriating, to discover that bad credit is better than no
credit at all: I was refused a Visa card on the grounds that I did not have
a credit profile. Speaking of credit cards, we are bemused by the relatively new fad of destroying the carbons. Back in Europe, people prefer
to keep their fingers clean.

Dreams. The American Dream, dented though it's been recently, is still 6
very much alive. Dreaming great dreams is what keeps American society
going—from the waitress who wants to become a car dealer to the street
kid who wants to become a basketball star. Europeans dream dreams too,
but don't seem to believe in them so much. See *Ambition.*

Exercise. A couple of years ago, I came to Washington in the slip-stream 7
of French President François Mitterrand. A cheer went up from the French
press corps as our bus passed a fitness center—and we saw body-
conscious Americans bending, stretching and leaping from side to side.
America's fetish for fitness amuses—and puzzles—Europeans.

First names. In Europe, there is a natural and orderly progression from 8
the use of last names to the use of first names. Here, it's first names at first
sight. This can create confusion. I have one acquaintance who calls me
Bill—and I am not quite sure how to correct him.

Gadgets. These can be addictive. It is difficult to imagine now how we 9
survived for so long without the cruise control, the automatic ice dis-
penser, the microwave and the cordless telephone.

Hechinger. If I were in charge of arranging the programs of visiting del- 10
egations from communist countries, I would include a compulsory visit
to Hechinger. We know Polish farmers who have to wait months to buy
fencing for their livestock. Their eyes would pop out of their heads in this
temple of American capitalism.

Insurance. Americans have a policy to cover every risk, both conceiv- 11
able and inconceivable. So far, we have refused rental reimbursement insurance for our car, death insurance for our mortgage and supplemen-
tary title insurance for our house. It gives us a feeling of living dangerously.

Junk food. Anyone who wants to understand why Americans suffer from 12
higher rates of cancer and arteriosclerosis only has to look at what they
eat.

Ketchup. I had to come to America to discover that it can be eaten with 13
anything—from french fries to French cheese.

Lines. American lines—beginning with the yellow line at immigration 14
control—are the most orderly and organized in the world. The British
queue, once internationally renowned, has begun to fray at the edges in
recent years. *La queue Française* was never very impressive, and *la linea
Italiana* is simply a mob.

Money. In Europe, money is something that everybody likes to have— 15
but is careful not to flaunt. Unless it has been in the family for several
generations, there is often an assumption that it has been acquired dis-
honestly. In America, the green justifies the means.

No smoking. No longer just a polite injunction in America, almost an 16
evangelical campaign. Nobody would dare ask a Frenchman to put out
his Gauloises in a restaurant.

Ollie North. What other major western democracy would allow a lieu- 17
tenant colonel to make foreign policy? A hero for some, a traitor for others, Ollie (see *First names*) is a wonderful example of the American go-
for-it attitude that both awes and alarms foreigners.

Patriotism. Exists everywhere, of course, but the American version is 18
brasher, louder, and more self-conscious than the European. In Britain, it
is taken for granted that a citizen or politician loves his country. Here, he
is expected to prove it.

Quiet. American cities are quieter than European cities—thanks to noise 19
controls on automobiles and the recent spate of environmental legislation. This was a major surprise for someone brought up to assume that
America was a noisy place.

Religion. It's difficult, somehow, to imagine an English version of Jim 20
and Tammy Bakker. When my parents came to visit recently, they were
startled at the sight of a fire-breathing Jimmy Swaggart denouncing the
Bakkers on live TV. That's not the kind of way they behave in our dear
old Church of England.

Sales. Ever since arriving in Washington, we have been hurrying to 21
take advantage of this week's unrepeatable *offer*—only to discover that it
is usually repeated next week. We are just catching on that there is always an excuse for a sale.

Television. How grown-ups can watch game shows and sitcoms at 11 22
A.M. mystifies me—but the national habit, day or night, is contagious. I
recently found myself nodding in full agreement with a professional type
who was saying that American kids watch too much television. It was
only later that I realized that I was watching him say this on television.

Ulcers. See *Work.*   23

Visas. Americans don't need visas to visit Britain (or most European 24
countries, for that matter). To get my entry permit for the United States, I
had to sign a document promising that I would not overthrow the government by force, had never been a member of the Communist Party, and
was not wanted for war crimes. I had to provide details of my affiliation
to labor unions as well as affidavits from four countries stating that I had
no criminal record. All this for cruise control and a cordless telephone.

Work. A leading Polish sociologist, Jan Szczepanski, once told me that 25
many Poles imagine that they will become rich simply by emigrating to

America. He tries to persuade whoever will listen that America became a rich society through work, work and more work. It is still true.

X-rated movies. We have them in Europe too, but not on motel room 26 TVs and not in most small towns.

Yuppies. The European counterpart remains a pale shadow of the all- 27 American original. The animal seems more driven, more ubiquitous on this side of the Atlantic.

Zillion. What other nation would have invented a number that is infi- 28 nitely more than a billion? America may not always be the best, but it is certainly the biggest.

Questions About the Reading

1. How long had the writer lived overseas before arriving in the United States?
2. What is the writer's nationality?
3. How does the writer feel about Americans' use of first names?
4. What is the writer's opinion of what Americans eat?
5. How does the European attitude toward money differ from the American attitude?

Questions About the Writer's Strategies

1. What is the tone of the essay? How does the writer achieve it?
2. What is the thesis of the essay?
3. What is the point of view in person of the essay? Is it consistent throughout the essay? If not, identify the paragraphs in which it differs.
4. In addition to classifying American characteristics, what other strategies does the writer use to support his thesis?

Writing Assignments

1. Write an essay in which you classify and explain the characteristics of a city you have visited.

2. Visit your college web site and the sites of several other colleges. Write an essay in which you classify the sites based on their effectiveness in explaining the academic programs the colleges offer. Include a list of the web site addresses you use.
3. *Working Together* Join with some classmates to write an essay in which you classify and explain the characteristics that are common either to people in a particular profession or to the students in your school.

Voice Mail and Fire Ants

Edward Tenner

A writer about technology, Edward Tenner believes that life has not been made easier nor can tasks be done faster by our ingenuity and technology. Indeed, Tenner maintains we have suffered unintended consequences.

Words to Know

defoliation   loss of leaves

ingenuity   cleverness, inventive skill

Isaac Newton   English mathematician and natural philosopher, famous for discovering the law of gravity

phenomenon   unique or unusual event or incident

Rube Goldberg   American cartoonist who drew complicated machines or inventions that do simple tasks

Getting Started

Are there some inventions that have complicated your life instead of made it easier?

Why do the seats get smaller as the airplanes get larger? Why does 1 voice mail seem to double the time to complete a telephone call? Why do filter-tip cigarettes often fail to reduce nicotine intake? Why has the leisure society gone the way of the leisure suit?

The world seems to be getting even with mankind, twisting our clev- 2 erness against us. Or we may be unconsciously twisting it ourselves. This is not a new phenomenon, but technology has magnified it. Wherever we look we face unintended consequences of mechanical, chemical, medical, social and financial ingenuity. They are revenge effects, and they are less the malignant ironies of a spiteful world than the results of a lack of human foresight. They fall into five major categories: repeating, recomplicating, recongesting, regenerating and rearranging.

Repeating occurs when a task is made easier or faster but becomes re- 3 quired more often. In the 1980s, companies spent billions of dollars on personal computers, yet in 1989 the service sector showed its smallest productivity growth of the postwar era. For example, when making a spreadsheet was laborious, people did it as seldom and as cautiously as possible. Computers have simplified them, but bosses demand them more often.

Recomplicating is another consequence of computer simplification. 4 Touch-tone telephones were introduced to increase dialing speed, but now the time saved by punching has been consumed by systems built to take advantage of it. Combining the telephone number, the carrier access code and credit card number, a call may require thirty digits—more if a voice mail machine answers.

In *recongesting*, an updated function becomes slower and less comfort- 5 able than the original. Technological change opens new frontiers only to clog them up again. Planners dreamed of the automobile-based suburb as an antidote to the crowding of cities and the power of railroads and urban landlords. But rapid traffic flow has turned out to be unrealistic, as cars inch down roads bumper to bumper.

The historian and philosopher Ivan Illich estimates that the average 6 American spends sixteen hundred hours driving or working to support transportation costs "to cover a year total of six thousand miles, four miles per hour." He says, "This is just as fast as a pedestrian and slower than a bicycle."

Regenerating appears after a problem seems to have been solved. In- 7 stead, the solution turns out to have revived or amplified the problem.

Pest control regenerates pests. In the 1950s and 1960s, the pesticides 8 heptachlor and Mirex killed the natural predators of fire ants, which then moved into their rivals' territory. DDT devastated wasps, the natural predators of Malaysian caterpillars, which flourished and caused large-scale defoliation.

Finally, *rearranging* is the revenge effect that delays a problem or moves 9 it physically, usually magnifying its effect. The geologist W. Barclay Kamb, in John McPhee's *The Control of Nature,* described efforts to channel the flow of debris from the San Gabriel Mountains in California: "You're not changing the source of the sediment. Those cribworks are less strong than nature's own constructs. . . . Sooner or later, a flood will wipe out those small dams and scatter the debris. Everything you store might come out in one event."

Likewise, suppressing forest fires builds up combustible materials for 10 even larger conflagrations. And disaster control and relief risk increasing casualties by encouraging occupation of unsafe areas.

The existence of revenge effects should not end the pursuit of conve- 11 nience and increased productivity. We should bear in mind that change never offers complete solutions, and be prepared to deal with its nega-tive consequences. Innovation involves both imperfect machines and unpredictable people. Revenge effects don't mean that progress is impossible, only that in planning for it we must look more to Rube Goldberg than to Isaac Newton.

Questions About the Reading

1. What does the writer mean by the "revenge effect"?
2. When does the writer say "repeating" occurs?
3. What causes "recomplicating"?
4. What revenge effect occurs when a function becomes slower and less comfortable?
5. What does the writer say has resulted from the use of pesticides?
6. Does the writer think the consequences of innovation should cause us to "end the pursuit of convenience and increased productivity"?

Questions About the Writer's Strategies

1. Is the essay objective, subjective, or both? Give examples to support your answer.
2. What is the point of view in person and tone of the essay?
3. What strategies does the writer use in addition to classification?
4. What is the thesis of the essay? State it in your own words.

Writing Assignments

1. Write an essay in which you classify the ways in which an invention has complicated your life or made life for others more difficult.
2. Write an essay in which you classify the ways in which an invention or a discovery has made your life easier or more pleasant.

Eggs, Twinkies and Ethnic Stereotypes

Jeanne Park

Jeanne Park, an Asian-American, found herself labeled as intelligent while in elementary school. In high school, she learned her intelligence did not set her apart in the classroom, but that outside the classroom her ethnic background did.

Words to Know

condescending   patronizing
metamorphose   change in nature

Getting Started

At lunchtime, do the students at your school segregate themselves according to their racial or ethnic background?

Who am I?   1

For Asian-American students, the answer is a diligent, hardworking   2
and intelligent young person. But living up to this reputation has secretly haunted me.

The labeling starts in elementary school. It's not uncommon for a teacher   3
to remark, "You're Asian, you're supposed to do well in math." The underlying message is, "You're Asian and you're supposed to be smarter."

Not to say being labeled intelligent isn't flattering, because it is, or not   4
to deny that basking in the limelight of being top of my class isn't ego-boosting, because frankly it is. But at a certain point, the pressure became crushing. I felt as if doing poorly on my next spelling quiz would stain the exalted reputation of all Asian students forever.

So I continued to be an academic overachiever, as were my friends. By   5
junior high school I started to believe I was indeed smarter. I became condescending toward non-Asians. I was a bigot; all my friends were Asians. The thought of intermingling occurred rarely if ever.

My elitist opinion of Asian students changed, however, in high school.   6
As a student at what is considered one of the nation's most competitive science and math schools, I found that being on top is no longer an easy feat.

I quickly learned that Asian students were not smarter. How could I   7
ever have believed such a thing? All around me are intelligent, ambitious
people who are not only Asian but white, black and Hispanic.

Superiority complexes aside, the problem of social segregation still   8
exists in the schools. With a few exceptions, each race socializes only with
its "own kind." Students see one another in the classroom, but outside
the classroom there remains distinct segregation.

Racist lingo abounds. An Asian student who socializes only with other   9
Asians is believed to be an Asian Supremacist or, at the very least, arrogant and closed off. Yet an Asian student who socializes only with whites
is called a "twinkie," one who is yellow on the outside but white on the
inside.

A white teenager who socializes only with whites is thought of as preju- 10
diced, yet one who socializes with Asians is considered an "egg," white
on the outside and yellow on the inside.

These culinary classifications go on endlessly, needless to say, leaving 11
many confused, and leaving many more fearful than ever of social ex-
perimentation. Because the stereotypes are accepted almost unanimously,
they are rarely challenged. Many develop harmful stereotypes of entire
races. We label people before we even know them.

Labels learned at a young age later metamorphose into more visible 12
acts of racism. For example, my parents once accused and ultimately fired
a Puerto Rican cashier, believing she had stolen $200 from the register at
their grocery story. They later learned it was a mistake. An Asian shopkeeper nearby once beat a young Hispanic youth who worked there with
a baseball bat because he believed the boy to be lazy and dishonest.

We all hold misleading stereotypes of people that limit us as individu- 13
als in that we cheat ourselves out of the benefits different cultures can
contribute. We can grow and learn from each culture whether it be Chinese, Korean or African-American.

Just recently some Asian boys in my neighborhood were attacked by a 14
group of young white boys who have christened themselves the Master
Race. Rather than being angered by this act, I feel pity for this generation
that lives in a state of bigotry.

It may be too late for our parents' generation to accept that each per- 15
son can only be judged for the characteristics that set him or her apart as
an individual. We, however, can do better.

Questions About the Reading

1. How did it affect the writer to be labeled as intelligent?
2. What did the writer learn about other students when she went to the competitive high school?
3. What is an Asian Supremacist? A "twinkie"? An "egg"?
4. According to the writer, how do the culinary classifications influence people's behavior?
5. According to the writer, how should we judge people?

Questions About the Writer's Strategies

1. Is the essay developed using classification or using division?
2. What mode of development does the writer use in paragraph 4?
3. What is the topic of paragraph 12? What mode of development does the writer use in the paragraph?
4. What are some transitional words the writer uses?
5. What is the thesis of the essay? Is it stated or implied?
6. Is the essay objective, subjective, or both?

Writing Assignments

1. Write an essay in which you classify the people in your neighborhood according to the cars they drive.
2. Write an essay in which you classify the students in your school according to what they eat for lunch.
3. Write an essay in which you divide a house, a car, or an item of clothing into its parts.

"Ever Et Raw Meat?"

Stephen King

Stephen King, best known for such horror novels and movies as Carrie *and* Misery, *classifies readers according to the questions they ask him.*

Words to Know

blasphemous   irreverent, profane
E. E. Cummings   American poet known for experimenting with form, punctuation, spelling, and syntax in his poetry
enumerate   name one by one
flagellate   beat, whip
kleptomaniac   a person who has an impulse or compulsion to steal
laconic   concise expression; expressed in few words
modicum   small amount
self-abnegation   self-denial, giving up of one's rights
Zen   Buddhist sect

Getting Started

What questions would you like to ask Stephen King?

It seems to me that, in the minds of readers, writers actually exist to serve two purposes, and the more important may not be the writing of books and stories. The primary function of writers, it seems, is to answer readers' questions. These fall into three categories. The third is the one that fascinates me most, but I'll identify the other two first.

The One-of-a-Kind Question

Each day's mail brings a few of these. Often they reflect the writer's field of interest—history, horror, romance, the American West, outer space, big business. The only thing they have in common is their uniqueness. Novelists are frequently asked where they get their ideas (see category No. 2), but writers must wonder where this relentless curiosity, these really strange questions, come from.

There was, for instance, the young woman who wrote to me from a penal institution in Minnesota. She informed me she was a kleptomaniac. She further informed me that I was her favorite writer, and she had stolen every one of my books she could get her hands on. "But after I stole *Different Seasons* from the library and read it, I felt moved to send it back," she wrote. "Do you think this means you wrote this one the best?" After due consideration, I decided that reform on the part of the reader has nothing to do with artistic merit. I came close to writing back to find out if she had stolen *Misery* yet but decided I ought to just keep my mouth shut.

From Bill V. in North Carolina: "I see you have a beard. Are you morbid of razors?"   4

From Carol K. in Hawaii: "Will you soon write of pimples or some other facial blemish?"   5

From Don G., no address (and a blurry postmark): "Why do you keep up this disgusting mother worship when anyone with any sense knows a MAN has no use to his mother once he is weaned?"   6

From Raymond R. in Mississippi: "Ever et raw meat?" (It's the laconic ones like this that really get me.)   7

I have been asked if I beat my children and/or my wife. I have been asked to parties in places I have never been and hope never to go. I was once asked to give away the bride at a wedding, and one young woman sent me an ounce of pot, with the attached question: "This is where I get my inspiration—where do you get yours?" Actually, mine usually comes in envelopes—the kind through which you can view your name and address printed by a computer—that arrive at the end of every month.   8

My favorite question of this type, from Anchorage, asked simply: "How could you write such a why?" Unsigned. If E. E. Cummings were still alive, I'd try to find out if he'd moved to the Big North.   9

The Old Standards

These are the questions writers dream of answering when they are collecting rejection slips, and the ones they tire of quickest once they start to publish. In other words, they are the questions that come up without fail in every dull interview the writer has ever given or will ever give. I'll enumerate a few of them: 10

Where do you get your ideas? (I get mine in Utica.)   11

How do you get an agent? (Sell your soul to the Devil.)   12

Do you have to know somebody to get published? (Yes; in fact, it helps to grovel, toady, and be willing to perform twisted acts of sexual depravity at a moment's notice, and in public if necessary.)   13

How do you start a novel? (I usually start by writing the number 1 in the upper right-hand corner of a clean sheet of paper.)   14

How do you write best sellers? (Same way you get an agent.)   15

How do you sell your book to the movies? (Tell them they don't want 16
it.)

What time of day do you write? (It doesn't matter; if I don't keep busy 17
enough, the time inevitably comes.)

Do you ever run out of ideas? (Does a bear defecate in the woods?)   18

Who is your favorite writer? (Anyone who writes stories I would have 19
written had I thought of them first.)

There are others, but they're pretty boring, so let us march on.   20

The Real Weirdies

Here I am, bopping down the street, on my morning walk, when some 21
guy pulls over in his pickup truck or just happens to walk by and says,
"Hi, Steve! Writing any good books lately?" I have an answer for this;
I've developed it over the years out of pure necessity. I say, "I'm taking
some time off." I say that even if I'm working like mad, thundering down
homestretch on a book. The reason why I say this is because no other
answer seems to fit. Believe me, I know. In the course of the trial and
error that has finally resulted in "I'm taking some time off," I have discarded about 500 other answers.

Having an answer for "You writing any good books lately?" is a good 22
thing, but I'd be lying if I said it solves the problem of *what the question
means.* It is this inability on my part to make sense of this odd query,
which reminds me of that Zen riddle—"Why is a mouse when it runs?"—
that leaves me feeling mentally shaken and impotent. You see, it isn't just
one question; it is a *bundle* of questions, cunningly wrapped up in one
package. It's like that old favorite, "Are you still beating your wife?"

If I answer in the affirmative, it means I may have written—how many 23
books? two? four?—(all of them good) in the last—how long? Well, how
long is "lately"? It could mean I wrote maybe three good books just last
week, or maybe two *on this very walk up to Bangor International Airport and
back!* On the other hand, if I say no, what does *that* mean? I wrote three or
four *bad* books in the last "lately" (surely "lately" can be no longer than a
month, six weeks at the outside)?

Or here I am, signing books at the Betts' Bookstore or B. Dalton's in the 24
local consumer factory (nicknamed "the mall"). This is something I do
twice a year, and it serves much the same purpose as those little bundles
of twigs religious people in the Middle Ages used to braid into whips
and flagellate themselves with. During the course of this exercise in mad-
ness and self-abnegation, at least a dozen people will approach the little
coffee table where I sit behind a barrier of books and ask brightly, "Don't
you wish you had a rubber stamp?"

I have an answer to this one, too, an answer that has been developed 25 over the years in a trial-and-error method similar to "I'm taking some time off." The answer to the rubber-stamp questions is: "No, I don't mind."

Never mind if I really do or don't (this time it's my own motivations I 26 want to skip over, you'll notice); the question is, Why does such an illogical query occur to so many people? My signature is actually stamped on the covers of several of my books, but people seem just as eager to get these signed as those that aren't so stamped. Would these questioners stand in line for the privilege of watching me slam a rubber stamp down on the title page of *The Shining* or *Pet Sematary?* I don't think they would.

If you still don't sense something peculiar in these questions, this one 27 might help convince you. I'm sitting in the cafe around the corner from my house, grabbing a little lunch by myself and reading a book (reading at the table is one of the few bad habits acquired in my youth that I have nobly resisted giving up) until a customer or maybe even a waitress sidles up and asks, "How come you're not reading one of your own books"?

This hasn't happened just once, or even occasionally; it happens *a lot.* 28 The computer-generated answer to this question usually gains a chuckle, although it is nothing but the pure, logical and apparent truth. "I know how they all come out," I say. End of exchange. Back to lunch, with only a pause to wonder why people assume you want to read what you wrote, rewrote, read again following the obligatory editorial conference and yet again during the process of correcting the mistakes that a good copy editor always prods, screaming, from their hiding places (I once heard a crime writer suggest that God could have used a copy editor, and while I find the notion slightly blasphemous, I tend to agree).

And then people sometimes ask in that chatty, let's-strike-up-a- 29 conversation way people have, "How long does it take you to write a book?" Perfectly reasonable question—at least until you try to answer it and discover there *is* no answer. This time the computer-generated answer is a total falsehood, but it at least serves the purpose of advancing the conversation to some more discussable topic. "Usually about nine months," I say, "the same length of time it takes to make a baby." This satisfies everyone but me. I know that nine months is just an average, and probably a completely fictional one at that. It ignores *The Running Man* (published under the name Richard Bachman), which was written in four days during a snowy February vacation when I was teaching high school. It also ignores *It* and my latest, *The Tommyknockers. It* is over 1,000 pages long and took four years to write. *The Tommyknockers* is 400 pages shorter but took five years to write.

Do I mind these questions? Yes . . . and no. Anyone minds questions 30 that have no real answers and thus expose the fellow being questioned to be not a real doctor but a sort of witch doctor. But no one—at least no one with a modicum of simple human kindness—resents questions from people who honestly want answers. And now and then someone will ask a really interesting question, like, Do you write in the nude? The answer— not generated by computer—is: I don't think I ever have, but if it works, I'm willing to try it.

Questions About the Reading

1. According to King, what seems to be the primary function of writers?
2. What do the one-of-a-kind questions have in common?
3. What does the writer mean when he says he gets his inspiration from what "comes in envelopes—the kind through which you can view your name and address printed by computer—that arrive at the end of every month"?
4. What are the writer's definitions of "old standards" and "real weirdies"?
5. What are the four "real weirdies" the writer has been asked?

Questions About the Writer's Strategies

1. What are the different modes of development that the writer uses in the essay?
2. What is the point of view in person and time? Are they consistent throughout the essay?
3. What is the tone of the essay? Is it consistent throughout?
4. What organizational pattern and modes of development does the writer use in describing "one-of-a-kind questions" and "old standards"?
5. What organizational pattern does the writer use in describing "real weirdies"?

Writing Assignments

1. Choose three or more famous writers and write an essay about the questions you would like to ask them.
2. *Working Together*   Join with some classmates to write an essay about the questions you would like to ask Babe Ruth, Michael Jordan, and Martina Navratilova.

Caution: Bumpy Road Ahead

Jeffrey Cummings (student)

Jeffrey Cummings makes an excellent point about college students need-ing to be taught how to handle some of the practical realities of life: credit, personal budgeting, and purchasing. Cummings decided that such knowl-edge was useful while he was still a student at California State Univer-sity in Bakersfield.

Word to Know

strategy   plan

Getting Started

Should colleges offer courses in personal financial planning?

Students graduating from colleges today are not fully prepared to deal 1 with the "real world." It is my belief that college students need to be taught more skills and information to enable them to meet the challenges that face everyone in daily life. The areas in which students need training are playing the credit game, planning their personal financial strategy, and consumer awareness.

Learning how to obtain and use credit is probably the most valuable 2 knowledge a young person can have. Credit is a dangerous tool that can be of tremendous help if it is handled with caution. Having credit can enable people to obtain material necessities before they have the money to purchase them outright. But unfortunately, many, many young people get carried away with their handy plastic cards and awake one day to find they are in serious financial debt. Learning how to use credit prop-erly can be a very difficult and painful lesson indeed.

Of equal importance is learning how to plan a personal budget. People 3 have to know how to control money; otherwise, it can control them. Stu-dents should leave college knowing how to allocate their money for liv-ing expenses, insurance, savings, and so forth in order to avoid the "Oh, no! I'm flat broke and I don't get paid again for two weeks!" anxiety syn-drome.

Along with learning about credit and personal financial planning, 4 graduating college students should be trained as consumers. The con-sumer market today is flooded with a variety of products and services of varying quality and prices. A young person entering the "real world" is suddenly faced with agonizing decisions about which product to buy or whose services to engage. He is usually unaware of such things as return policies, guarantees, or repair procedures. Information of this sort is vital knowledge to everyday living.

For a newly graduated college student, the "real world" can be a scary 5 place to be when he or she is faced with such issues as handling credit, planning a budget, or knowing what to look for when making a purchase and whom to purchase it from. Entering this "real world" could be made less traumatic if persons were educated in dealing with these areas of daily life. What better place to accomplish this than in college?

Questions About the Reading

1. Cummings says that students need training in three areas. What are the three areas?
2. Why does Cummings say young people need to learn how to handle credit?
3. Why should students learn how to plan a personal budget?

Questions About the Writer's Strategies

1. Does Cummings state the thesis of the essay? If so, identify the sentence(s).
2. Identify the paragraphs that develop the thesis.
3. What is the topic of paragraph 2? Of paragraph 3? Of paragraph 4?
4. Cummings uses some transitions to link the body paragraphs. What are they?
5. What is the dominant mode of development in the essay?

Writing Assignments

1. Suppose you have been asked to organize a course for your fellow students on obtaining and using credit and credit cards. Identify and explain the topics you would cover in the course.
2. Write an essay in which you identify and explain the topics you would cover in a course on preparing and managing personal budgets.
3. *Working Together*   Join with some classmates to write a paper in which you identify topics not normally handled at your college but that you feel should be covered, such as legal rights of employees.

Connections

1. Two of the writers in this chapter (Paul Gallico and Jeanne Park) have organized people into different categories. What categories do these writers use? What connections can you make between their essays and Robert MacNeil's essay, which deals with how people use different levels of language?

2. Some of the selections in this chapter are informative as well as humorous. Describe two of the humorous selections you liked and explain why you enjoyed them. Cite details and examples from the selections to support your opinions.

6

Comparison
and Contrast

To COMPARE IS to show how items are alike. To **contrast** is to show how items are different. Thus comparison and contrast involve pointing out the similarities or differences between two (or more) items. Birdwatchers, for instance, may compare bird A with bird B according to their common color, but contrast them according to their difference in size.

In the preceding chapter, you learned about the **modes of development** called **classification** and **division.** The comparison and contrast modes are related to those modes. In deciding what to compare or contrast, you will want to make sure that the items share points in common. Thus the items are usually the same kind or **class** of thing, and in comparing or contrasting them, you essentially establish at least two categories, showing the differences or similarities between them. For instance, you can compare two passenger cars—a Ford and a Chevrolet—with more precision than you can a Ford and a helicopter. Fords are compared with Chevrolets because they have many features in common—features that you can pinpoint. Similarly, you can usually compare two paintings more precisely than you can a novel and a painting.

Once you have selected the closely related items, you will want to explain as clearly as possible the ways in which the items are alike or different. In any one piece of writing, you may want to use comparison only—or contrast only. Or you may decide to use both in the same essay. These three possibilities are illustrated in the following paragraphs. Notice, in each case, how the writer compares or contrasts *specific* points.

Comparison

A Buick and a Cadillac, both built by General Motors, are alike in many ways. A Buick, which measures over 200 inches in length and weighs over 3,000 pounds, is large and holds the road well. A Cadillac is similar in length and weight. Like a Buick, a Cadillac gets relatively low gas mileage compared with smaller economy cars made by the same manufacturer. The Buick provides an unusually comfortable ride, especially on cross-country trips on the highway, as does a Cadillac. And both cars enjoy a certain status as a luxury automobile.

Contrast

The twins are as different as two people can be. Sally, who is always hoping someone will have a party, has black hair, brown eyes, and an outgoing personality. She wants to be an actress or a popular singer. Susan, more serious and studious, has blonde hair, blue eyes, and a somewhat shy manner. Since she has done well in all her classes in graphic arts and math, she plans to become an architect or an engineer.

Mixed Comparison and Contrast

Most Americans would say it is not really possible to establish an ideal society. But time after time, a small dedicated group of people will drop out of the mainstream of American society to try, once more, to live according to the group's concept of an ideal society. Most of these groups have believed in holding their property in common. Most have used the word *family* to refer to all members of the group. Many of these groups, however, have differed widely in their attitudes toward sex and marriage.

Notice that all three of these paragraphs supply information but do not try to claim that one of the compared items is better or worse than the other. Notice, too, the **objective** tone of these paragraphs. However, writers also use comparison and contrast to support their opinions about subjects or to show how a certain thing or idea is superior to others in the same class. The writer of the paragraph about twins, for instance, could have used her information to support an opinion, as in the following revised paragraph.

Opinion

The twins are as different as two people can be. Sally, who has black hair, brown eyes, and an outgoing, flighty personality, is always hoping someone will have a party. She fritters away her time and money shopping for the latest clothes, and she dreams of being an actress or a popular singer. But until she settles down and applies her energy to something useful, she will probably not be successful at anything. Susan, more serious and studious, has blonde hair, blue eyes, and a somewhat shy manner. Since she works hard and makes good use of her time, she has done well in all her classes in graphic arts and math. She plans to become an architect or an engineer and will no doubt be a good one.

Opinion

As you plan a comparison-and-contrast composition, it is very useful to **brainstorm** for items of comparison. That is, as described in chapter 1, think about the subjects of your composition and briefly jot down whatever comes to mind about them. You can then use your list in deciding on the content of your paragraph.

Organization

You should organize your comparison (or contrast) by whichever method suits your material best. One simple method is to explain a characteristic of item A, perhaps its cost, and then immediately compare it with the same characteristic of item B—and then go on to compare the two items point by point. For example, in contrasting two chocolate cakes, you may first want to say cake A is more expensive to prepare than cake B. Second, you may say that cake A, which requires more steps and ingredients, takes more time to make than cake B. Third, cake A is richer—almost too rich—and sweeter than cake B. You may conclude by saying that you recommend cake B. In this manner, you move back and forth, mentioning the specific differences between cake A and cake B in an orderly manner.

When the writer compares (or contrasts) two objects item by item, it is called the **alternating** or **point-by-point method.** The following diagram shows how this method works in the paragraph comparing Buicks and Cadillacs.

Alternating (or point-by-point) method

Topic sentence: "A Buick and a Cadillac . . . are alike in many ways."

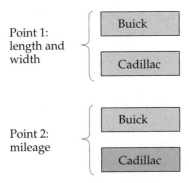

Point 1:
length and
width
Buick
Cadillac

Point 2:
mileage
Buick
Cadillac

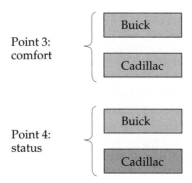

If the writer prefers a second type of organization, the **block method,** he or she explains all the characteristics of the first item together in a block and then explains all the characteristics of the second item in the same order in a corresponding block. The paragraphs contrasting the twins Sally and Susan (pages 144–145) are organized in this block method.

Block method

Topic sentence: "The twins are as different as two people can be."

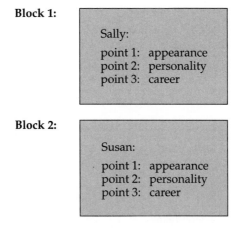

A third method, the **mixed method,** is useful when the writer wants to both compare and contrast in the same paragraph. All the similarities of the two items may first be explained and then all the differences. (Or, if the writer chooses, the differences may be explained first and then the similarities.) The following diagram shows this third method of organization, which was used in the paragraph on ideal societies (page 144).

Mixed comparison-and-contrast method

Topic sentence: "people . . . drop out of the mainstream of American society . . . to live according to the group's concept of an ideal society."

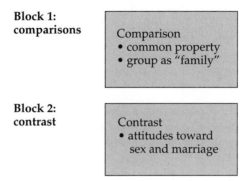

Block 1:
comparisons

Comparison
- common property
- group as "family"

Block 2:
contrast

Contrast
- attitudes toward sex and marriage

You will want to use these same three methods—alternating, block, and mixed—in writing longer essays. In the following essay, the writer uses the alternating method of organization to contrast types of people.

There are only two types of people in the world, Type A and Type Z. It isn't hard to tell which type you are. How long before the plane leaves do you arrive at the airport?

Point 1: catching a plane

Early plane-catchers, Type A, pack their bags at least a day in advance, and they pack neatly. If they're booked on a flight that leaves at four in the afternoon, they get up at 5:30 that morning. If they haven't left the house by noon, they're worried about missing the plane.

Late plane-catchers, Type Z, pack hastily at the last minute and arrive at the airport too late to buy a newspaper.

Point 2: reading a book

What do you do with a new book? Type A reads more carefully and finishes every book, even though it isn't any good.

Type Z skims through a lot of books and is more apt to write in the margins with a pencil.

Point 3: eating breakfast

Type A eats a good breakfast; Type Z grabs a cup of coffee.

Point 4: turning off lights

Type As turn off the lights when leaving a room and lock the doors when leaving a house. They go back to make sure they've locked it, and they worry later about whether they left the iron on or not. They didn't.

Type Zs leave the lights burning and if they lock the door at all when they leave the house, they're apt to have forgotten their keys.

Point 5: seeing the dentist

Type A sees the dentist twice a year, has an annual physical checkup and thinks he may have something.

Type Z has been meaning to see a doctor.

Point 6: using toothpaste

> Type A squeezes a tube of toothpaste from the bottom, rolls it very carefully as he uses it and puts the top back on every time.
> Type Z squeezes the tube from the middle, and he's lost the cap under the radiator.

Point 7: other characteristics

> Type Zs are more apt to have some Type A characteristics than Type As are apt to have any Type Z characteristics.

Point 8: marriage

> Type As always marry Type Zs.
> Type Zs always marry Type As.

Andy Rooney,
"Types"

The comparison and contrast mode of development gives Rooney a framework for making use of **irony.** Irony is a device used by writers to imply something different or the opposite from what is actually stated. Here, Rooney uses irony for its humorous effect, with the ultimate irony being that Type As and Type Zs always marry their opposites.

Comparison and contrast, like classification and division, is a useful mode of development for writing on the academic subjects you will study in college courses. You will encounter it in textbooks, with comparison indicated by such transitional words as *similarly* and *by comparison* and contrast by *however, on the other hand,* and *on the contrary.* If you become comfortable with this mode, it will come in handy in your writing for other courses. Be alert, for example, to essay assignments and exam questions that begin "Compare and contrast . . ."

In the readings that follow, you will find the alternating, block, and mixed methods of comparison-and-contrast development. You will also see the variety of ideas that writers express through comparison and contrast.

Yin and Yang

Mary Paumier Jones

The yin-yang symbol comes from ancient Chinese cosmology. It repre-
sents both the dark and the light, or shaded and sunlit, sides of a moun-
tain. The "yin" represents the female or shaded aspects of the symbol
such as the earth, darkness, and passivity. The "yang" represents the
male aspects of the symbol, such as light, sun, and activity. In this para-
graph from her essay, "The Opposite of Saffron," Mary Paumier Jones
explains that the yin and yang movements in T'ai Chi, a Chinese form of
exercise, form a perfect balance. (Adapted from **http://www2.cybernex**
.net/~jefkirsh/symbol.html.)

Words to Know

inscrutably   obscurely, mysteriously

intercourse   communication

simultaneous   at the same time

Getting Started

How are walking and running alike? How are they different?

In T'ai Chi class Dr. Young talked about yin and yang. In the beginning
square form, each movement is followed by a pause: the movement is
yin, the pause yang. To my Western ears this smacks of sexism; the mas-
culine principle acting, the feminine doing nothing. But I eventually begin to learn the pause is not nothing. Given its proper weight, gravity,
and time, the pause does its work, its stretch, its subtle modification of
the quality of the move before and the one to come. Later in the round
form, the movement is continuous. Yin and yang, though still opposite,
are inscrutably simultaneous, engaged in an ancient abstract intercourse.

Questions About the Reading

1. What is yin and what is yang in the beginning square form of T'ai Chi?
2. Why does the writer think yin and yang "smacks of sexism"?
3. What is the purpose of the pause?
4. How does the round form of T'ai Chi differ from the square?

Questions About the Writer's Strategies

1. What is the main idea of the paragraph? Is it stated or implied?
2. What is the point of view (person, time, tone) of the paragraph?
3. Is the point of view consistent throughout the paragraph? If not, where and in what way does it change?
4. If the point of view in the paragraph changes, is the change acceptable? Why or why not?

Writing Assignments

1. Write an essay about two sports you have played, explaining how the sports are alike and how they are different.
2. Write an essay about two subjects you have studied in school and explain how they are alike and how they are different.

Good Girl, Bad Girl

Anna Quindlen

Understanding why two people become friends is sometimes difficult. In this paragraph, essayist Anna Quindlen provides a candid assessment of an unbalanced friendship from her days at a boarding school for girls.

Words to Know

dialectical   having to do with two opposite or contradictory forces

naïve   innocent

refectory   cafeteria, dining hall

Getting Started

What is it that attracts two friends to each other?

She was my best friend, and hard as it may have been to figure by the looks of us, she was the good girl, I the bad. I suppose everyone has at least one friendship like this in their lives. We were dialectical, she the thesis, I the antithesis. She was direct, trustworthy, kind, and naïve; I was manipulative, selfish, and clever. She laughed at all my jokes, took part in all my schemes, told everyone that I was the smartest and the funniest and the best. Like a B movie of boarding school life, we stole peanut butter from the refectory, short-sheeted beds, called drugstores and asked them if they had Prince Albert in a can. Whenever I hear a mother say, "If so-and-so told you to jump off the Brooklyn Bridge, would you do it?" I think of her. On my order, she would have jumped.

Questions About the Reading

1. How do you imagine the author and her friend looked? Reread the first sentence before you describe the two girls.
2. What does the writer mean when she says that her exploits were "like a B movie of boarding school life"?
3. Does the writer believe she and her friend had a healthy relationship? Why or why not?

Questions About the Writer's Strategies

1. Is the writer's mode of development comparison, contrast, or a combination of the two?
2. What other mode of development does the writer use?
3. What words does the writer use to describe herself? What words does she use to describe how her friend thought of her?
4. What simile does the author use to describe the friendship?

Writing Assignments

1. Write a narrative paragraph that compares your personality with that of one of your closest friends.
2. Write a paragraph in which you compare and contrast a childhood friendship with a current friendship.
3. In a paragraph, compare and contrast a relationship between friends with one between brothers and sisters. Use examples from your own experience to illustrate similarities and differences.

Sports Talk

Scott Russell Sanders

We're all familiar with the idea that men and women feel differently about watching sports events—the men glued to the TV, the women ignoring it. In this paragraph, Scott Russell Sanders suggests that men and women also have different reactions to sports talk.

Words to Know

indifference   lack of interest
scoffing   sneering, making fun of
vicinity   area
yearn   long for, want

Getting Started

Do you think men and women have different attitudes toward sports?

In many households and offices, gossip about games and athletes breaks down along gender lines, the men indulging in it and the women scoffing. Those on each side of the line may exaggerate their feelings, the men pumping up their enthusiasm, the women their indifference, until sport becomes a male mystery. No locker room, no sweat lodge is needed to shut women out; mere talk will do it. Men are capable of muttering about wins and losses, batting averages and slam dunks, until the flowers on the wallpaper begin to wilt and every woman in the vicinity begins to yearn for a supply of gags. A woman friend of mine, an executive in a computing firm, has been driven in self-defense to scan the headlines of the sports pages before going to work, so that she can toss out references to the day's contests and stars, like chunks of meat, to feed the appetites of her male colleagues. After gnawing on this bait, the men may consent to speak with her of things more in keeping with her taste, such as books, birds, and the human condition.

Questions About the Reading

1. According to the writer, how do women react to men's gossip about athletic games and athletes?

2. What does the writer mean when he says men can talk about sports "until the flowers on the wallpaper begin to wilt."
3. How does the woman executive in a computing firm handle the sports talk of her male coworkers?
4. According to the last line of the paragraph, what subjects are women interested in talking about?

Questions About the Writer's Strategies

1. What is the main idea of the paragraph? Is it stated or implied?
2. Is the paragraph mainly comparison or mainly contrast?
3. What method of comparison/contrast does the writer use?
4. What is the metaphor in the paragraph?

Writing Assignments

1. Write a paragraph in which you compare and contrast coverage of men's and women's sports on television.
2. Write a paragraph in which you compare and contrast two friends who have different opinions about one of the following topics: music, work, or sports.

Mrs. vs. Ms.

Anne Roiphe

Anne Roiphe tells us that the feminist movement of the 1960s changed women's view of themselves and freed them from being just a "Mrs." to being themselves and expressing their own desires and abilities.

Words to Know

denigrating   insulting
hypochondria   persistent, neurotic conviction that one is ill or becoming ill

Getting Started

Is there such a thing as a "right" role for women or men?

Shortly after my mother's funeral as the sixties began its Punch and Judy show, the this-time-around feminist movement rose from behind the curtain. You could virtually hear the whoop of relief that rolled over the country. The first and most important message was that you didn't have to, you didn't need to, you had other choices, whether this was a turn against marriage, a turn against cooking, a turn against babies as destiny, it was all about not having to, not being coerced into, about not polishing the furniture till it shone, about searching for meaning outside the home. What wonderful fresh air this feminist wind brought to the choking lady in the apron holding her cookies on a hot baking tray. Now she could see her children, her always needing to be chauffeured children, with tennis rackets and piano lessons, with Little League and skating competitions and play dates, as sucking the life out of her, as draining her of her own dreams, as eating at the promise that had been. Now she could see that always giving and never getting were not divinely ordained. She was not just a Mrs., someone's wife, and not just a mom, someone's mother. She breathed her own desires, expressed her own anger, and suddenly everything was changed. All over America consciousness raised its own rooftops and fled the house. Women remembered that they had once run like crazy, climbed trees, planned to visit Istanbul, intended to ride a motorbike or go to graduate school. Women took courses, learned karate, let their body hair grow as nature intended. They became aware of all the denigrating images in the culture, all the insults to their brains and bravery that blared at them from magazines, books, movies, children's readers, billboards. Seeing the insult defused its power. The madwomen in the attic gave up their delusions, depressions, hypochondria and made plans to become potters or neurosurgeons. By the end of the nineteen sixties if a woman put her head to her own pillow she could hear the band playing, the coming of freedom, the hope of power returned, of self-expression, of self-fulfillment, of her intelligence newly awake, in love again with life.

Questions About the Reading

1. What does the writer say was the "message" of the feminist movement of the 1960s?
2. How does the writer portray women before the movement? Do you agree with her description?
3. How does the writer portray women after the movement? Do you agree with her description?
4. What does the writer mean by "All over America consciousness raised its own rooftops and fled the house"? Do you think the generalization is accurate?

Questions About the Writer's Strategies

1. Does the writer use any mode of development other than comparison and contrast?
2. What is the tone of the paragraph?
3. What is the point of view in person of the paragraph?
4. What method of comparison and contrast does the writer use?
5. What is the main idea of the paragraph? Is it stated? If so, identify it; if not, state it in your own words.

Writing Assignments

1. Write a paragraph in which you discuss the effect of the feminist movement on your mother, sister, or girlfriend.
2. Write a paragraph in which you discuss the effect of the feminist movement on your father, brother, or boyfriend.

Conversational Ballgames

Nancy Masterson Sakamoto

The difference between Western and Japanese conversation styles is like the difference between tennis or volleyball and bowling, according to Nancy Sakamoto in this essay from her book Polite Fictions. *She is an American married to a Japanese man and is a professor of American Studies at a Japanese university.*

Words to Know

elaboration   further information; additional details
indispensable   necessary, essential
unconsciously   unknowingly

Getting Started

Is there a difference between the way you talk to a friend and the way you talk to a teacher, a stranger, or an older person?

After I was married and had lived in Japan for a while, my Japanese 1 gradually improved to the point where I could take part in simple conversations with my husband and his friends and family. And I began to notice that often, when I joined in, the others would look startled, and the conversational topic would come to a halt. After this happened several times, it became clear to me that I was doing something wrong. But for a long time, I didn't know what it was.

Finally, after listening carefully to many Japanese conversations, I dis- 2 covered what my problem was. Even though I was speaking Japanese, I was handling the conversation in a western way.

Japanese-style conversations develop quite differently from western- 3 style conversations. And the difference isn't only in the languages. I realized that just as I kept trying to hold western-style conversations even when I was speaking Japanese, so my English students kept trying to hold Japanese-style conversations even when they were speaking English. We were unconsciously playing entirely different conversational ballgames.

A western-style conversation between two people is like a game of 4 tennis. If I introduce a topic, a conversational ball, I expect you to hit it back. If I agree with me, I don't expect you simply to agree and do nothing more. I expect you to add something—a reason for agreeing,

157

another example, or an elaboration to carry the idea further. But I don't expect you always to agree. I am just as happy if you question me, or challenge me, or completely disagree with me. Whether you agree or disagree, your response will return the ball to me.

And then it is my turn again. I don't serve a new ball from my original starting line. I hit your ball back again from where it has bounced. I carry your idea further, or answer your questions or objections, or challenge or question you. And so the ball goes back and forth, with each of us doing our best to give it a new twist, an original spin, or a powerful smash. 5

And the more vigorous the action, the more interesting and exciting the game. Of course, if one of us gets angry, it spoils the conversation, just as it spoils a tennis game. But getting excited is not at all the same as getting angry. After all, we are not trying to hit each other. We are trying to hit the ball. So long as we attack only each other's opinions, and do not attack each other personally, we don't expect anyone to get hurt. A good conversation is supposed to be interesting and exciting. 6

If there are more than two people in the conversation, then it is like doubles in tennis, or like volleyball. There's no waiting in line. Whoever is nearest and quickest hits the ball, and if you step back, someone else will hit it. No one stops the game to give you a turn. You're responsible for taking your own turn. 7

But whether it's two players or a group, everyone does his best to keep the ball going, and no one person has the ball for very long. 8

A Japanese-style conversation, however, is not at all like tennis or volleyball. It's like bowling. You wait for your turn. And you always know your place in line. It depends on such things as whether you are older or younger, a close friend or a relative stranger to the previous speaker, in a senior or junior position, and so on. 9

When your turn comes, you step up to the starting line with your bowling ball, and carefully bowl it. Everyone else stands back and watches politely, murmuring encouragement. Everyone waits until the ball has reached the end of the alley, and watches to see if it knocks down all the pins, or only some of them, or none of them. There is a pause, while everyone registers your score. 10

Then, after everyone is sure that you have completely finished your turn, the next person in line steps up to the same starting line, with a different ball. He doesn't return your ball, and he does not begin from where your ball stopped. There is no back and forth at all. All the balls run parallel. And there is always a suitable pause between turns. There is no rush, no excitement, no scramble for the ball. 11

No wonder everyone looked startled when I took part in Japanese conversations. I paid no attention to whose turn it was, and kept snatching 12 the ball halfway down the alley and throwing it back at the bowler. Of course the conversation died. I was playing the wrong game.

This explains why it is almost impossible to get a western-style con- 13 versation or discussion going with English students in Japan. I used to think that the problem was their lack of English language ability. But I finally came to realize that the biggest problem is that they, too, are playing the wrong game.

Whenever I serve a volleyball, everyone just stands back and watches 14 it fall, with occasional murmurs of encouragement. No one hits it back. Everyone waits until I call on someone to take a turn. And when that person speaks, he doesn't hit my ball back. He serves a new ball. Again, everyone just watches it fall.

So I call on someone else. This person does not refer to what the previ- 15 ous speaker has said. He also serves a new ball. Nobody seems to have paid any attention to what anyone else has said. Everyone begins again from the same starting line, and all the balls run parallel. There is never any back and forth. Everyone is trying to bowl with a volleyball.

And if I try a simpler conversation, with only two of us, then the other 16 person tries to bowl with my tennis ball. No wonder foreign English teachers in Japan get discouraged.

Now that you know about the difference in the conversational ball- 17 games, you may think that all your troubles are over. But if you have been trained all your life to play one game, it is no simple matter to switch to another, even if you know the rules. Knowing the rules is not at all the same thing as playing the game.

Even now, during a conversation in Japanese I will notice a startled 18 reaction, and belatedly realize that once again I have rudely interrupted by instinctively trying to hit back the other person's bowling ball. It is no easier for me to "just listen" during a conversation, than it is for my Japanese students to "just relax" when speaking with foreigners. Now I can truly sympathize with how hard they must find it to try to carry on a western-style conversation.

If I have not yet learned to do conversational bowling in Japanese, at 19 least I have figured out one thing that puzzled me for a long time. After his first trip to America, my husband complained that Americans asked him so many questions and made him talk so much at the dinner table that he never had a chance to eat. When I asked him why he couldn't talk and eat at the same time, he said that Japanese do not customarily think that dinner, especially on fairly formal occasions, is a suitable time for extended conversation.

Since westerners think that conversation is an indispensable part of 20 dining, and indeed would consider it impolite not to converse with one's dinner partner, I found this Japanese custom rather strange. Still, I could accept it as a cultural difference even though I didn't really understand it. But when my husband added, in explanation, that Japanese consider it extremely rude to talk with one's mouth full, I got confused. Talking with one's mouth full is certainly not an American custom. We think it very rude, too. Yet we still manage to talk a lot and eat at the same time. How do we do it?

For a long time, I couldn't explain it, and it bothered me. But after I 21 discovered the conversational ballgames, I finally found the answer. Of course! In a western-style conversation, you hit the ball, and while someone else is hitting it back, you take a bite, chew, and swallow. Then you hit the ball again, and then eat some more. The more people there are in the conversation, the more chances you have to eat. But even with only two of you talking, you still have plenty of chances to eat.

Maybe that's why polite conversation at the dinner table has never 22 been a traditional part of Japanese etiquette. Your turn to talk would last so long without interruption that you'd never get a chance to eat.

Questions About the Reading

1. How did the writer's Japanese husband, family, and friends react to her participation in conversations?
2. What does the writer say was wrong with how she was handling the conversations?
3. How does the writer characterize Western-style conversation? To what does she compare Western-style conversation?
4. How does the writer characterize Japanese-style conversation? To what does she compare Japanese-style conversation?
5. What did the writer's Japanese husband complain about after his first trip to America?

Questions About the Writer's Strategies

1. What is the thesis of the essay?
2. What method of comparison-and-contrast organization does the writer use?
3. What is the simile the writer uses for a Western-style conversation between two people? What simile does she use for a conversation among several people?
4. What simile does the writer use for a Japanese-style conversation?

5. How do Westerners manage to carry on a conversation while they are eating and not talk with their mouths full?
6. Does the writer use any mode of development in addition to contrast? If so, what is it and in which paragraphs is it found?

Writing Assignments

1. Write an essay in which you contrast the way you talk to your best friends with the way you talk to neighborhood or school friends. Use dialogue to illustrate the differences.
2. Go to a shopping mall and listen to the people who are walking around or working in the stores. Classify the different people you see and write an essay in which you compare and/or contrast their conversations.

Aiming for Success?

Marvin Olasky

Marvin Olasky, a professor at the University of Texas, uses two sports figures—Kevin Mitchell and Michael Jordan—to advise incoming students about what it takes to succeed. He shared his advice in this article, written in the fall of 1997.

Words to Know

exhilaration   excitement
predestining   deciding in advance

Getting Started

What do you think you need to do to successfully reach your career goal? What do you need not to do?

Students will be heading off to college soon, and as a professor I know   1
the pattern. For the first few weeks, the exhilaration of new beginnings reigns. Then the grind commences. I know a little about sports, so when they start muttering about their workload, I'm ready to ask, "Who do you want to be—Kevin Mitchell or Michael Jordan"?

I've encountered each of those talented athletes twice, once up close   2
and once from afar. Each time, I was impressed with the difference.

My first encounters came in 1993 and 1994, when I was visiting spring-   3
training camps with my sons, interviewing players and writing magazine articles about what they believed concerning God.

Kevin Mitchell (no longer a household name) was so out of shape that   4
the other players made jokes about him. He said, "Whatever I do, the Big Man Upstairs takes care of me." Mitchell had been the 1989 National League Most Valuable Player, and his raw talent was the stuff of legend. Often he took no batting practice. Before a 1994 game in Chicago, his coaches gave him a scouting report on the pitcher. He didn't even look at it. He just walked to the plate and hit a home run.

Also in 1994, history's greatest basketball player tried to transform into   5
a baseball player. Michael Jordan took batting practice for hours on end, just as he'd taken shots at the basket. He said, "Every time I read something negative about my being here, I think about God giving me the opportunity to do something that I really like to do. I want to work hard."

In basketball, natural ability plus hard work helped Jordan excel. In baseball, despite hard work, he just couldn't hit.

My next encounter with them was this past June. Millions saw Jordan 6
play a game of hard-charging basketball with the flu as he led the Chicago Bulls to another championship. He told reporters, "It's a great feeling, I'm tired, I'm weak. I have a whole summer to recuperate."

Kevin Mitchell, meanwhile, was being released by the Cleveland Indi- 7
ans. This spring they signed him for a half-million dollars, plus another $100,000 if he stayed under 240 pounds, plus another million if he played regularly. The goal was to get the 5-foot-11 player in shape, but he showed up at spring training weighing 270 and was unable to complete a half-mile training run. Jordan played championship basketball with a high temperature, but Mitchell missed game after game of relatively stationary baseball with minor complaints. (Once, predestining himself, he showed up at the ballpark wearing slippers and pajamas.)

A *Sports Illustrated* story about Mitchell early this year played his saga 8
for laughs. "Oft-injured Kevin Mitchell," Tom Verducci wrote, "loves toys and clubhouse high jinks." The overweight Mitchell, we were told, "Showed up late for spring training because he needed emergency dental work after munching on a microwaved chocolate donut."

The Mitchell story, however, is a tragedy of talent wasted. Former 9
manager Davey Johnson used to tell him, "Kevin, don't put on too much weight. . . . It will take a toll on your legs. Make a few sacrifices now." Mitchell did not make any sacrifices. His extra poundage made him vulnerable. He played in at least 150 games only once, the year he was voted MVP. As teams were awed by his talent and then frustrated by his sloth, Mitchell had a total of 10 stops, including one in Japan.

He went to Japan out of shape in 1995, hit the first pitch for a grand 10
slam, and then twisted his knee and was done. He joined the Boston Red Sox in 1996, sat out 10 days with a strained hamstring, had three hits, including a home run in his first game back, then reinjured the hamstring in the same game and spent six weeks on the disabled list.

Sports Illustrated excused some of his conduct: poor background, abu- 11
sive father; what can you expect? Puh-leeze: Mitchell had great opportunity—now he's not only out of shape but also out of baseball. My students have great opportunity: They are in the state's top university with time to learn and hours to burn. Some may have talent like Michael Jordan's in particular spheres, but they'll never make full use of it unless, in their work habits, they kick out the Kevin and be like Mike.

Questions About the Reading

1. What was the fundamental cause of Kevin Mitchell's failure?
2. Why does the writer tell his students about Mitchell and Michael Jordan?
3. When did the writer interview the players and what was he interviewing them for? How did the players answer the writer?
4. What did Mitchell do that caused his release by the Cleveland Indians?
5. What does the writer mean when he says his students need to "kick out the Kevin and be like Mike"?

Questions About the Writer's Strategies

1. What method(s) of comparison and contrast does the writer use?
2. Does the writer use any other modes of development in the essay? If so, what are they? Identify sentences and paragraphs to support your answer.
3. What is the thesis of the essay? Is it stated? If so, identify it; if not, state the thesis in your own words.
4. What is the tone of the essay?
5. Is the essay objective, subjective, or both? Support your answer with examples.

Writing Assignments

1. Write an essay in which you compare and/or contrast the work habits of two of your friends.
2. Write an essay in which you compare and/or contrast what you must and must not do to meet your career goals.

Glittering Alice and Sad Eleanor

Richard Cohen

In his essay, Richard Cohen compares and contrasts Alice Roosevelt Longworth and Eleanor Roosevelt, who were cousins, on the basis of their looks and intelligence. Cohen ordinarily writes on national affairs for the Washington Post. *("Glittering Alice and Sad Eleanor" by Richard Cohen,* The Washington Post, *February 4, 1980. © 1980, The Washington Post Writers Group. Reprinted with permission.)*

Words to Know

appurtenance   an attachment, addition, accessory
formidable   awe-inspiring, important
gilding   a covering of gold
indomitability   the inability to be conquered or subdued
manifestly   clearly, obviously
obituaries   death notices or biographies
proclaimed   declared, made clear

Getting Started

Do you have close friends who are very different from each other?

It is one of those coincidences of history that Alice Roosevelt Longworth, 1 daughter of the grand and unforgettable Teddy and wife of the totally forgettable Nicholas, died the very same week two more books were published about her cousin, Eleanor. The two hated each other—at least Alice hated Eleanor—thinking probably that they had little in common but a family name. They had something else: They were prisoners of their looks.

Alice, of course, was radiant and pretty—daughter of a president, a 2 Washington debutante, a standard of style and grace, the one who gave the color Alice Blue to the nation as surely as her father gave his name to a certain kind of stuffed toy bear.

She married in the White House, took the speaker of the House of Rep- 3 resentatives for her husband, and stayed pretty much at the center of things Washingtonian for something like 70 years. She was, as they say, formidable.

Eleanor, on the other hand, was homely. She had a voice pitched at the 4 level of chalk on a blackboard, and the teeth of a beaver. She was awkward in both speech and manner and when she talked—when she rose to speak—the experience was both painful to her and her audience. She had a husband, but there is reason to believe that she was unloved by him. There is about Eleanor Roosevelt an aura of aching sadness, yet in her own way she, too, was formidable. She certainly endures.

It is interesting to consider how their looks—the way they looked to   5 the world—shaped these two women. It is interesting because in some ways they were so similar. They were both Roosevelts—one of the Oyster Bay branch, the other of the Hyde Park—both well-off, both of the aristocracy, and both manifestly bright.

Eleanor's intelligence proclaimed itself. She threw herself into causes.   6 She spoke for people who had no spokesperson and she spoke well. She championed the poor, the black, women and other minorities. She campaigned and lectured and gave speeches and she did this with such intensity and such effect that it is not too much to say that before her death she was either a goddess or a witch to most Americans.

I am partial to the goddess side, thinking that the worst you can call a   7 person is not "do-gooder" but rather "do-nothinger." That is something you could never call Eleanor Roosevelt.

As for Alice, she showed her intelligence in her wit. It was she who   8 said, "The secret of eternal youth is arrested development," and who commented on Wendell Willkie after he received the presidential nomination: "He sprang from the grass roots of the country clubs of America."

Her most admired remark, the one about Thomas Dewey looking like   9 the "bridegroom on a wedding cake," was not hers at all. The reason we know is that she admitted it. She borrowed it, popularized it, but did not invent it.

No matter. She invented enough so that Washington adored her and   10 presidents more or less routinely elbowed themselves to her side so that they could hear what she had to say.

Yet with Alice, there it stopped. She was what she was, and what she   11 was was beautiful. She did more or less what was expected of pretty girls. She was perfect just being—just being Alice and being pretty—and in the America of both her youth and her maturity there was nothing better than to be rich and pretty and well-married.

That she was also intelligent was almost beside the point, like the gild-   12 ing on a lily. And while she later became cherished for her wit, it was not because she could use it for any purpose, but because it was like her beauty itself: something of a jewel. She was the perfect appurtenance, the one men wanted seated next to them.

With Eleanor, the story is different. Her looks were not her strong suit   13 and so she had to declare herself in another way—by intellect, character, indomitability. She did this well, found causes, gave purpose to her life and left this earth with the certainty that she had mattered.

The conventional view is to see Eleanor as sad and Alice as glittering. 14
To an extent, I'm sure, that's true. But in reading the obituaries, in reading how Alice cruelly imitated Eleanor and mocked her good causes, you
get the sense that Alice herself realized that something ironic had happened, that she had somehow become trapped by her own good looks,
by her perfection, by her wit—that she had become the eternal debutante, frozen in time. Eleanor was actually doing something.

So now Eleanor and Alice are dead. One led a sad life, the other a glit- 15
tering one. But one suspects that as the books came out on Eleanor, Alice
realized the tables had turned. There is something sad about being an
ugly duckling, but there is something sadder yet about being the belle of
the ball after the music has stopped, the guests have gone home and the
rest of the world has gone to work.

———————————

Questions About the Reading

1. What coincidence related to Alice's death does the writer point out?
2. How did Alice and Eleanor feel about each other?
3. What words does the writer use to describe Alice's looks? How does
   he describe Eleanor's looks?
4. What toy is named after Alice's father, Theodore Roosevelt?
5. In what ways were Alice and Eleanor alike?
6. How did most Americans feel about Eleanor before her death?
7. Which woman does the writer think is sadder? Why?

Questions About the Writer's Strategies

1. What is the writer's thesis?
2. What are the topic sentences of paragraphs 6 and 8?
3. What method of comparison-and-contrast organization does the writer
   use? Does the writer maintain the same order in describing the looks
   and intelligence of each woman?
4. What is the point of view in person, time, and tone of the essay? Is the
   point of view in time consistent throughout the essay? If not, in which
   paragraphs does it change, and is each change necessary?
5. Is the essay objective, subjective, or both? If both, give an example of
   each.
6. Identify a metaphor in paragraph 4 and a simile in paragraph 9.

Writing Assignments

1. Write an essay in which you compare and/or contrast two people who are famous in television, movies, or sports. Identify the method of organization you use.
2. Write an essay in which you compare and/or contrast houses in your neighborhood. Identify the method of organization you use.

Neat People vs. Sloppy People

Suzanne Britt

In this essay from her book Show and Tell, *Suzanne Britt explains the differences between neat and sloppy people, claiming—surprisingly— that neat people are lazier and meaner than sloppy people.*

Words to Know

cavalier   easygoing, offhand
meticulously   excessively
métier   occupation
rectitude   character, principles

Getting Started

How would you characterize neat people and sloppy people?

I've finally figured out the difference between neat people and sloppy 1
people. The distinction is, as always, moral. Neat people are lazier and
meaner than sloppy people.

Sloppy people, you see, are not really sloppy. Their sloppiness is merely 2
the unfortunate consequence of their extreme moral rectitude. Sloppy
people carry in their mind's eye a heavenly vision, a precise plan, that is
so stupendous, so perfect, it can't be achieved in this world or the next.

Sloppy people live in Never-Never Land. Someday is their métier. 3
Someday they are planning to alphabetize all their books and set up home
catalogs. Someday they will go through their wardrobes and mark certain items for tentative mending and certain items for passing on to relatives of similar shape and size. Someday sloppy people will make family
scrapbooks into which they will put newspaper clippings, postcards, locks
of hair, and the dried corsage from their senior prom. Someday they will
file everything on the surface on their desk, including the cash receipts
from coffee purchases at the snack shop. Someday they will sit down and
read all the back issues of *The New Yorker.*

For all these noble reasons and more, sloppy people never get neat. 4
They aim too high and wide. They save everything, planning someday to
file, order, and straighten out the world. But while these ambitious plans
take clearer and clearer shape in their heads, the books spill from the
shelves onto the floor, the clothes pile up in the hamper and closet, the

family mementos accumulate in every drawer, the surface of the desk is buried under mounds of paper, and the unread magazines threaten to reach the ceiling.

Sloppy people can't bear to part with anything. They give loving at- 5 tention to every detail. When sloppy people say they're going to tackle the surface of the desk, they really mean it. Not a paper will go unturned; not a rubber band will go unboxed. Four hours or two weeks into the excavation, the desk looks exactly the same, primarily because the sloppy person is meticulously creating new piles of papers with new headings and scrupulously stopping to read all the old book catalogs before he throws them away. A neat person would just bulldoze the desk.

Neat people are bums and clods at heart. They have cavalier attitudes 6 toward possessions, including family heirlooms. Everything is just another dust-catcher to them. If anything collects dust, it's got to go and that's that. Neat people will toy with the idea of throwing the children out of the house just to cut down on the clutter.

Neat people don't care about process. They like results. What they want 7 to do is get the whole thing over with so they can sit down and watch the rasslin' on TV. Neat people operate on two unvarying principles: Never handle any item twice, and throw everything away.

The only thing messy in a neat person's house is the trash can. The 8 minute something comes to a neat person's hand, he will look at it, try to decide if it has immediate use and, finding none, throw it in the trash.

Neat people are especially vicious with mail. They never go through 9 their mail unless they are standing directly over a trash can. If the trash can is beside the mailbox, even better. All ads, catalogs, pleas for charitable contributions, church bulletins and money-saving coupons go straight into the trash can without being opened. All letters from home, postcards from Europe, bills and paychecks are opened, immediately responded to, then dropped in the trash can. Neat people keep their receipts only for tax purposes. That's it. No sentimental salvaging of birthday cards or the last letter a dying relative ever wrote. Into the trash it goes.

Neat people place neatness above everything, even economics. They 10 are incredibly wasteful. Neat people throw away several toys every time they walk through the den. I knew a neat person once who threw away a perfectly good dish drainer because it had mold on it. The drainer was too much trouble to wash. And neat people sell their furniture when they move. They will sell a La-Z-Boy recliner while you are reclining in it.

Neat people are no good to borrow from. Neat people buy everything 11 in expensive little single portions. They get their flour and sugar in two-pound bags. They wouldn't consider clipping a coupon, saving a leftover, reusing plastic non-dairy whipped cream containers or rinsing off tin foil and draping it over the unmoldy dish drainer. You can never borrow a neat person's newspaper to see what's playing at the movies. Neat people have the paper all wadded up and in the trash by 7:05 A.M.

Neat people cut a clean swath through the organic as well as the inor- 12 ganic world. People, animals, and things are all one to them. They are so insensitive. After they've finished with the pantry, the medicine cabinet, and the attic, they will throw out the red geranium (too many leaves), sell the dog (too many fleas), and send the children off to boarding school (too many scuff marks on the hardwood floors).

Questions About the Reading

1. What is the reason, according to the writer, that people are sloppy?
2. What do sloppy people intend to do with everything they keep?
3. Why do sloppy people never get neat?
4. Why are people neat?
5. How do neat people handle their mail?

Questions About the Writer's Strategies

1. What is the comparison/contrast method used by the writer?
2. What is the topic of each paragraph, beginning with the second?
3. Is each topic stated in a sentence? If so, what are the topic sentences?
4. What is the tone of the essay? Is it consistent throughout?

Writing Assignments

1. Write an essay in which you compare/contrast shopping in different grocery stores.
2. *Working Together*   Join with some classmates to compare/contrast how people in different neighborhoods keep their yards.

The Seattle-to-Hattiesburg Shuttle Bus

Dixielynn Gleason (student)

What could be more different? A big, bustling city in the Pacific North-west is miles from a small, slow Southern town—both in distance and way of life. But a bus station is a bus station, and it attracts the same kinds of people everywhere. Dixielynn Gleason, a student at the College of the Virgin Islands, discovered this on a trip from Seattle, Washington, to Hattiesburg, Mississippi.

Words to Know

garishly   flashily, with tasteless sense of color
relics   something old or values from the past

Getting Started

What differences have you noticed between two cities in your travels?

The big silver bus glides into the grubby depot and stops smoothly. 1
The passengers stand up, stretch their cramped muscles, shuffle down the aisle and walk out into the fresh air to greet a friend or flag a cab. This scene takes place every day in almost every town and city in America. I am well acquainted with buses and, as a consequence, with bus depots. The two I am most familiar with are at opposite ends of the country. They differ in many ways, yet they are also similar.

The Greyhound station in Seattle, Washington, is always bustling. Even 2
at two o'clock in the morning people are going in and out. Shopping-bag ladies huddle in their chairs; college boys squint at the arrival/departure board, trying to get oriented. The station itself is high-ceilinged, garishly lit with fluorescent tubes, and many-levelled. One goes up steps to claim baggage, down steps to the restaurant, down even more steps to the lock-ers. When I need to warm up, it is freezing inside; when bare feet sizzle on the sidewalk, the depot is an oven.

Now I'm in the quiet dim cave of the Hattiesburg, Mississippi, bus 3
depot, waiting for my grandmother to pick me up. Fanning myself in the eternally warm, moist air, I observe the old black men who spend their lives sitting here. Their gnarled hands hang limply between their thighs,

172

their age-yellowed eyes refuse to meet mine; like the shoeshine stand I sit upon, they are relics from a bygone era. The voices inquiring at the ticket counter are soft, even in dispute. Two very angry Yankees are standing outside for a taxi. They are having no success because the only taxi in this tiny town has already picked up and left with the only other strangers. The Hattiesburg bus station is a bowl of blackstrap molasses, slow and dark and foreign-smelling, but as familiar to me as my first doll.

The quick efficient anthill of the Seattle depot is 1500 miles away from   4
this sleepy place. Yet the metropolitan loonies reach out and call the ancient silent loungers "brothers," the frustrated Yankees can sympathize with the college kid who missed the bus to Portland, and I can relate to anyone trying to be physically comfortable in either of the stations.

Questions About the Reading

1. The author says that the two bus depots she describes are both different and similar. List the ways in which they are alike and unlike.
2. Are bus depots the same all over the country?
3. Describe the people found in the Seattle bus depot. Describe the people found in the Hattiesburg one.
4. Contrast the appearance of the two bus depots. If you had to wait for someone, in which would you rather be?

Questions About the Writer's Strategies

1. This essay contains an introduction, a thesis statement, support for the thesis statement, and a conclusion. Where is the thesis statement in this essay?
2. Identify a simile and a metaphor in paragraph 3.
3. What method of organization does the writer use in contrasting the bus depots?
4. Does the conclusion of the essay emphasize the similarities or the differences between the two depots? What ideas are stated in the conclusion?

Writing Assignments

1. Write an essay in which you compare and contrast two modes of travel—for example, by car and by bus. Do the advantages of one mode of travel outweigh its disadvantages? Which do you prefer?

2. Using the Internet, compare and contrast fares for air and bus transportation between two cities. Include a list of the web site addresses you use. To get started, try **http://www.lowestfare.com/** for information on air fares and Greyhound's web site (**http://www.greyhound.com/**) for information on bus fares.
3. *Working Together* Join with some classmates to write an essay in which you compare and contrast the schools in different cities or neighborhoods.

Connections

1. Although the comparisons vary from selection to selection, most of the writers in this chapter have written about people. Describe some of the connections among these readings. How are the people described? Are individuals or groups compared?
2. What connections can you make between the individuals that Anne Roiphe and Richard Cohen contrast?
3. What connections can you make between the Marvin Olasky and Richard Cohen selections? What do the people they write about have in common?

7

Process

IF YOU WANT to hook up your new computer, you will probably follow the directions, or a **process,** provided by the manufacturer. A **process** is a method of doing a task or a job, usually in orderly steps, to achieve a desired result. For example, directions and recipes are both detailed explanations of processes. So are all articles and essays that tell how to prepare for a job interview, assemble a stereo system, dress for success, or operate a personal computer. So, too, are essays that describe how someone else used a process to accomplish something or complete a task.

In an essay explaining how to carry out a process, the writer needs to give clear and accurate guidance or directions, making the steps as simple as possible for the reader to follow. To do this, the writer must decide exactly what the reader already knows and what he or she needs to be told. The burden is on the writer to provide complete information to enable the reader to perform the task. If the writer forgets to mention how long the cookies should bake, the cook may be left with burned chocolate-chip cookies and disappointed friends.

The written explanation of such a process must be organized with particular care. Each step or part of the directions should be discussed in the same order as it occurs in the process. The following sample paragraph is a recipe for shrimp—one you might want to try. Notice that the writer begins with the purchase of the shrimp and then proceeds, step by step, through preparing, cooking, and serving the shrimp.

Topic sentence   ⌐ When fresh shrimp can be had, have it. What size? Medium for reasons of economy and common sense. Huge shrimps

Step 1: choose size	⌐ are magnificently expensive while small ones come in such
	⌐ numbers per pound that shelling them becomes slave labor.
Step 2: choose quantity	⌐ Buy two pounds of fresh shrimp and shell them. First, with
	⌐ a thumbnail pinch the tail shell hard crosswise (so the tail
Step 3: shell shrimp	segments will come out intact), then handle the headless
	animals like so many pea pods; split them lengthwise, save
	⌐ the contents, and throw the husks away. Sauté the shrimp
	with three crushed garlic cloves in two-thirds of a stick of
	butter. When the shrimp turn pink, add a 12-ounce can of
	Italian tomatoes (which taste better than the fresh supermar-
Step 4: cooking directions	ket kind), two bay leaves, a teaspoon of dried oregano, a half-
	cup of dry white wine, and the juice of a lemon. Simmer for
	ten minutes, sprinkle with chopped parsley and serve with
	⌐ rice.

Philip Kopper,
"Delicacies de la Mer"

Because this paragraph is telling the reader what to do, the **point of view** is **second person** (you), and it is in the present tense (*come, buy, save, throw,* and so forth). But the word *you* is unstated, which makes the paragraph seem to address the reader even more directly. This **tone** is commonly used in process writing that instructs the reader.

Not all process essays are such clear-cut models of process writing as the previous example. In some cases, a paragraph or essay describing a process may serve a purpose similar to that of a **narrative** or a **description.** That is, whereas strictly process writing is intended primarily to **instruct,** process writing also can be adapted to situations in which the writer mainly wants to **inform** or **describe.** In such cases, a process is often combined with narration and description, as in the following example. Notice that in describing the process—the way the woman packs her suitcases and leaves the house—the writer describes her character. You also know, by the contrast between her habits and those of her husband, that her basic character differs sharply from his. By detailing the process of packing and combining it with other narrative details, the writer tells you indirectly what has previously happened in the woman's life.

Introduction— narrative	⌐ He slammed the door angrily behind him, and she heard the	1
	squeal of the tires as he raced off in the car. For a moment,	
	she felt her usual fear. She knew he shouldn't drive after he'd	
	⌐ been drinking heavily.	
Step 1: preparation	⌐ But then she turned, went to the linen closet, and took	2
	out a clean towel. She spread the towel out on her neatly	
	⌐ made bed.	
Step 2: finding suitcases	⌐ Next, she got her overnight bag and a larger suitcase from	3
	⌐ the closet and put them carefully on the towel on her bed.	

Methodically, she took neatly folded underwear, stockings, and nightgowns from her drawers and packed them in neat rows in the two bags. One set in the overnight bag, and five in the larger suitcase. She laid aside a nightgown with a matching robe to pack last.

Next, she lifted dresses and suits, carefully hung on the hangers and buttoned up so they wouldn't wrinkle, from her closet and folded them into the larger suitcase. Two extra blouses and a dress went into the overnight bag. She'd wear the suit she had on.   4

Step 3: packing suitcases

She brought plastic bags from the kitchen and put her shoes into them. One pair went into the overnight bag; two pairs, one for the dresses and one for the suits, went into the larger bag. Then she put her bedroom slippers and the night-gown with the matching robe on top of the other clothes in the overnight bag. She would take only the overnight bag into her parents' house, at least at first. No need for them to know right away that this time was for more than one night. They'd always said that she wasn't going to change him and that the marriage wouldn't last.   5

Step 4: final check and look around

She sighed again, closed the suitcases, carried them out to her car, and then went back into the house for one last look around. Almost ready, she took her coat from the hall closet, folded it carefully over her arm, and took a last look at his shoes and socks left beside his chair and the newspaper flung across the couch where it would leave newsprint on the upholstery. She left the shoes and socks but couldn't resist folding the newspaper and putting it on a table. Finally, she went out, closed the door silently behind her, got into her car, and drove quietly and slowly away.   6

As you started reading this essay, you probably realized right away that it would be more narrative and descriptive than instructive of a process. Two signals that alerted you are that the point of view is **third person** (*she*) and past tense (*took, packed, lifted, laid,* and so on). Think, for a minute, about writing a clear process explanation using that person and tense. Experienced writers may use varying **points of view** in process writing, but for clear point-by-point process explanations, the **second person** (*you*), the present tense (*take, pour, measure*), and a straightforward tone are the most common.

Although a process approach can sometimes be useful in writing narratives and descriptions that deal with significant activities or accomplishments, you usually will use process for giving directions, describing how a mechanical gadget works, or reporting on science experiments. In these situations you may combine process with other modes like **definition** (chapter 9), **examples** (chapter 4), and **cause and effect** (chapter 8).

Always remember that three factors are essential to an effective process essay. First, be sure that the steps or procedures are carefully organized, step by step—usually in the same order as they should be carried out—so that the reader can understand and follow your explanation. Second, be sure that you include any information that the reader needs about any special materials or preliminary steps. And, third, include *all* the specific steps in the process.

Bear Attack

William McGinnis

In this paragraph from his book Whitewater Rafting, *William McGinnis tells us how to avoid an attack by a bear. But don't try it. According to recent reports, bears have become more aggressive, so it is best to stay away from areas where they live.*

Words to Know

pursuit chase

sprint run

Getting Started

What process would you follow if you had a flat tire on a highway?

Most bears will sprint away at the first sight of man. But if, on a side hike, you come across a bear that stands his ground, don't panic and run, for this may excite the bear and invite pursuit. Slowly put down any food or candy you might be carrying and retreat, keeping downhill from the bear and glancing around for escape routes and nearby trees to climb. If the bear advances in a threatening manner, either scoot up a tree or lie still on the ground, with knees drawn up and hands protecting the back of your head. In either case, stay put until you are certain the bear has gone.

Questions About the Reading

1. What does the writer say a bear will do if it sees a person?
2. According to the writer, what is the first thing you should not do if a bear "stands his ground"?
3. What should you do next?
4. What should you do if the bear advances?

Questions About the Writer's Strategies

1. What is the point of view (person, time, tone) of the paragraph?
2. What is the main idea of the paragraph? Is it stated or implied?
3. What is the order the writer uses?

Writing Assignments

1. Write a paragraph in which you explain the process of changing a tire.
2. Write a paragraph in which you explain the process of finding information on the Internet.

How Not to Make a Bow and Arrow

Leslie Marmon Silko

A best-selling author, poet, and essayist, Leslie Marmon Silko grew up at Laguna Pueblo in New Mexico. In this paragraph from her story "Uncle Tony's Goat," Silko's narrator is a mischievous young boy, growing up at Laguna Pueblo, who is undertaking a special project with his friends: making their first bows and arrows.

Getting Started

When you were a child, did you and your friends ever try to build or make something special? What was the process you undertook and what were the results of your efforts?

———

We had a hard time finding the right kind of string to use. We knew we needed gut to string our bows the way the men did, but we were little kids and we didn't know how to get any. So Kenny went to his house and brought back a ball of white cotton string that his mother used to string red chili with. It was thick and soft and it didn't make very good bowstring. As soon as we got the bows made we sat down again on the sand bank above the stream and started skinning willow twigs for arrows. It was past noon, and the tall willows behind us made cool shade. There were lots of little minnows that day, flashing in the shallow water, swimming back and forth wildly like they weren't sure if they really wanted to go up or down the stream; it was a day for minnows that we were always hoping for—we could have filled our rusty coffee cans and old pickle jars full. But this was the first time for making bows and arrows, and the minnows weren't much different from the sand or the rocks now. The secret is the arrows. The ones we made were crooked, and when we shot them they didn't go straight—they flew around in arcs and curves; so we crawled through the leaves and branches, deep into the willow groves, looking for the best, the straightest willow branches. But even after we skinned the sticky wet bark from them and whittled the knobs off, they still weren't straight. Finally we went ahead and made notches at the end of each arrow to hook in the bowstring, and we started practicing, thinking maybe we could learn to shoot the crooked arrows straight.

———

Questions About the Reading

1. Where did the group of friends get the string they needed for their bows? Why didn't it make very good bowstring?
2. What did the group use to make the arrows?
3. Why does the narrator say, "it was a day for minnows that we were always hoping for"? Why didn't the youngsters fish for minnows?
4. According to the narrator, why didn't their arrows shoot straight?
5. Why did the children crawl through the willow groves?
6. Describe the step-by-step process the group of friends went through to make their bows and arrows.
7. Do you think the youngsters ever learned to shoot the crooked arrows straight? Why or why not?
8. What does this paragraph tell you about what it would be like to grow up at Laguna Pueblo? Pick out details that help you visualize growing up there.

Questions About the Writer's Strategies

1. Is there a topic sentence in this paragraph? If so, where is it? If not, state the main idea in a sentence of your own.
2. What order does the writer use to organize her information in the process? Support your answer with examples from the paragraph.
3. Does the writer use any other modes of development in this paragraph? If so, what are they and where in the paragraph are they used?
4. Why do you think the writer uses an informal tone in this paragraph?

Writing Assignments

1. Have you ever made something you were proud of? Write a paragraph describing the step-by-step process. Remember to present all the steps in sequential order so that your readers can understand and follow your explanation.
2. Write a paragraph in which you describe your own process of studying for an exam. Be sure to include all the steps and use examples, details, or images that help your reader understand exactly what you do.

The Right Way to Eat
an Ice-Cream Cone

L. Rust Hills

Rust Hills was fiction editor of Esquire *and the* Saturday Evening Post, *and is now a free-lance writer. In this paragraph, taken from his book* How To Do Things Right, *he explains his technique, which was perfected through years of taking his children to ice-cream cone stands. Having told us the preliminary pitfalls—melted ice cream on car upholstery, choosing a flavor, holding more than one cone—he delivers the ultimate instructions on eating the cone.*

Words to Know

forgoing   deciding against
jostling   bumping together
molecules   very small particles
stance   way of standing

Getting Started

What is the best or right way to eat spaghetti?

Grasp the cone with the right hand firmly but gently between thumb and at least one but not more than three fingers, two-thirds of the way up the cone. Then dart swiftly away to an open area, away from the jostling crowd at the stand. Now take up the classic ice-cream-cone-eating stance: feet from one to two feet apart, body bent forward from the waist at a twenty-five-degree angle, right elbow well up, right forearm horizontal, at a level with your collarbone and about twelve inches from it. But don't start eating yet! Check first to see what emergency repairs may be necessary. Sometimes a sugar cone will be so crushed or broken or cracked that all one can do is gulp at the thing like a savage, getting what he can of it and letting the rest drop to the ground, and then evacuating the area of catastrophe as quickly as possible. Checking the cone for possible trouble can be done in a second or two, if one knows where to look and does it systematically. A trouble spot some people overlook is the bottom tip of the cone. This may have been broken off. Or the flap of the cone material at the bottom, usually wrapped over itself in that funny spiral construction, may be folded in a way that is imperfect and leaves an opening. No need to say that through this opening—in a matter of perhaps thirty or, at most, ninety seconds—will begin to pour hundreds of thousands of sticky molecules of melted ice cream. You know in this case that you must instantly get the paper napkin in your left hand under and around the bottom of the cone to stem the forthcoming flow, or else be doomed to eat the cone far too rapidly. It is a grim moment. No one wants to eat a cone under that kind of pressure, but neither does anyone want to end up with the bottom of the cone stuck to a messy napkin. There's one other alternative—one that takes both skill and courage: Forgoing any cradling action, grasp the cone more firmly between thumb and forefinger and extend the other fingers so that they are out of the way of the dripping from the bottom, then increase the waist-bend angle from twenty-five to thirty-five degrees, and then eat the cone, *allowing* it to drip out of the bottom onto the ground in front of you! Experienced and thoughtful cone-eaters enjoy facing up to this kind of sudden challenge.

Questions About the Reading

1. How many ways are there to eat an ice-cream cone?
2. Despite all of the problems with ice-cream cones, does the writer like to eat them?

Questions About the Writer's Strategies

1. When faced with having to write a clear and easy-to-understand description of a complicated process (how to prepare income-tax returns, do minor home repairs, or operate a computer), writers must use very precise language. Which words or phrases in this paragraph have a technical precision that makes this process clear to the reader?
2. The writer describes a number of problems associated with ice-cream cones. Which words or phrases does he use to help the reader know when he is about to identify these problems?

Writing Assignments

1. Choose another popular yet sometimes hard-to-eat food, e.g., spaghetti and meatballs, and imagine that you have to write directions for eating this food for someone who is wearing a new white suit and has never eaten this before. Write a paragraph of directions.
2. Choose some simple, everyday activity such as making a peanut-butter sandwich or brushing your teeth and write a short essay describing the *process* (steps, necessary equipment) involved. Imagine that your reader has never handled jars, sliced bread, and toothbrush and toothpaste.

The Cook

Barbara Lewis (student)

Barbara Lewis takes us through the process of preparing dinner at a busy restaurant. She juggles meat, potatoes, and a seemingly endless stream of sauces and other delectables in a two-hour race with the dinner bell. And she does all this after a day of classes at Cuyahoga Community College in Cleveland, Ohio.

Words to Know

au jus   natural, unthickened juices or gravy
escargots   snails
requisition   a formal written order
sauté   to fry food quickly in a little fat
scampi   shrimp

Getting Started

At what times in your life have you felt like the busiest, most pressured person in the world? What factors contributed to your state of mind?

Preparing food for the sauté line at the restaurant where I work is a hectic two-hour job. I come to work at 3:00 P.M. knowing that everything must be done by 5:00 P.M. The first thing I do is to check the requisition for the day and order my food. Then I have to clean and season five or six prime rib roasts and place them in the slow-cooking oven. After this, I clean and season five trays of white potatoes for baking and put them in the fast oven. Now I have two things cooking, prime ribs and potatoes, at different times and temperatures, and they both have to be watched very closely. In the meantime, I must put three trays of bacon in the oven. The bacon needs very close watching, too, because it burns very easily. Now I have prime ribs, potatoes, and bacon all cooking at the same time—and all needing constant watching. Next, I make popovers, which are unseasoned rolls. These also go into an oven for baking. Now I have prime ribs, baking potatoes, bacon, and popovers cooking at the same time and all of them needing to be closely watched. With my work area set up, I must make clarified butter and garlic butter. The clarified butter is for cooking liver, veal, and fish. The garlic butter is for stuffing escargots. I have to make ground meat stuffing also. Half of the ground meat will be mixed with wild rice and will be used to stuff breast of chicken. The other half of the ground meat mixture will be used to stuff mushrooms. I have to prepare veal, cut and season scampi, and clean and sauté mushrooms and onions. In the meantime, I check the prime ribs and potatoes, take the bacon and the popovers out of the oven, and put the veal and chicken into the oven. Now I make au jus, which is served over the prime ribs, make the soup for the day, and cook the vegetables and rice. Then I heat the bordelaise sauce, make the special for the day, and last of all, cook food for the employees. This and sometimes more has to be done by five o'clock. Is it any wonder that I say preparing food for the sauté line at the restaurant where I work is a very hectic two-hour job!

Questions About the Reading

1. Run through the cook's list again. For about how many people do you think she is preparing food?
2. Classify the food the cook is responsible for.
3. Do you think the cook likes her job? Explain your answer.

Questions About the Writer's Strategies

1. Where is the topic sentence of the paragraph? Does the writer restate the topic sentence anywhere in the paragraph? If so, where? Does the sentence then serve a second purpose? What is that purpose?
2. Do you think *hectic* is an effective word for describing this job?
3. The cook states at the beginning that she has two things to watch carefully. The list of things she watches continues to grow during the paragraph. Identify the sentences where she reemphasizes this point. Does this help support her statement that the job is hectic?
4. What order does the writer use to organize her information in the paragraph?

Writing Assignments

1. We all have moments when we feel under pressure. Write a process paragraph illustrating one of your busy days.
2. Imagine that the restaurant has decided to hire a helper for the cook and that you are to be that helper. Write a process paragraph explaining the steps you would take to assist the cook and how you would blend your activities with hers.

How to Write a Personal Letter

Garrison Keillor

Writing personal letters is an activity that many people believe they do not have the time to undertake. However, as Garrison Keillor explains in this essay, letter writing is a step-by-step process that leads to a unique kind of two-way communication.

Words to Know

anonymity   namelessness, obscurity
declarative   serving to state, announce, or say
obligatory   required, necessary

Getting Started

In what ways is letter writing a unique form of communication?

We shy persons need to write a letter now and then, or else we'll dry   1
up and blow away. It's true. And I speak as one who loves to reach for the
phone and talk. The telephone is to shyness what Hawaii is to February,
it's a way out of the woods. *And yet:* a letter is better.

Such a sweet gift—a piece of handmade writing, in an envelope that is   2
not a bill, sitting in our friend's path when she trudges home from a long
day spent among wahoos and savages, a day our words will help repair.
They don't need to be immortal, just sincere. She can read them twice
and again tomorrow: *You're someone I care about, Corinne, and think of often,
and every time I do, you make me smile.*

We need to write, otherwise nobody will know who we are. They will   3
have only a vague impression of us as A Nice Person, because, frankly,
we don't shine at conversation, we lack the confidence to thrust our faces
forward and say, "Hi, I'm Heather Hooten, let me tell you about my week."
Mostly we say "Uh-huh" and "Oh really." People smile and look over
our shoulder, looking for someone else to talk to.

So a shy person sits down and writes a letter. To be known by another   4
person—to meet and talk freely on the page—to be close despite distance.
To escape from anonymity and be our own sweet selves and express the
music of our souls.

We want our dear Aunt Eleanor to know that we have fallen in love,   5
that we quit our job, that we're moving to New York, and we want to say

a few things that might not get said in casual conversation: *Thank you for what you've meant to me. I am very happy right now.*

The first step in writing letters is to get over the guilt of *not* writing. 6 You don't "owe" anybody a letter. Letters are a gift. The burning shame you feel when you see unanswered mail makes it harder to pick up a pen and makes for a cheerless letter when you finally do. *I feel bad about not writing, but I've been so busy,* etc. Skip this. Few letters are obligatory, and they are *Thanks for the wonderful gift* and *I am terribly sorry to hear about George's death.* Write these promptly if you want to keep your friends. Don't worry about the others, except love letters, of course. When your true love writes *Dear Light of My Life, Joy of My Heart,* some response is called for.

Some of the best letters are tossed off in a burst of inspiration, so keep 7 your writing stuff in one place where you can sit down for a few minutes and—*Dear Roy, I am in the middle of an essay but thought I'd drop you a line. Hi to your sweetie too*—dash off a note to a pal. Envelopes, stamps, address book, everything in a drawer so you can write fast when the pen is hot.

A blank white 8" x 11" sheet can look as big as Montana if the pen's not 8 so hot—try a smaller page and write boldly. Get a pen that makes a sensuous line, get a comfortable typewriter, a friendly word processor—whichever feels easy to the hand.

Sit for a few minutes with the blank sheet of paper in front of you, and 9 let your friend come to mind. Remember the last time you saw each other and how your friend looked and what you said and what perhaps was unsaid between you; when your friend becomes real to you, start to write.

Write the salutation—*Dear You*—and take a deep breath and plunge in. 10 A simple declarative sentence will do, followed by another and another. As if you were talking to us. Don't think about grammar, don't think about style, just give us your news. Where did you go, who did you see, what did they say, what do you think?

If you don't know where to begin, start with the present: *I'm sitting at* 11 *the kitchen table on a rainy Saturday morning. Everyone is gone and the house is quiet.* Let the letter drift along. The toughest letter to crank out is one that is meant to impress, as we all know from writing job applications; if it's hard work to slip off a letter to a friend, maybe you're trying too hard to be terrific. A letter is only a report to someone who already likes you for reasons other than your brilliance. Take it easy.

Don't worry about form. It's not a term paper. When you come to the 12 end of one episode, just start a new paragraph. You can go from a few lines about the sad state of rock 'n' roll to the fight with your mother to your fond memories of Mexico to the kitchen sink and what's in it. The more you write, the easier it gets, and when you have a True True Friend to write to, a soul sibling, then it's like driving a car; you just press on the gas.

Don't tear up the page and start over when you write a bad line—try 13
to write your way out of it. Make mistakes and plunge on. Let the letter
cook along and let yourself be bold. Outrage, confusion, love—whatever
is in your mind, let it find a way to the page. Writing is a means of discovery,
always, and when you come to the end and write *Yours ever* or *Hugs and
Kisses,* you'll know something you didn't when you wrote *Dear Pal.*

Probably your friend will put your letter away, and it'll be read again a 14
few years from now—and it will improve with age.

And forty years from now, your friend's grandkids will dig it out of 15
the attic and read it, a sweet and precious relic of the ancient Eighties that
gives them a sudden clear glimpse of the world we old-timers knew. You
will have then created an object of art. Your simple lines about where you
went, who you saw, what they said, will speak to those children and they
will feel in their hearts the humanity of our times.

You can't pick up a phone and call the future and tell them about our 16
times. You have to pick up a piece of paper.

Questions About the Reading

1. Why does Keillor believe a letter is better than a phone call?
2. Why is it especially important for shy people to write letters?
3. Why does the writer believe that style and grammar aren't important in a personal letter?
4. What is the first step to letter writing that Keillor suggests most people never get past?
5. What do you think the writer means when he says that "writing is a means of discovery"? Do you agree or disagree? Why?
6. How do you feel about writing—and receiving—letters?

Questions About the Writer's Strategies

1. Is the author's purpose to inform, describe, or instruct? What is it about the point of view of this essay that makes it more than a set of instructions?
2. What kind of order does the writer use in listing his points?
3. Why is this labeled a process essay? List the steps in the process that Keillor suggests.
4. The writer uses the mode of comparison and contrast in the beginning and conclusion of the essay. To what does he compare writing letters?

Writing Assignments

1. In a process paragraph, explain how to plan a party, go on a first date, or invite someone new to dinner. Try to use a casual, friendly tone.
2. Write a process essay that describes how to respond to a very friendly letter from someone you wish hadn't written to you.
3. Rewrite "How to Write a Personal Letter" in a purely instructional manner. Use numbered steps and the second-person point of view.

The Beekeeper

Sue Hubbell

Preparing for a job as a beekeeper is a painstaking process that actually requires, as Sue Hubbell shows us, taking pain.

Words to Know

anaphylactic   severe reaction with possible collapse or death
supers   wooden boxes that contain the bees' honey

Getting Started

Do you follow a process in getting ready to do your homework?

The time to harvest honey is summer's end, when it is hot. The temper 1
of the bees requires that we wear protective clothing: a full set of overalls,
a zippered bee veil and leather gloves. Even a very strong young man
works up a sweat wrapped in a bee suit in the heat, hustling 60-pound
supers while being harassed by angry bees. It is a hard job, harder even
than haying, but jobs are scarce here and I've always been able to hire
help.

This year David, the son of a friend of mine, is working for me. He is 2
big and strong and used to labor, but he was nervous about bees. After
we had made the job arrangement I set about desensitizing him to bee
stings. I put a piece of ice on his arm to numb it and then, holding a bee
carefully by its head, I put it on the numbed spot and let it sting him. A
bee stinger is barbed and stays in the flesh, pulling loose from the body of
the bee as it struggles to free itself. The bulbous poison sac at the top of
the stinger continues to pulsate after the bee has left, pumping the venom
and forcing the stinger deeper into the flesh.

That first day I wanted David to have only a partial dose of venom, so 3
after a minute I scraped the stinger out. A few people are seriously sensitive to bee venom; each sting they receive can cause a more severe reaction than the one before—reactions ranging from hives, breathing difficulties, accelerated heart beat and choking to anaphylactic shock and
death. I didn't think David would be allergic in that way, but I wanted to
make sure.

We sat down and had a cup of coffee and I watched him. The spot 4
where the stinger went in grew red and began to swell. That was a normal reaction, and so was the itching that he felt later on.

The next day I coaxed a bee into stinging him again, repeating the pro- 5
cedure, but I left the stinger in place for 10 minutes, until the venom sac
was empty. Again the spot was red, swollen and itchy but had disappeared in 24 hours. By that time David was ready to catch a bee himself
and administer his own sting. He also decided that the ice cube was a
bother and gave it up. I told him to keep to one sting a day until he had
no redness or swelling and then to increase to two stings. He was ready
for them the next day. The greater amount of venom caused redness and
swelling for a few days, but soon his body could tolerate it without reaction and he increased the number of stings once again.

Today he told me he was up to six stings. His arms look as though they 6
have track marks on them, but the fresh stings are having little effect. I'll
keep him at it until he can tolerate 10 a day with no reaction and then I'll
not worry about taking him out to the bee yard.

Questions About the Reading

1. When is the honey harvested? Why is the honey harvested then?
2. How much do the supers that hold the honey weigh?
3. Why is the beekeeper able to hire help in harvesting the honey?
4. How many stings per day does the beekeeper want her helper to tolerate before taking him to the bee yard?

Questions About the Writer's Strategies

1. Identify the steps in the desensitizing process.
2. Could the selection as a whole or the sentences within it be classified
   by any other modes of development? If so, which modes and which
   sentences?
3. What is the thesis of the selection? Is it stated? If so, identify it; if not,
   state the thesis in your own words.

Writing Assignments

1. Write an essay in which you explain the process you follow in getting
   ready for work, doing your laundry, or repairing your car or some
   household item.
2. Write an essay in which you explain the process you follow in preparing to buy groceries and then in buying them.

The Wine Experience

Leo Buscaglia

In contemporary life we often are too far removed from the actual process of growing and making things. We buy all our food and clothes in stores without any knowledge of their original sources. This essay describes the joyful step-by-step procedure of wine making in a traditional Italian-American home.

Words to Know

connoisseur   someone with shrewd, clever discrimination concerning matters of taste; an expert

cylindrical   circular and tubelike

dissertation   a speech, lecture, or long essay on a specific subject

oenophile   someone who loves the study of wine

precariously   without stability, without balance

prelude   an introduction

Getting Started

Why is it so satisfying to make something from scratch?

Like all good Italians, Papa loved his wine, although I never knew him 1 to drink to excess. A glass or two of wine to accompany his dinner was his limit. He never touched hard liquor.

Papa's love of wine went far beyond the simple enjoyment of drinking 2 it. He was truly an oenophile, a connoisseur. He always made his own wine, from ripened grapes to dated label. His cool, dark cellar was full of dusty bottles and cylindrical, wooden barrels of varying sizes, all carefully marked to indicate the type of grape and the year of the harvest.

When I was growing up, we had many festivities in our home. None, 3 except Christmas and Easter, topped the one night each year that we made the new wine. The anticipation and preparation began in July and August, long before the eventful September evening when the truckload of grapes was delivered. By then Papa had made several visits to his friends—grape growers in Cucamonga, about forty miles from our home—to observe the progress of his grapes. He had spent hours scouring the barrels in which the wine would be made and stored, and applying antirust varnish on every visible metal part of the wine-making equipment. The fermenting vat had been filled with water to swell the wood.

On the appointed evening, the truck would arrive after nightfall, brimming with small, tough-skinned, sweet-smelling Cabernet grapes. The boxes of grapes were hand-carried about two hundred feet to the garage, where a giant empty vat awaited. A hand-powered crusher was positioned precariously on top of the vat, ready to grind noisily into the night, as thousands of grapes were poured into it. It was an all-male operation that included Papa, his relatives, and friends. Dressed in their undershirts, bodies glistening with perspiration, they took turns cranking the crusher handle. My job was to stack the empty crates neatly out of the way as a prelude to what for me was the most exciting part of the evening. 4

After all the grapes had been mashed and the empty boxes stacked, it was time for us to remove our shoes, socks, and pants and slip into the cool, dark moisture for the traditional grape stomping. This was done, of course, to break up the skins, but I couldn't have cared less why it was necessary. For me it was a sensual experience unlike any other, feeling the grape residue gushing between my toes and watching as the new wine turned my legs the rich, deep color of Cabernet Sauvignon. 5

While this "man's work" was being accomplished, the "woman's work" was progressing in the kitchen. The heady fragrance of the crushed grapes, mingled with the savory aromas of dinner wafting from the house, caused our feet to move in step with our growing appetites. The traditional main course for our wine-making dinner was gnocchi, a small, dumplinglike pasta that would be cooked to perfection and topped with a wonderful sauce that had been simmering for hours. 6

Like Christmas Eve, this particular night was unique in many ways. Throughout the rest of the year, we routinely sat down to dinner by 5:30 each evening. But for this occasion dinner was never served until the wine making was finished, sometimes as late as 10 P.M. By then, we were all purple from grape juice, exhausted, and famished. 7

No matter how tired and hungry we were, however, Papa always prefaced the dinner with a dissertation on "the wine experience." This ceremony called for his finest wines, which had been aging in his modest but efficient wine cellar. Drinking wine, he would remind us, was a highly respected activity, not to be taken lightly. The nectar of the grape had brought joy to human beings long before recorded history. 8

"Wine is a delight and a challenge and is never meant to be drunk quickly. It's to be savored and sipped slowly," he'd tell us. "All the senses are awakened when you drink wine. You drink with your eyes, your tongue, your throat, your nose. Notice the colors the wine makes in the glass—all the way from dark purple, like a bishop's robe, to the golden amber of an aspen leaf." 9

He would hold up the glass to the light as if we were about to share a 10
sacrament, then swirl the wine around in his glass, guiding us through
the whole ritual, from the first sip to the final, all-important swallow.

  "Alla salute!"   11

Questions About the Reading

1. How do you think the writer feels about his father? What leads you to
   this conclusion?
2. How often did the Buscaglia family make wine?
3. What happened to the grapes after they were crushed?
4. What did wine making and Christmas have in common to the writer
   as a child?

Questions About the Writer's Strategies

1. What is the writer's thesis? Can you identify the thesis statement, or is
   the thesis implied?
2. What is the point of view in the essay? Could another point of view be
   used?
3. In what ways is this paragraph subjective? In what ways is it objective?
4. Is the writer's purpose to instruct a beginner in how to make wine? If
   so, what are the main steps? If not, what else would you need to know?

Writing Assignments

1. Write a first-person essay about a family tradition in your home that
   involves a holiday or a special event. Write it as a process so that your
   readers could try to duplicate the celebration at home.
2. Choose a skill you have learned from one of your parents and write a
   second-person process essay describing it.
3. *Working Together* Join with some classmates and think of an item
   that all of you have eaten, worn, or used recently. Write an essay in
   which you explain the process involved in producing the item (for
   example, a spiral-bound notebook, a pair of tennis shoes, or a blackboard).

How Dictionaries Are Made

S. I. Hayakawa

When we look at familiar, everyday objects, we rarely think, "Someone made this." How often have you looked up a word in your dictionary this year? Did you ever wonder, "Who wrote this definition? What makes it correct?" S. I. Hayakawa, who has been a teacher, a university president, the author of several books on language, and a United States senator, here tells us how the definitions that appear in a dictionary are determined.

Words to Know

context   statements that occur before or after a word and that determine its meaning

decreed   ruled

disseminate   distribute

docility   passiveness

grammarian   person who is an expert in grammar

prophecy   ability to see into the future

Getting Started

What process do you follow in doing your homework?

It is an almost universal belief that every word has a "correct meaning,"   1
that we learn these meanings principally from teachers and grammarians (except that most of the time we don't bother to, so that we ordinarily speak "sloppy English"), and that dictionaries and grammars are the "supreme authority" in matters of meaning and usage. Few people ask by what authority the writers of dictionaries and grammars say what they say. The docility with which most people bow down to the dictionary is amazing, and the person who says, "Well, the dictionary is wrong!" is looked upon with smiles of pity and amusement which say plainly, "Poor fellow! He's really quite sane otherwise."

Let us see how dictionaries are made and how the editors arrive at   2
definitions. What follows applies, incidentally, only to those dictionary offices where first-hand, original research goes on—not those in which editors simply copy existing dictionaries. The task of writing a dictionary begins with the reading of vast amounts of the literature of the period or subject that it is intended to cover. As the editors read, they copy on cards

every interesting or rare word, every unusual or peculiar occurrence of a common word, a large number of common words in their ordinary uses, and also the sentences in which each of these words appears, thus:

> pail
> The dairy *pails* bring home increase of milk
> Keats, *Endymion*
> I, 44–45

That is to say, the context of each word is collected, along with the   3
word itself. For a really big job of dictionary writing, such as the *Oxford English Dictionary* (usually bound in about twenty-five volumes), millions of such cards are collected, and the task of editing occupies decades. As the cards are collected, they are alphabetized and sorted. When the sorting is completed, there will be for each word anywhere from two or three to several hundred illustrative quotations, each on its card.

To define a word, then, the dictionary editor places before him the stack   4
of cards illustrating that word; each of the cards represents an actual use of the word by a writer of some literary or historical importance. He reads the cards carefully, discards some, re-reads the rest, and divides up the stack according to what he thinks are the several senses of the word. Finally, he writes his definitions, following the hard-and-fast rule that each definition must be based on what the quotations in front of him reveal about the meaning of the word. The editor cannot be influenced by what he thinks a given word ought to mean. He must work according to the cards, or not at all.

The writing of a dictionary, therefore, is not a task of setting up au-   5
thoritative statements about the "true meanings" of words, but a task of recording, to the best of one's ability, what various words have meant to authors in the distant or immediate past. The writer of a dictionary is a historian, not a law-giver. If, for example, we had been writing a dictionary in 1890, or even as late as 1919, we could have said that the word "broadcast" means "to scatter," seed and so on; but we could not have decreed that from 1921 on, the commonest meaning of the word should become "to disseminate audible messages, etc., by wireless telephony." To regard the dictionary as an "authority," therefore, is to credit the dictionary writer with gifts of prophecy which neither he nor anyone else possesses. In choosing our words when we speak or write, we can be guided by the historical record afforded us by the dictionary, but we cannot be bound by it, because new situations, new experiences, new inven-

tions, new feelings, are always compelling us to give new uses to old words. Looking under a "hood," we should ordinarily have found, five hundred years ago, a monk; today, we find a motorcar engine.

Questions About the Reading

1. Describe the process used to write a dictionary.
2. Do meanings of words change over time?
3. How does the editor of a dictionary decide what meaning a word should have?
4. Do you think a dictionary from the 1880s would be useful for writing college papers now? Why or why not?

Questions About the Writer's Strategies

1. Which sentences in the essay state how to make a dictionary? Are they arranged in chronological order?
2. What is the tone of this essay? Is this a good model for college writing? Why or why not?
3. Divide this essay into introductory, development, and concluding paragraphs. (See chapter 1.) Does the author restate his thesis in the concluding paragraph?

Writing Assignments

1. There are some similarities between organizing a dictionary and organizing a term paper. What are the steps you would recommend for writing a term paper?
2. *Working Together*   With some classmates imagine you are planning to write a short biography of Abraham Lincoln or another president you all admire. Write an essay in which you describe possible ways of finding information, making sure to include several methods.

Pithing a Frog

Irene Szurley (student)

Irene Szurley is offering us more than instructions here. Her running commentary on the process she is describing leaves us asking more questions than just "Are we doing it right?" She wants us to wonder, "Are we right to do this?" Be careful. After she gets through with you, you may never want to go to biology class again.

Words to Know

anaesthesis   deadening of pain or sensation
annihilation   death
cephalic   of the head
cranial   pertaining to the brain
dubiously   questionably
flaccid   soft, limp
grotesque   distorted
intricate   complex
middorsal   middle of the back
occipital   the back part of the head
posteriorly   along the back part of the body
procure   to obtain
vertebrae   the bones of the spinal column

Getting Started

How does humor or sarcasm help you endure unpleasant tasks?

During the course of biological events, it often becomes necessary to 1
kill in order to learn about life. Biologists have devised many intricate
procedures to accomplish this annihilation, and pithing is one of these.

This procedure is used as a means of destroying the central nervous 2
system in order to eliminate sensation and response in the frog, so that it
can be properly dissected. Anaesthesis cannot possibly be used as an alternative method, because it wears off, and that could prove disastrously
disadvantageous.

To begin this dubiously humane procedure, you, the aspiring muti- 3
lationist, must hold the cool, dry frog in your left fist, positioning your
fingers and thumbs in the grotesque attitude of a vise-like grip. The in-

dex finger must press down on top of the poor, defenseless frog's head, exerting pressure so that the spinal cord will be bent at the neck.

Next, take your right index finger and use your nail—the longer, the 4 better tactile response—to find the junction of the frog's vertebral column with its occipital bone. If a nail doesn't work, bring the point of a dull dissecting needle—we don't want any more pain than is absolutely necessary—posteriorly along the animal's middorsal line until the first bulge of a vertebra can be felt twinging through the skin.

Now cast aside your dull needles. You are ready to begin the actual 5 rupturing—the mutilation. Procure a sharp needle and puncture the skin at the junction you have just located. Neatness is important, so remember to make only a *hole* in the skin; no lengthy gashes, please.

Retrieve your dull needle and insert it through this gaping hole, plung- 6 ing it into the spinal cord as far as it will go. Don't be timid now. At this point, the frog will become totally limp and flaccid, as he is in a state of spinal shock. You will no longer have to worry about his squirming and wiggling efforts to free himself, all in vain. Tsk.

As soon as the probe is in the cord up to the hilt, turn it and direct it 7 forward into the cranial cavity. Move it parallel to the external surface, which by this time is awash with cephalic blood, but don't let this minor problem deter you. If the needle is positioned correctly in the cranial cavity, it will be possible to feel bone on all sides of the needle.

Begin, slowly at first, then progressively more rapidly, to twist the 8 needle; thrash it right and left. Complete destruction of the brain is inevitable, even if you are clumsy.

After this step, the frog is single-pithed. Since our knowledge must 9 know no bounds, we must invariably explore further. Place the needle at right angles to the body surface, turn its handle towards the vacant head, parallel to the external surface. *Gently,* since we must maintain the essence of humanity at all times, push the needle into the spinal cord. A quick way to test your aim, and to amuse your friends, is to see if the frog's legs have spastically jerked out straight. If so, then you may proceed to slowly rotate your implement of destruction until all the nerves are disconnected and frayed. The frog is now double-pithed and unable to offer any resistance to your further exploratory efforts in the name of science.

Questions About the Reading

1. What does the writer mean by the phrase "kill in order to learn about life" (paragraph 1)?

2. What is *pithing*? First describe it as you understand it from the essay and then check a dictionary.
3. What is the purpose of destroying the frog's brain?
4. What further steps are necessary to double-pith?

Questions About the Writer's Strategies

1. What tone is established in this essay? What words or phrases establish the tone? What is the effect of this tone on the reader?
2. Is the technical terminology clearly defined for the nonscientist? What additional terms would you like to see defined by the writer?
3. Where does the writer define *pithing*? Is the definition necessary? Is that the most effective place for it?
4. In what order does the writer organize her material?

Writing Assignments

1. Describe any other common procedure, using descriptive words to convey your personal feeling about the procedure. For example, tell how to iron a shirt, wash the car, clean the bathtub, or take out the garbage. Tell your feelings and reactions after each step.
2. Rewrite the paragraph, eliminating the emotionally charged or sarcastic words, and compare the effectiveness of the two paragraphs.
3. Give a new owner an explanation of how to housebreak a dog or how to care for a bird or cat. Describe some of the less pleasant parts of these tasks.

——————— Connections ———————

1. Choose two of the selections in this chapter and discuss the similarities and differences between the processes they describe.
2. Some of the selections in this chapter offer how-to advice on topics ranging from being desensitized to bee stings to making a dictionary. What connections can you make between any two of these pieces? How are the selections alike? How are they different?
3. The selections in this chapter by Leslie Marmon Silko and L. Rust Hills are humorous in tone. Of what are these pieces making fun? How are they alike? How are they different? Which selection do you prefer? Why? Cite details and examples from the selections to support your opinions.

8

Cause and Effect

IN YOUR LOCAL newspaper you notice a story about a car accident that took place late on a Saturday night. The driver missed a curve, slammed into a tree, and was badly injured. Police investigators reported that the young victim had been drinking heavily with friends and lost control of the car on the way home. This news article is a relatively clear example of a **cause,** heavy consumption of alcohol, and an **effect,** a serious accident.

Sometimes you can recognize immediately that cause and effect is part of a writer's **mode of development** because the writer uses words that signal a cause-and-effect relationship—transitional words like *because, therefore, as a result,* and *consequently.* However, writers will not necessarily indicate cause and effect so directly. Sometimes a cause-and-effect relationship will be clear only from the arrangement of ideas or the narrative sequence of events. Usually, though, the **topic sentence** or **thesis statement** will indicate that the writer is describing a cause-and-effect situation.

A cause-and-effect explanation tells *why* something turns out the way it does. In some cases, a single cause may contribute to one or more effects. In the following paragraph, the writer says that a single cause—the early release of prisoners—led to an increase in crimes.

Cause | To save money in the early 1980s, Illinois released 21,000 prisoners an average of three months early. James Austin of the
Effects | National Council on Crime and Delinquency calculates that the early releases produced 23 homicides, 32 rapes, 262 arsons, 681 robberies, 2,472 burglaries, 2,571 assaults and more than 8,000 other crimes. According to Harvard researchers

Effect
> David P. Cavanaugh and Mark A. R. Kleiman, the $60 mil-
> lion the state saved cost Illinois crime victims $304 million,
> directly or indirectly.

Eugene H. Methvin,
"Pay Now—Or Pay Later"

A writer may also say that several causes contributed to or resulted in a particular effect.

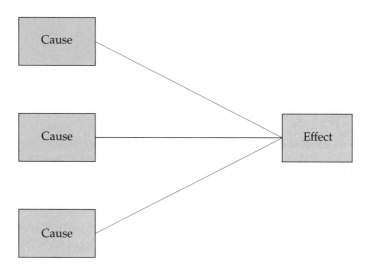

For example, in the following essay, the writer suggests three causes for the disappearance of moonshining—the secret manufacturing of whiskey—as a fine art.

The manufacture of illicit whiskey in the mountains is not   1
dead. Far from it. As long as the operation of a still remains
so financially rewarding, it will never die. There will always
be men ready to take their chances against the law for such
an attractive profit, and willing to take their punishment
when they are caught.

Effect
> Moonshining as a fine art, however, effectively disap-   2
> peared some time ago. There were several reasons. One was

Cause 1: decline
in use of home
remedies contain-
ing corn whiskey
> the age of aspirin and modern medicine. As home doctoring
> lost its stature, the demand for pure corn whiskey as an es-
> sential ingredient of many home remedies vanished along
> with those remedies. Increasing affluence was another rea-

Cause 2: young
people finding
easier ways to
make money
> son. Young people, rather than follow in their parents' foot-
> steps, decided that there were easier ways to make money,
> and they were right.

Cause 3: greed
causing producers
to care more for
quantity than
quality

Third, and perhaps most influential of all, was the arrival,   3
even in moonshining, of that peculiarly human disease
known to most of us as greed. One fateful night, some force
whispered in an unsuspecting moonshiner's ear, "Look.
Add this gadget to your still and you'll double your production. Double your production, and you can double your
profits."

Soon the small operators were being forced out of busi-   4
ness, and moonshining, like most other manufacturing en-
terprises, was quickly taken over by a breed of men bent on
making money—and lots of it. Loss of pride in the product,
and loss of time taken with the product increased in direct
proportion to the desire for production; and thus moonshining as a fine art was buried in a quiet little ceremony attended
only by those mourners who had once been the proud artists, known far and wide across the hills for the excellence of
their product. Too old to continue making it themselves, and
with no one following behind them, they were reduced to
reminiscing about "the good old days when the whiskey that
was made was *really* whiskey, and no questions asked."

Suddenly moonshining fell into the same category as faith   5
healing, planting by the signs, and all the other vanishing
customs that were a part of a rugged, self-sufficient culture
that is now disappearing.

Eliot Wigginton,
"Moonshining as a Fine Art"

In still other cases, one cause may have several effects.

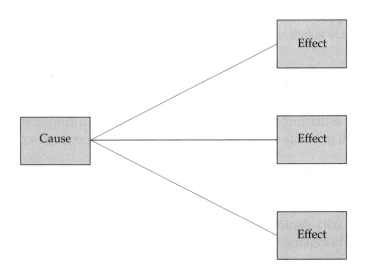

In the following paragraph, the writer explains that the explosion of a nuclear bomb (the cause) has five primary effects. Notice as you read that the writer combines **process** with the cause-and-effect explanation.

Topic	Whereas most conventional bombs produce only one destructive effect—the shock wave—nuclear weapons produce many
Cause	destructive effects. At the moment of the explosion, when the temperature of the weapon material, instantly gasified, is at the superstellar level, the pressure is millions of times the normal atmospheric pressure. Immediately, radiation, consisting mainly of gamma rays, which are a very high-
Effect 1: initial nuclear radiation	energy form of electromagnetic radiation, begins to stream outward into the environment. This is called the "initial nuclear radiation," and is the first of the destructive effects of a nuclear explosion. In an air burst of a one-megaton bomb—a bomb with the explosive yield of a million tons of TNT, which is a medium-sized weapon in present-day nuclear arsenals—the initial nuclear radiation can kill unprotected human beings in an area of some six square miles.
Effect 2: electromagnetic pulse	Virtually simultaneously with the initial nuclear radiation, in a second destructive effect of the explosion, an electromagnetic pulse is generated by the intense gamma radiation acting on the air. In a high-altitude detonation, the pulse can knock out electrical equipment over a wide area by inducing a powerful surge of voltage through various conductors, such as antennas, overhead power lines, pipes, and railroad tracks. . . . When the fusion and fission reactions have blown themselves out, a fireball takes shape. As it expands, energy
Effect 3: thermal pulse	is absorbed in the form of X rays by the surrounding air, and then the air re-radiates a portion of that energy into the environment in the form of the thermal pulse—a wave of blinding light and intense heat—which is the third of the destructive effects of a nuclear explosion. . . . The thermal pulse of a one-megaton bomb lasts for about ten seconds and can cause second-degree burns in exposed human beings at a distance of nine and a half miles, or in an area of more than two hundred and eighty square miles. . . . As the fireball expands, it
Effect 4: blast wave	also sends out a blast wave in all directions, and this is the fourth destructive effect of the explosion. The blast wave of an air-burst one-megaton bomb can flatten or severely damage all but the strongest buildings within a radius of four and a half miles. . . . As the fireball burns, it rises, condensing water from the surrounding atmosphere to form the characteristic mushroom cloud. If the bomb has been set off on the ground or close enough to it so that the fireball touches the surface, a so-called ground burst, a crater will be formed, and tons of dust and debris will be fused with the intensely radioactive fission products and sucked up into the mush-
Effect 5: radioactive fallout	room cloud. This mixture will return to earth as radioactive fallout, most of it in the form of fine ash, in the fifth destruc-

⌐ tive effect of the explosion. Depending upon the composition of the surface, from 40 to 70 percent of this fallout—
often called the "early" or "local" fallout—descends to earth
within about a day of the explosion, in the vicinity of the
blast and downwind from it, exposing human beings to radiation disease, an illness that is fatal when exposure is intense.

Jonathan Schell,
The Fate of the Earth

You should notice still another characteristic in this sample paragraph:
the writer describes both main causes and subordinate causes, and main
effects and subordinate effects. One main cause, the explosion of the bomb,
causes a series of five initial (main) effects. However, these effects become the causes for still other effects. The initial nuclear radiation (effect
1), for example, is also a cause that results in the death of unprotected
human beings in a six-square-mile area (a subordinate effect). The elec-
tromagnetic pulse (effect 2) that is generated by the explosion is the cause,
in turn, of the knocking out of electrical equipment (a subordinate effect).
The thermal pulse (effect 3) causes second-degree burns (a subordinate
effect) in exposed humans in a 280-square-mile area. The blast wave (effect 4) causes the destruction of buildings (a subordinate effect), and the
radioactive fallout (effect 5) causes radiation disease (a subordinate effect) in humans. As the following chart shows, cause-and-effect relationships can be complicated.

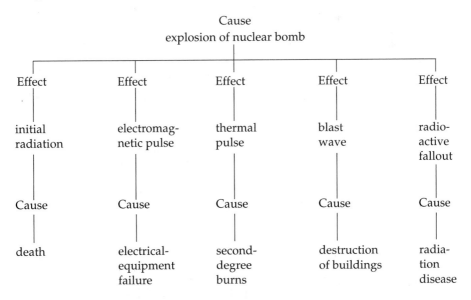

You should keep two factors in mind when you are writing and **revising** a cause-and-effect essay. First, be sure that you have actually thought

through the causes and effects very carefully. You should not be satisfied with considering only obvious or simple causes. For example, we tend to oversimplify and cite one cause as the reason for a war—the attack on Pearl Harbor for the United States entering World War II, the firing on Fort Sumter for the start of the Civil War, and so on. For the most part, these tend to be the last of many contributing causes that have led to the war. A thoughtful discussion of such a topic in your writing would include an explanation of some of the contributing, less obvious but perhaps more important, causes.

Second, you should be careful that you do not mistake an event as a cause simply because it preceded a particular effect. For instance, if a child swallows a coin and then comes down with measles, it would be inaccurate and faulty reasoning, a *fallacy*—in this case, a *post hoc* (meaning "after this, therefore because of this") *fallacy*—to assume that swallowing the coin was a cause of the measles. Other common fallacies you should guard against in both your reading and your writing include the

- *Hasty generalization,* which is reasoning based on too few examples or insufficient evidence. "The cause of World War II was the Japanese bombing of Pearl Harbor."
- *Non sequitur,* which is claiming an effect that does not necessarily follow from the stated cause. "He believes in the supernatural because he has read the Harry Potter books."

Even though you need to guard against fallacies, you should also be aware that writers do not always state a cause-and-effect relationship directly. Sometimes they **imply** the relationship and leave it to the reader to infer the relationship. That is, the writer does not state the relationship, but arranges certain information in such a way that the reader will be able to conclude that the relationship exists, as in the following sentences.

> On the ground next to the parked Jeep, the compass glinted in the moonlight. Deep in the woods, shielded from the moon, the hungry teenager circled in the dark with little idea where he had been or how to get where he wanted to go.

Although the writer does not directly state what happened, it is not hard to infer that the teenager dropped his compass without realizing it, with the effect that he is now lost.

You will need to make inferences when you read cause-and-effect writing as well as other **modes of development.** When you make an inference, be sure that you can pinpoint the information and trace the logic on which your inference is based. When you are writing about cause and effect, be sure to give enough information, directly or indirectly, so that your reader can determine the cause-and-effect relationship.

You use cause-and-effect reasoning every day in solving problems and making decisions. Legislators create laws to address the causes of certain problems. In a similar way, scientists find cures for diseases when they are able to isolate the causes of those diseases. Understanding the relation between causes and effects is extremely important in both day-to-day living and long-range planning. Communicating your understanding in writing is significant evidence of your ability to reason clearly and accurately.

The Power of Place

Winifred Gallagher

There are many ways in which the physical environment in which we live and work affects our well-being. In this paragraph about the effect of computer screens on computer operators, journalist Winifred Gallagher explains why you can't always blame your boss for a bad day at the office.

Words to Know

clarity   clearness

irritants   things that cause annoyance or physical discomfort

microanalysis   analysis of quantities weighing one milligram or less

noxious   harmful to health

occupational   pertaining to jobs and work

overtly   openly, not hidden

stressor   something that causes stress

VDTs   video display terminals or computer screens

Getting Started

What are the factors that cause you the most physical stress in your daily life?

Few places are as overly stimulating as the rush-hour subway, yet some of the less overtly jittery spots where we spend far more time exact their tolls as well. As we move further into the postmodern age of information, the workplace is changing fast, causing occupational safety specialists to focus on problems that would have seemed light-weight to their predecessors. Not long ago, for example, "industrial fatigue" meant the hard-hat exhaustion of steelworkers and coal miners. Now it is just as likely to refer to the weariness, eyestrain, and aches and pains of computer operators who spend long periods with poorly designed VDTs, desks, and chairs. Environmental psychologists have shown that the proper adjustment of a single element at a computer station calls for painstaking microanalysis. To evaluate the screen, for example, one must consider its height, tilt, and distance from the operator, the size and clarity of its characters, and its brightness, glare, and flickering. Because its effects are often subtle, combined with other irritants, and bother us after exposure ceases, trying to pinpoint an environmental stressor is difficult for the layman. As a result, we often end up blaming its noxious influence on something else—the project, the boss, or "stress" in general—thus perpetuating the dilemma.

Questions About the Reading

1. What are the most common complaints of computer operators?
2. What are the variations in screen design and use that environmental psychologists evaluate?
3. What do you think the writer means by "hard-hat exhaustion"? What would be a good name for the more modern industrial fatigue the writer describes?
4. In what ways does the author show that circumstances are rapidly changing in the field of occupational safety? Give examples.

Questions About the Writer's Strategies

1. Identify the cause-and-effect elements in this paragraph.
2. Besides cause and effect, what other mode of development does the writer use in this paragraph?
3. According to the writer, why is it difficult for the average worker to pinpoint environmental stressors?
4. Is this paragraph written subjectively or objectively? Use words and phrases from the paragraph to support your answer.

Writing Assignments

1. Do you think the government should spend more money researching the effects of VDTs on workers' stress levels? Using cause-and-effect elements, write a paragraph discussing why it is important to keep office environments safe.
2. Write a paragraph in which you identify some of the effects on your body of your own work and study environments.
3. Do some experimenting with the lighting, chair position, and screen position in your own computer environment. Then write a paragraph about the effects of these changes on your stress level while you work at the computer.

A Momentous Arrest

Martin Luther King, Jr.

Martin Luther King, Jr., was catapulted into international fame when, working for the Southern Christian Leadership Conference, he organized blacks in Montgomery, Alabama, to boycott that city's segregated buses in 1955 and 1956. King, preaching nonviolent resistance to segregation, became the most important leader in the civil rights movement that changed American life so radically over the next decade. Here, in a simple matter-of-fact tone, King tells of the incident that sparked the Montgomery bus boycott.

Words to Know

accommodate   to make space for, oblige
complied   carried out willingly

Getting Started

Have you ever disobeyed a rule because you thought it was unfair?

On December 1, 1955, an attractive Negro seamstress, Mrs. Rosa Parks, boarded the Cleveland Avenue Bus in downtown Montgomery. She was returning home after her regular day's work in the Montgomery Fair—a leading department store. Tired from long hours on her feet, Mrs. Parks sat down in the first seat behind the section reserved for whites. Not long after she took her seat, the bus operator ordered her, along with three other Negro passengers, to move back in order to accommodate boarding white passengers. By this time every seat in the bus was taken. This meant that if Mrs. Parks followed the driver's command she would have to stand while a white male passenger, who had just boarded the bus, would sit. The other three Negro passengers immediately complied with the driver's request. But Mrs. Parks quietly refused. The result was her arrest.

Questions About the Reading

1. Was Mrs. Parks breaking any law or custom in sitting where she did?
2. Why didn't Mrs. Parks move when the bus driver asked her to? Do

you think she would have moved if the white passenger had been a woman instead of a man?

3. Was Mrs. Parks thinking about the civil rights movement when she refused to move? Explain your answer.
4. What is it about Mrs. Park's action that seems so symbolic of the early civil rights movement?

Questions About the Writer's Strategies

1. Which sentence states the cause in this paragraph? Which one states the effect?
2. Do you think the writer presents the incident objectively or subjectively? Use words and phrases from the paragraph to support your answer.
3. Other than cause and effect, what mode of development dominates in this paragraph?
4. What is the order in which the incidents in the paragraph are arranged?
5. Do you sympathize with Mrs. Parks? Explain your answer, citing examples from the essay that influence your feelings.

Writing Assignments

1. Think of a situation that made you angry enough to defy authority and risk discipline or even arrest. Perhaps you protested an unfair grade, a school rule, an unjust traffic ticket, or something of more consequence, like contamination of your city's water supply. Using cause and effect as your mode of development, describe in a paragraph what happened. Try to write objectively.
2. The civil rights movement of the 1950s and 1960s brought about many positive changes in our country's attitude toward minorities. There are, however, still steps that can be taken. In a paragraph, suggest one possible change the country can make, and speculate on the effects it could have on the lives of minority citizens.

An Eyewitness Account

Jack London

Jack London (1876–1916) is best known for such adventure novels as
The Call of the Wild. *In this paragraph from an essay published in May,*
1906, in Collier's Weekly, *he describes the effects of the devastating San*
Francisco earthquake of April 16, 1906.

Words to Know

conflagration   destructive fire
imperial   magnificent, majestic
nabobs   rich men
wrought   caused

Getting Started

Have you ever seen a fire, flood, or other natural disaster?

The earthquake shook down in San Francisco hundreds of thousands of
dollars' worth of walls and chimneys. But the conflagration that followed
burned up hundreds of millions of dollars' worth of property. There is no
estimating within hundreds of millions the actual damage wrought. Not
in history has a modern imperial city been so completely destroyed. San
Francisco is gone! Nothing remains of it but memories and a fringe of
dwelling houses on its outskirts. Its industrial section is wiped out. Its
social and residential section is wiped out. The factories and warehouses,
the great stores and newspaper buildings, the hotels and the palaces of
the nabobs, are all gone. Remains only the fringe of dwelling houses on
the outskirts of what was once San Francisco.

Questions About the Reading

1. According to the writer, how many dollars' worth of property were
   destroyed by the earthquake?
2. If the earthquake shook down walls and chimneys, what do you think
   caused the devastating fire that followed?
3. What happened to the San Francisco industrial section?

4. What were the only things that remained of San Francisco after the earthquake?

Questions About the Writer's Strategies

1. What is the tone of the paragraph?
2. Is the paragraph objective, subjective, or both?
3. Identify the cause-and-effect elements in the paragraph.
4. What modes of development does the writer use in addition to cause and effect?

Writing Assignments

1. Watch your local news report and write a paragraph in which you suggest the cause and effects of a reported fire, flood, robbery, or accident.
2. Write a paragraph in which you identify some of the effects of the closing of a business that employs many people in your city or town.
3. Write a paragraph in which you explain the possible effects on a business of its product being determined harmful.

On Being Unemployed

Nelliejean Smith (student)

*In the paragraph that follows, we learn of the many effects that unem-
ployment can have on a person's life. The writer makes us see—and feel
with her—that unemployment is a traumatic experience. Nelliejean Smith
has proven, however, that she can cope with it, for she wrote this paragraph as a student at Cuyahoga Community College.*

Words to Know

bureaucracy   an administrative section of government that is
   often impersonal and inflexible; red tape
evoke   to summon or call forth; to elicit

Getting Started

In what ways do the effects of unemployment reach deeper than
an empty bank account?

Being unemployed creates many problems for my family and me. First
of all, there are financial problems. We have cut back on the quality of
groceries we purchase. We now buy two pounds of hamburger in place
of two pounds of sirloin. This hamburger is also divided into quantities
sufficient for three meals: one may be creole beef, one chili, and the other
spaghetti. There is also less money for clothing. Dresses must be altered
and made into blouses; pants make nice skirts after some alteration. I
have two more very sticky problems. I've fallen behind in the rental payments for our apartment, and now I am experiencing difficulties trying
to pay the back rent. The other sticky problem is my son's tuition payments. There does not seem to be any way that I can send a complete
payment to his college. These are not the only problems I face. I also have
psychological problems as a result of unemployment. Often I wonder
why this has happened to me. Then depression and confusion take over,
and I feel drained of all my abilities. The one question that fills my mind
most often is the following: Why can't I get employment? This question
evokes in me a lack of self-confidence and self-worth. I am haunted by an
overall feeling of uselessness. My other problems center on trying to cope
with the bureaucracy of the Employment Bureau. Once I get to the Employment Bureau, I stand in line to sign up. I then wait in another line to
which I must report. Once I go through all of this, I am sent out for job

interviews, only to find that the employer wants someone with more experience. To top everything off, I had to wait almost six months to receive my first unemployment check. As you can see, there is often a frustratingly long delay in receiving benefits. My family and I have suffered through many problems because of my unemployment.

Questions About the Reading

1. What do you think makes the inability to pay rent and her son's tuition particularly "sticky" problems for the writer?
2. What makes the writer feel "drained" of her abilities?
3. What psychological effects do you think the writer's unsuccessful job interviews have on her?

Questions About the Writer's Strategies

1. What is the main idea of this paragraph? Where is this idea first introduced? Where is it repeated?
2. Transitional words and phrases provide a bridge between points in this paragraph. Identify the writer's transitions.
3. The writer uses many examples to illustrate the effects of her unemployment. Identify two effects and two examples for each of these effects.
4. What order does the writer use in discussing the problems?

Writing Assignments

1. Is the employment bureau the writer describes doing a good job? In a paragraph, describe the effects of the bureau's procedures.
2. *Working Together*   Discuss with some classmates the effects unemployment has on the American people as a whole. Do you think it has changed our image of ourselves as a nation? Then collaborate to write a cause-and-effect paragraph or essay in which you describe some of the social effects of unemployment. You may want to read some articles on this topic in the library before you write.
3. Although being employed has more positive than negative effects, work does have effects that may not always be pleasant. Write a paragraph on how a particular job or certain types of jobs can have negative effects.

It Took This Night to Make Us Know

Bob Greene

Eleven Israeli athletes were murdered by Palestinian terrorists at the 1972 summer Olympics in Munich, in what was then West Germany. The news shocked and horrified the world. It also made at least one man— Chicago newspaper columnist Bob Greene—look deep inside himself and think, for perhaps the first time, about where he came from, who he was, and what it means to be born Jewish in today's world.

Words to Know

abstraction   a remote, unreal idea

patronized   treated in an offensive, condescending manner

Getting Started

In what ways can prejudice and violence be seen as integral parts of the human experience?

W<small>ASHINGTON</small>—It is not supposed to be very strong in us, for we cannot 1 remember. We are the young Jews, born after Hitler, and we have never considered the fact that we are Jewish to be a large part of our identity. A lot of us have not been near a temple in ten years, and we laugh along with the Jewish jokes to show that we are very cool about the whole thing. We are Americans, we have told ourselves, we do not go around calling ourselves Jews: that is for the elderly men with the tortured faces, the old Jews we feel a little embarrassed to be around. Let them recall the centuries of hurt, we think; it is over now, so let them recall those years while we live our good todays.

It is not supposed to be very strong in us, and yet I am sitting at a 2 typewriter in a hotel room hundreds of miles from home trying to write a story about a presidential campaign, and I cannot do it. For the television has just got done telling the story, the story of how once again people who hate the Jews have knocked on a door in the middle of the night and done their killing, and I can think of nothing else. Now the lesson is being taught all over again; it is not up to us to decide how to treat our Jewishness. That was decided for us centuries ago.

It is not supposed to be very strong in us, because all the barriers are 3 down now, and a hotel will not turn us away or a restaurant will not deny

218

us a table if our name does not sound right. And yet when the killings began, they thought to get a young man named Mark Spitz out of Germany, because he may be the best swimmer in the world, but first of all he is a Jew, and no one wanted to think what might happen to him. Many of the people who thrilled as he won his gold medals were very surprised to find out now that Spitz is a Jew. Later they will say that of course it doesn't matter what his religion is. But Spitz knew that it mattered; we all knew that it mattered, and that it would be smarter for him to go.

It is not supposed to be very strong in us, and we have heard the term   4
"six million Jews are dead" so often that it is just an abstraction to us. And yet if the Dachau concentration camp, just a few miles from the Olympic site, was not enough to remind us, the killers in the Munich darkness made sure that we remembered. There is a hate for us that goes back centuries, and every time it seems to have weakened with the years there is another band of men ready to show us that the hate is still strong enough to make them kill in the night.

When the news was certain, when there was no question but that the   5
young Jewish men were dead, I called some friends and we talked about it. They were thinking the same way I was. For all these years we have acted bored with the Jewish traditions, smirked at the ancient, detailed ceremonies, patronized the old ones who insisted on showing their link with the past.

And for us, it took this one night to make us know that maybe it will   6
never go away. We are all Jews who were born into a world where money and education and parents who speak with no accent were part of the package, and that can fool you. But this is the oldest hate the world has ever seen, and 25 years of Jewish prosperity in the United States are hardly enough to erase it from the earth.

It is nothing that we young ones have ever talked much about, and   7
there are not many words to tell it now. Words cannot tell it as well as the look we have seen for years in the faces of the oldest Jews, the look of deepest sorrow that has been there for as many centuries as the hate.

This time the look is there because of a group of Arab terrorists. But it   8
goes so far beyond Middle Eastern politics; the look was there in this same Germany 30 years ago, it was there in Egypt centuries ago, it has been there in every place there have ever been Jews who were not wanted because they were Jews. And because there have been so many of these places, the look has been reborn and reborn and reborn.

There are young men who are dead this week who should be alive,   9
and it would be a horrible thing no matter who they were. But of course they were Jews; the reason that they are dead is because they were Jews, and that is why on this night there are so many of us starting to realize for the first time what that means.

It is not supposed to be very strong in us, for we cannot remember. We 10
grew up laughing at the solemn old Jewish phrases that sounded so
mournful and outmoded and out of date in the second half of the twentieth century. Ancient, outmoded phrases from the temples, phrases like
"Let my people go." Phrases that we chose to let mean nothing, because
it is not supposed to be very strong in us.

Questions About the Reading

1. Why, according to the writer, are young Jews embarrassed to be around
   old Jews with "tortured faces" (paragraph 1)?
2. Why is the writer having difficulty writing a story about a presidential
   campaign?
3. What effect does the killing of several Jewish men at the Olympics
   have on the young Jewish people living in the United States?
4. What "is not supposed to be very strong" in young American Jews?
5. Consider the title of the essay. What is it that the writer and his con-
   temporaries now know?

Questions About the Writer's Strategies

1. In your own words, express the main idea or thesis of the essay. Does
   the writer ever state this idea explicitly in a single sentence, or must
   the reader infer it?
2. What is the writer's tone in the essay? What attitude does he have
   toward the event described—and toward himself and his friends as a
   result of the event?
3. Identify the cause-and-effect elements in the essay.
4. How does the writer use repetition in the essay? What is its effect?

Writing Assignments

1. *Working Together*   Join with some classmates to write an essay in
   which you discuss what you perceive to be the causes of racial violence and their effects on society.
2. Do the Olympic Games decrease tensions among people of different
   nations, cultures, and races? Write a cause-and-effect essay on this topic.
3. Recall an incident in which you were ridiculed, harassed, or mistreated
   for no apparent reason other than groundless hostility. If you have
   never experienced anything like this, maybe someone among your
   friends could describe such an incident for you. Using the incident as
   the cause, write an essay about its effects on you or your friend.

Black Men and Public Space

Brent Staples

Journalist Brent Staples offers his readers a rare opportunity to trade places with another human being. Staples's forceful words and images allow each of us to walk in the shoes of a young black male in today's urban environment, where fear and racism are intricately linked.

Words to Know

ad hoc   with a specific purpose or cause

bandolier   a belt soldiers wear over the shoulder to carry cartridges

bravado   courage, defiance

constitutional   a walk taken regularly

dicey   dangerous, risky

errant   wrong

labyrinthine   like a maze

mark   victim

quarry   object of a hunt; prey

SoHo   an area of New York City with many art galleries, restaurants, and specialty shops

unwieldy   difficult to carry or manage

warrenlike   overcrowded

Getting Started

If you have ever been judged solely on the basis of your gender, skin color, ethnic origin, or external appearance, how did it feel?

My first victim was a woman—white, well dressed, probably in her 1
early twenties. I came upon her late one evening on a deserted street in Hyde Park, a relatively affluent neighborhood in an otherwise mean, impoverished section of Chicago. As I swung onto the avenue behind her, there seemed to be a discreet, uninflammatory distance between us. Not so. She cast back a worried glance. To her, the youngish black man—a broad six feet two inches with a beard and billowing hair, both hands shoved into the pockets of a bulky military jacket—seemed menacingly close. After a few more quick glimpses, she picked up her pace and was soon running in earnest. Within seconds she disappeared into a cross street.

That was more than a decade ago. I was twenty-two years old, a gradu- 2
ate student newly arrived at the University of Chicago. It was in the echo of that terrified woman's footfalls that I first began to know the unwieldy

inheritance I'd come into—the ability to alter public space in ugly ways. It was clear that she thought herself the quarry of a mugger, a rapist, or worse. Suffering a bout of insomnia, however, I was stalking sleep, not defenseless wayfarers. As a softy who is scarcely able to take a knife to a raw chicken—let alone hold it to a person's throat—I was surprised, embarrassed, and dismayed all at once. Her flight made me feel like an accomplice in tyranny. It also made it clear that I was indistinguishable from the muggers who occasionally seeped into the area from the surrounding ghetto. That first encounter, and those that followed, signified that a vast, unnerving gulf lay between nighttime pedestrians—particularly women—and me. And I soon gathered that being perceived as dangerous is a hazard in itself. I only needed to turn a corner into a dicey situation, or crowd some frightened, armed person in a foyer somewhere, or make an errant move after being pulled over by a policeman. Where fear and weapons meet—and they often do in urban America—there is always the possibility of death.

In that first year, my first away from my hometown, I was to become   3 thoroughly familiar with the language of fear. At dark, shadowy intersections in Chicago, I could cross in front of a car stopped at a traffic light and elicit the *thunk, thunk, thunk, thunk* of the driver—black, white, male, or female—hammering down the door locks. On less traveled streets after dark, I grew accustomed to but never comfortable with people who crossed to the other side of the street rather than pass me. Then there were the standard unpleasantries with police, doormen, bouncers, cabdrivers, and others whose business is to screen out troublesome individuals *before* there is any nastiness.

I moved to New York nearly two years ago and I have remained an   4 avid night walker. In central Manhattan, the near-constant crowd cover minimizes tense one-on-one street encounters. Elsewhere—visiting friends in SoHo, where sidewalks are narrow and tightly spaced buildings shut out the sky—things can get very taut indeed.

Black men have a firm place in New York mugging literature. Norman   5 Podhoretz in his famed (or infamous) 1963 essay, "My Negro Problem— And Ours," recalls growing up in terror of black males; they "were tougher than we were, more ruthless," he writes—and as an adult on the Upper West Side of Manhattan, he continues, he cannot constrain his nervousness when he meets black men on certain streets. Similarly, a decade later, the essayist and novelist Edward Hoagland extols a New York where once "Negro bitterness bore down mainly on other Negroes." Where some see mere panhandlers, Hoagland sees "a mugger who is clearly screwing up his nerve to do more than just *ask* for money." But Hoagland has "the New Yorker's quick-hunch posture for broken-field maneuvering," and the bad guy swerves away.

I often witness that "hunch posture," from women after dark on the 6
warrenlike streets of Brooklyn where I live. They seem to set their faces
on neutral and, with their purse straps strung across their chests bandolier style, they forge ahead as though bracing themselves against being
tackled. I understand, of course, that the danger they perceive is not a
hallucination. Women are particularly vulnerable to street violence, and
young black males are drastically overrepresented among the perpetra-
tors of that violence. Yet these truths are no solace against the kind of
alienation that comes of being ever the suspect, against being set apart, a
fearsome entity with whom pedestrians avoid making eye contact.

It is not altogether clear to me how I reached the ripe old age of twenty- 7
two without being conscious of the lethality nighttime pedestrians attributed to me. Perhaps it was because in Chester, Pennsylvania, the small,
angry industrial town where I came of age in the 1960s, I was scarcely
noticeable against a backdrop of gang warfare, street knifings, and murders. I grew up one of the good boys, had perhaps a half-dozen fistfights.
In retrospect, my shyness of combat has clear sources.

Many things go into the making of a young thug. One of those things 8
is the consummation of the male romance with the power to intimidate.
An infant discovers that random flailings send the baby bottle flying out
of the crib and crashing to the floor. Delighted, the joyful babe repeats
those motions again and again, seeking to duplicate the feat. Just so, I
recall the points at which some of my boyhood friends were finally se-
duced by the perception of themselves as tough guys. When a mark cow-
ered and surrendered his money without resistance, myth and reality
merged—and paid off. It is, after all, only manly to embrace the power to
frighten and intimidate. We, as men, are not supposed to give an inch of
our lane on the highway; we are to seize the fighter's edge in work and in
play and even in love; we are to be valiant in the face of hostile forces.

Unfortunately, poor and powerless young men seem to take all this 9
nonsense literally. As a boy, I saw countless tough guys locked away; I
have since buried several, too. They were babies, really—a teenage cousin,
a brother of twenty-two, a childhood friend in his mid-twenties—all gone
down in episodes of bravado played out in the streets. I came to doubt
the virtues of intimidation early on. I chose, perhaps even unconsciously,
to remain a shadow—timid, but a survivor.

The fearsomeness mistakenly attributed to me in public places often 10
has a perilous flavor. The most frightening of these confusions occurred
in the late 1970s and early 1980s when I worked as a journalist in Chicago. One day, rushing into the office of a magazine I was writing for
with a deadline story in hand, I was mistaken for a burglar. The office
manager called security and, with an ad hoc posse, pursued me through
the labyrinthine halls, nearly to my editor's door. I had no way of prov-

ing who I was. I could only move briskly toward the company of someone who knew me.

Another time I was on assignment for a local paper and killing time 11
before an interview. I entered a jewelry store on the city's affluent Near
North Side. The proprietor excused herself and returned with an enormous red Doberman pinscher straining at the end of a leash. She stood,
the dog extended toward me, silent to my questions, her eyes bulging
nearly out of her head. I took a cursory look around, nodded, and bade
her good night. Relatively speaking, however, I never fared as badly as
another black male journalist. He went to nearby Waukegan, Illinois, a
couple of summers ago to work on a story about a murderer who was
born there. Mistaking the reporter for the killer, police hauled him from
his car at gunpoint and but for his press credentials would probably have
tried to book him. Such episodes are not uncommon. Black men trade
tales like this all the time.

In "My Negro Problem—and Ours," Podhoretz writes that the hatred 12
he feels for blacks makes itself known to him through a variety of avenues—one being his discomfort with that "special brand of paranoid
touchiness" to which he says blacks are prone. No doubt he is speaking
here of black men. In time, I learned to smother the rage I felt at so often
being taken for a criminal. Not to do so would surely have led to mad-
ness—via that special "paranoid touchiness" that so annoyed Podhoretz
at the time he wrote the essay.

I began to take precautions to make myself less threatening. I move 13
about with care, particularly late in the evening. I give a wide berth to
nervous people on subway platforms during the wee hours, particularly
when I have exchanged business clothes for jeans. If I happen to be entering a building behind some people who appear skittish, I may walk by,
letting them clear the lobby before I return, so as not to seem to be following them. I have been calm and extremely congenial on those rare occasions when I've been pulled over by the police.

And on late-evening constitutionals along streets less traveled by, I 14
employ what has proved to be an excellent tension-reducing measure: I
whistle melodies from Beethoven and Vivaldi and the more popular classical composers. Even steely New Yorkers hunching toward nighttime
destinations seem to relax, and occasionally they even join in the tune.
Virtually everybody seems to sense that a mugger wouldn't be warbling
bright, sunny selections from Vivaldi's *Four Seasons*. It is my equivalent
of the cowbell that hikers wear when they know they are in bear country.

Questions About the Reading

1. What does the title of this essay mean?
2. Why does Staples describe the woman in paragraph 1 as his "first victim"?
3. What are some examples of what Staples refers to, in paragraph 3, as the "language of fear?" At what age did he become familiar with this new language?
4. List the things that Staples believes go into the making of a "young thug."
5. What are some of the precautions Staples takes to make himself appear less threatening in public places?
6. What conclusions can you draw about the writer's attitude about his predicament? Does he like or dislike his "ability to alter public space"? Give specific details from the essay to support your opinion.

Questions About the Writer's Strategies

1. What type of order does Staples use to organize his essay? List the biographical details the writer includes that support this kind of order.
2. Does the writer state the thesis of this essay? If so, in which sentence(s)? If not, state the thesis in a sentence of your own.
3. What is the point of view of this essay? Could the writer have used another point of view? Do you think the essay would have been more or less effective if written from another point of view? Why?
4. What is the cause and what is the effect in the essay?
5. At the end of his essay, Staples compares his humming classical music to a hiker's wearing a cowbell in bear country. What does this comparison mean?

Writing Assignments

1. Have you ever done something that caused your friends to react to you in a way you didn't like? Write an essay about the incident. Include both objective details about the incident and subjective details about your feelings.
2. Have you ever had an experience that made you very fearful? Write an essay about the experience.

The Bounty of the Sea

Jacques Cousteau

Jacques Cousteau, the famous French oceanographer, brought the world of the oceans to us through his books and television documentaries. His love for the oceans extended to a lifelong concern for protecting and conserving the marine environment. In the following essay, written in the mid-1960s, he vividly describes the sickening of the ocean and the effects that the death of the oceans would have on humankind.

Words to Know

buffer   something that protects
cheek by jowl   very close together
effluents   outflows of waste, sewage
insupportable   unbearable
plankton algae   microscopic plant life that grows in water
remorseless   without regret or pity
stench   stink, bad smell
teemed   swarmed
trawlers   fishing boats that drag large nets along the bottom of
    the ocean

Getting Started

How can the world community understand—and undo—the effects of pollution before it's too late?

During the past thirty years, I have observed and studied the oceans   1
closely, and with my own two eyes I have seen them sicken. Certain reefs that teemed with fish only ten years ago are now almost lifeless. The ocean bottom has been raped by trawlers. Priceless wetlands have been destroyed by landfill. And everywhere are sticky globs of oil, plastic refuse, and unseen clouds of poisonous effluents. Often, when I describe the symptoms of the oceans' sickness, I hear remarks like "they're only fish" or "they're only whales" or "they're only birds." But I assure you that our destinies are linked with theirs in the most profound and fundamental manner. For if the oceans should die—by which I mean that all life in the sea would finally cease—this would signal the end not only for marine life but for all other animals and plants of this earth, including man.

With life departed, the ocean would become, in effect, one enormous 2
cesspool. Billions of decaying bodies, large and small, would create such
an insupportable stench that man would be forced to leave all the coastal
regions. But far worse would follow.

The ocean acts as the earth's buffer. It maintains a fine balance between 3
the many salts and gases which make life possible. But dead seas would
have no buffering effect. The carbon dioxide content of the atmosphere
would start on a steady and remorseless climb, and when it reached a
certain level a "greenhouse effect" would be created. The heat that normally radiates outward from the earth to space would be blocked by the
CO_2, and sea level temperatures would dramatically increase.

One catastrophic effect of this heat would be melting of the icecaps at 4
both the North and South Poles. As a result, the ocean would rise by 100
feet or more, enough to flood almost all the world's major cities. These
rising waters would drive one-third of the earth's billions inland, creating famine, fighting, chaos, and disease on a scale almost impossible to
imagine.

Meanwhile, the surface of the ocean would have scummed over with a 5
thick film of decayed matter, and would no longer be able to give water
freely to the skies through evaporation. Rain would become a rarity, creating global drought and even more famine.

But the final act is yet to come. The wretched remnant of the human race 6
would now be packed cheek by jowl on the remaining highlands, bewildered, starving, struggling to survive from hour to hour. Then would be
visited upon them the final plague, anoxia (lack of oxygen). This would
be caused by the extinction of plankton algae and the reduction of land
vegetation, the two sources that supply the oxygen you are now breathing.

And so man would finally die, slowly gasping out his life on some 7
barren hill. He would have survived the oceans by perhaps thirty years.
And his heirs would be bacteria and a few scavenger insects.

Questions About the Reading

1. How does Cousteau know that the oceans are sick? What evidence
   does he give?
2. What is the "greenhouse effect" (paragraph 3)?
3. What is CO_2?

Questions About the Writer's Strategies

1. What is the thesis of this essay? Is it directly stated or implied? If it is
   directly stated, where in the essay is it stated?

2. Identify the cause-and-effect elements of this essay.
3. Apart from cause and effect, does the writer use any other modes of development?
4. How are you affected by the use of such words as "scummed over," "thick film of decayed matter," and "cesspool" to describe the ocean?

Writing Assignments

1. Use the Internet to research the causes and effects of air pollution, and then write an essay based on your findings. Include a list of the website addresses you use. To find helpful sites, use a search engine such as AltaVista (**http://www.altavista.com/**), Yahoo! (**http://www.yahoo .com/**), or Excite (**http://www.excite.com/**) and type in keywords such as "air pollution."
2. What personal steps can you take to stop pollution? Write an essay that describes what you as an individual can do and what effects you think your actions would have.
3. Why do people pollute? Write an essay identifying some of the things that cause people to harm the environment and the types of pollution that result.

The Thirsty Animal

Brian Manning

In this personal essay, Brian Manning recounts how he developed into a problem drinker and describes his life now as an alcoholic who has quit drinking. Straightforwardly, he tells of his bittersweet memories of drinking and of his struggle, successful so far, to keep the thirsty "animal living inside" locked in its cage.

Words to Know

accouterments   the items and sensations accompanying a certain activity

Bordeaux   a type of French wine, usually red

lolling   lounging, relaxing

Getting Started

Can you describe some of the negative effects of alcohol on you or someone you know?

I was very young, but I still vividly remember how my father fascinated my brothers and me at the dinner table by running his finger around the rim of his wineglass. He sent a wonderful, crystal tone wafting through the room, and we loved it. When we laughed too raucously, he would stop, swirl the red liquid in his glass and take a sip. 1

There was a wine cellar in the basement of the house we moved into when I was eleven. My father put a few cases of Bordeaux down there in the dark. We played there with other boys in the neighborhood, hid there, made a secret place. It was musty and cool and private. We wrote things and stuck them in among the bottles and imagined someone way in the future baffled by our messages from the past. 2

Many years later, the very first time I drank, I had far too much. But I found I was suddenly able to tell a girl at my high school that I was mad about her. 3

When I drank in college with the men in my class, I was trying to define a self-image I could feel comfortable with. I wanted to be "an Irishman," I decided, a man who could drink a lot of liquor and hold it. My favorite play was Eugene O'Neill's *Long Day's Journey into Night,* my model the drunken Jamie Tyrone. 4

I got out of college, into the real world, and the drunk on weekends 5
started to slip into the weekdays. Often I didn't know when one drunk
ended and another began. The years were measured in hangovers. It took
a long time to accept, and then to let the idea sink in, that I was an
alcoholic.

It took even longer to do anything about it. I didn't want to believe it, 6
and I didn't want to deny myself the exciting, brotherly feeling I had
whenever I went boozing with my friends. For a long time, in my relationships with women, I could only feel comfortable with a woman who
drank as much as I did. So I didn't meet many women and spent my time
with men in dark barrooms, trying to be like them and hoping I'd be
accepted.

It is now two years since I quit drinking, and that, as all alcoholics 7
know who have come to grips with their problem, is not long ago at all.
The urge to have "just one" includes a genuine longing for all the accouterments of drink: the popping of a cork, the color of Scotch through a
glass, the warmth creeping over my shoulders with the third glass of
stout. Those were joys. Ever since I gave them up I remember them as
delicious.

I go to parties now and start off fine, but I have difficulty dealing with 8
the changing rhythms as the night wears on. Everyone around me seems
to be having a better time the more they drink, and I, not they, become
awkward. I feel like a kid with a broken chain when everyone else has
bicycled around the corner out of sight. I fight against feeling sorry for
myself.

What were the things I was looking for and needed when I drank? I 9
often find that what I am looking for when I want a drink is not really the
alcohol, but the memories and laughter that seemed possible only with a
glass in my hand. In a restaurant, I see the bottle of vintage port on the
shelf, and imagine lolling in my chair, swirling the liquid around in the
glass, inhaling those marvelous fumes. I think of my neighbor, Eileen,
the funniest woman I ever got smashed with, and I want to get up on a
bar stool next to her to hear again the wonderful stories she told. She
could drink any man under the table, she claimed, and I wanted to be one
of those men who tried. She always won, but it made me feel I belonged
when I staggered out of the bar, her delighted laughter following me.

I had found a world to cling to, a way of belonging, and it still attracts 10
me. I pass by the gin mills and pubs now and glance in at the men lined
up inside, and I don't see them as suckers or fools. I remember how I felt
sitting there after work, or watching a Sunday afternoon ball game, and I
long for the smell of the barroom and that ease—toasts and songs, jokes
and equality. I have to keep reminding myself of the wasting hangovers,
the lost money, the days down the drain.

I imagine my problem as an animal living inside me, demanding a 11
drink before it dies of thirst. That's what it says, but it will never die of
thirst. The fact an alcoholic faces is that this animal breathes and waits. It
is incapable of death and will spring back to lustful, consuming life with
even one drop of sustenance.

When I was eighteen and my drinking began in earnest, I didn't play 12
in the wine cellar at home anymore; I stole there. I sneaked bottles to my
room, sat in the window and drank alone while my parents were away. I
hated the taste of it, but I kept drinking it, without the kids from the
neighborhood, without any thought that I was feeding the animal. And
one day, I found one of those old notes we had hidden down there years
before. It fell to the ground when I pulled a bottle from its cubbyhole. I
read it with bleary eyes, then put the paper back into the rack. "Beware,"
it said, above a childish skull and crossbones, "all ye who enter here." A
child, wiser than I was that day, had written that note.

I did a lot of stupid, disastrous, sometimes mean things in the years 13
that followed, and remembering them is enough to snap me out of the memories and back to the reality that I quit just in time. I've done something I
had to do, something difficult and necessary, and that gives me satisfaction
and the strength to stay on the wagon. I'm very lucky so far. I don't get
mad that I can't drink anymore; I can handle the self-pity that overwhelmed
me in my early days of sobriety. From time to time, I daydream about
summer afternoons and cold beer. I know such dreams will never go away.
The thirsty animal is there, getting a little fainter every day. It will never
die. A lot of my life now is all about keeping it in a very lonely cage.

Questions About the Reading

1. What went along with drinking for the writer? Why did he need alcohol to get those effects?
2. Why are parties difficult for the writer?
3. Why did the writer stop drinking?
4. When you finished reading the essay, what opinions had you formed
   of the writer's personality and character? Cite specific details from the
   essay to support your opinions.

Questions About the Writer's Strategies

1. What is the main idea of this essay? In which sentences is it most clearly
   stated?
2. What are the causes in this essay? What are the effects? Do they overlap at all?

3. Other than cause and effect, what modes of development does the writer use? Cite paragraphs in which he uses other modes.
4. The "animal" introduced in paragraph 11 is a metaphor. What does it stand for? Interpret it in your own words.
5. Identify the simile in paragraph 8. Is it effective in helping you understand how the writer feels?

Writing Assignments

1. Describe in an essay the effects that alcohol has on you. If you do not drink, describe the effects that you have seen it have on others.
2. Do you know anyone who abuses alcohol or other substances? If not, you have surely come across the lure of drugs in the media or in school awareness programs. On the basis of what you know and what you have learned from reading this essay, write an essay describing the causes and effects of substance abuse.

Halfway to Dick and Jane

Jack Agueros

Jack Agueros tells us that his first seven years of life in a New York City neighborhood were much like those of the storybook characters Dick and Jane. Then, he says, his life changed.

Words to Know

chenille   soft, tufted fabric
compensation   payment
declaim   speak, orate
plantain   a kind of banana
Victrola   early record player

Getting Started

Did your life change when you moved to a new neighborhood or started a new school?

I am an only child. My parents and I always talked about my becoming 1
a doctor. The law and politics were not highly regarded in my house. Lawyers, my mother would explain, had to defend people whether they were guilty or not, while politicians, my father would say, were all crooks. A doctor helped everybody, rich and poor, white and black. If I became a doctor, I could study hay fever and find a cure for it, my godmother would say. Also, I could take care of my parents when they were old. I like the idea of helping, and for nineteen years my sole ambition was to study medicine.

My house had books, not many, but my parents encouraged me to read. 2
As I became a good reader they bought books for me and never refused me money for their purchase. My father once built a bookcase for me. It was an important moment, for I had always believed that my father was not too happy about my being a bookworm. The atmosphere at home was always warm. We seemed to be a popular family. We entertained frequently, with two standing parties a year—at Christmas and for my birthday. Parties were always large. My father would dismantle the beds and move all the furniture so that the full two rooms could be used for dancing. My mother would cook up a storm, particularly at Christmas. *Pastels, lechon asado, arroz con gandules,* and a lot of *coquito* to drink (meat-

stuffed plantain, roast pork, rice with pigeon peas, and coconut nog). My father always brought in a band. They played without compensation and were guests at the party. They ate and drank and danced while a Victrola covered the intermissions. One year my father brought home a whole pig and hung it in the foyer doorway. He and my mother prepared it by rubbing it down with oil, orègano, and garlic. After preparation, the pig was taken down and carried over to a local bakery where it was cooked and returned home. Parties always went on till daybreak, and in addition to the band, there were always volunteers to sing and declaim poetry.

My mother kept an immaculate household. Bedspreads (chenille 3 seemed to be very in) and lace curtains, washed at home like everything else, were hung up on huge racks with rows of tight nails. The racks were assembled in the living room, and the moisture from the wet bedspreads would fill the apartment. In a sense, that seems to be the lasting image of that period of my life. The house was clean. The neighbors were clean. The streets, with few cars, were clean. The buildings were clean and uncluttered with people on the stoops. The park was clean. The visitors to my house were clean, and the relationships that my family had with other Puerto Rican families, and the Italian families that my father had met through baseball and my mother through the garment center, were clean. Second Avenue was clean and most of the apartment windows and awnings. There was always music, there seemed to be no rain, and snow did not become slush. School was fun, we wrote essays about how grand America was, we put up hunchbacked cats at Halloween, we believed Santa Claus visited everyone. I believed everyone was Catholic. I grew up with dogs, nightingales, my godmother's guitar, rocking chair, cat, guppies, my father's occasional roosters, kept in a cage on the fire escape. Laundry delivered and collected by horse and wagon, fruits and vegetables sold the same way, windowsill refrigeration in winter, iceman and box in summer. The police my friends, likewise the teachers.

In short, the first seven or so years of my life were not too great a varia- 4 tion on Dick and Jane, the schoolbook figures who, if my memory serves me correctly, were blond Anglo-Saxons, not immigrants, not migrants like the Puerto Ricans, and not the children of either immigrants or migrants.

My family moved in 1941 to Lexington Avenue into a larger apartment 5 where I could have my own room. It was a light, sunny, railroad flat on the top floor of a well-kept building. I transferred to a new school, and whereas before my classmates had been mostly black, the new school had few blacks. The classes were made up of Italians, Irish, Jews, and a sprinkling of Puerto Ricans. My block was populated by Jews, Italians, and Puerto Ricans.

And then a whole series of different events began. I went to junior 6
high school. We played in the backyards, where we tore down fences to
build fires to cook stolen potatoes. We tore up whole hedges, because the
green tender limbs would not burn when they were peeled, and thus
made perfect skewers for our stolen "mickies." We played tag in the abandoned buildings, tearing the plaster off the walls, tearing the wire lath off
the wooden slats, tearing the wooden slats themselves, good for fires, for
kites, for sword fighting. We ran up and down the fire escapes playing
tag and over and across many rooftops. The war ended and the heavy
Puerto Rican migration began. The Irish and the Jews disappeared from
the neighborhood. The Italians tried to consolidate east of Third Avenue.

What caused the clean and open world to end? Many things. Into an 7
ancient neighborhood came pouring four to five times more people than
it had been designed to hold. Men who came running at the promise of
jobs were jobless as the war ended. They were confused. They could not
see the economic forces that ruled their lives as they drank beer on the
corners, reassuring themselves of good times to come while they were
hell-bent toward alcoholism. The sudden surge in numbers caused new
resentments, and prejudice was intensified. Some were forced to live in
cellars, and were then characterized as cave dwellers. Kids came who
were confused by the new surroundings; their Puerto Rican-ness forced
us against a mirror asking, "If they are Puerto Ricans, what are we?" and
thus they confused us. In our confusion we were sometimes pathetically
reaching out, sometimes pathologically striking out. Gangs. Drugs. Wine.
Smoking. Girls. Dances and slow-drag music. Mambo. Spics, Spooks, and
Wops. Territories, brother gangs, and war councils establishing rules for
right of way on blocks and avenues and for seating in the local theater.
Pegged pants and zip guns. Slang.

Dick and Jane were dead, man. Education collapsed. Every classroom 8
had ten kids who spoke no English. Black, Italian, Puerto Rican relations
in the classroom were good, but we all knew we couldn't visit one
another's neighborhoods. Sometimes we could not move too freely within
our own blocks. On 109th, from the lamp post west, the Latin Aces, and
from the lamp post east, the Senecas, the "club" I belonged to. The kids
who spoke no English became known as Marine Tigers, picked up from a
popular Spanish song. (The Marine Tiger and the Marine Shark were two
ships that sailed from San Juan to New York and brought over many,
many migrants from the island.)

The neighborhood had its boundaries. Third Avenue and east, Italian. 9
Fifth Avenue and west, black. South, there was a hill on 103rd Street known
locally as Cooney's Hill. When you got to the top of the hill, something
strange happened: America began, because from the hill south was where

the "Americans" lived. Dick and Jane were not dead: they were alive and well in a better neighborhood.

When, as a group of Puerto Rican kids, we decided to go swimming to 10 Jefferson Park Pool, we knew we risked a fight and a beating from the Italians. And when we went to La Milagrosa Church in Harlem, we knew we risked a fight and a beating from the blacks. But when we went over Cooney's Hill, we risked dirty looks, disapproving looks, and questions from the police like, "What are you doing in this neighborhood?" and "Why don't you kids go back where you belong?"

Where we belonged! Man I had written compositions about America. 11 Didn't I belong on the Central Park tennis courts, even if I didn't know how to play? Couldn't I watch Dick play? Weren't these policemen working for me too?

Questions About the Reading

1. What career did the writer want to have? Why? Did he follow that career? How do you know?
2. Why was it an important moment when the writer's father built him a bookcase?
3. What was the "atmosphere" in the writer's home? What were the family's parties like?
4. What was the main impression the writer had of his parents' household (paragraph 3)?
5. What reason does the writer give for the change in the neighborhood where his family moved (paragraph 7)?

Questions About the Writer's Strategies

1. In addition to cause and effect, what other modes of development does the writer use? Identify the sentences or paragraphs in which other modes are used.
2. What is the thesis of the essay? State it in your own words.
3. What technique does the writer use in the first sentence of paragraph 7?
4. What is the tone of the essay?
5. What is the point of view in person of the essay? Would it be as effective if it were third person? Why or why not?

Writing Assignments

1. *Working Together*   Join with some classmates to write an essay in

which you describe the careers you wanted to have when you were in grade school and explain what caused you to decide on different careers.
2. Write an essay in which you explain how you felt when your friends left you out of a party or some activity.

Connections

1. What connections can you make between the selections by Jack Agueros and Bob Greene? How are they alike? How are they different?
2. Both Nelliejean Smith and Brian Manning write about battling a problem that seems insurmountable. In what ways are their stories similar? In what ways are they different?
3. The selections by Bob Greene, Brent Staples, and Brian Manning deal with young men who have been affected by discrimination or alcohol. How do the writers portray these young men? What point of view do they use? What did you learn about the causes and effects of discrimination and alcoholism?

9

Definition

W HEN WRITERS USE words that they think may be unfamiliar to their readers, they usually will define the words. A **definition** is an explanation of the meaning of a word or term.

In its shortest form, the definition may be simply a **synonym**—a familiar word or phrase that has the same meaning as the unfamiliar word. For example, in "she shows more *empathy* for, or true understanding of, older people than her sister," the word *understanding* is a synonym for *empathy*. Or the writer may choose to use an **antonym**—a word or phrase that has the opposite meaning of the unfamiliar word—as in "she is a compassionate rather than an *inconsiderate* person." Here the word *inconsiderate* gives the reader the opposite meaning of *compassionate*.

The writer may also choose to use the kind of precise definition found in dictionaries, called a **formal definition.** In a formal definition, the writer first uses a form of **classification,** assigning the word to the **class** of items to which it belongs, and then describing the characteristics that distinguish it from other items of that class. Here is an example of a formal definition.

Word defined: tiger; class: cat family | A tiger, a member of the <u>cat family</u>, is native to Asia, usually
Description of characteristics | weighs over 350 pounds, and has tawny and black-striped fur.

Connotation, which refers to the impressions or qualities we associate with a word, and **denotation,** the dictionary definition of a word, are

239

important in writing a definition. Think of the word *pig,* for instance. The dictionary may tell you that a pig is simply a domestic animal with hooves, short legs, bristly hair, and a blunt snout; and a farmer may tell you that a pig is relatively smarter and cleaner than other farm animals. However, the negative connotations of this word are so strong that you are likely to have trouble thinking of a pig without thinking of filth, fat, and greed.

In writing definitions, it is particularly important to choose your words in such a way that their connotations as well as their denotations will give your readers the correct impression of what you are defining. As you are writing and **revising,** remember to search for the single best word for conveying your ideas.

When you search for connotative words and expressions to use in your writing, beware of **clichés.** Clichés are words or phrases—such as "rosy red," "silly goose," "bull in a china shop," "weird," or "outrageous"—which have become so overused that they indicate a lack of imagination and thought on the part of the writer who uses them. Symbols, too, can be clichés. If you are defining *courage,* for example, using Superman as a symbol to enhance your definition is unlikely to impress your readers. You should also be aware that many clichés take the form of **similes:** "as filthy as a pig," for example. Try to make sure your similes are always of your own creation, not ones you have heard before.

Many complex words and abstract ideas—such as *truth* and *justice*—require longer and more detailed explanations, which are called **extended definitions.** In an extended definition, the writer may use one or more of the methods of development—description, examples, classification, and so forth—that you have learned about in the earlier chapters of this book. For example, the writer might use **process, description,** or **narration**—or all three—as the method of development in an extended definition.

Topic sentence: formal definition	A glacier is an accumulation of snow and ice that continually flows from a mountain ice field toward sea level. Gla-
Process	ciers are formed when successive snowfalls pile up, creating pressure on the bottom layers. Gradually, the pressure causes the snow on the bottom to undergo a structural change into an extremely dense form of ice called glacier ice, a process that may take several years.
Extended definition: descriptive narration	Once the ice begins to accumulate, gravity causes the mass to move downhill. Glaciers usually take the path of least resistance, following stream beds or other natural channels down the mountainside. As they move, they scrape along the surface of the earth, picking up rocks and other sediment on the way. The ice and the debris carve a deep U-shaped valley as they proceed down the mountain. If they advance far enough, they will eventually reach the sea and become tidewater glaciers that break off, or calve, directly into salt water. Southeast Alaska is one of

> only three places in the world where tidewater glaciers exist. (They also are found in Scandinavia and Chile.) Other glaciers, called hanging glaciers, spill out of icy basins high up on valley walls and tumble toward the valley floor.
>
> Sarah Eppenbach,
> *Alaska's Southeast*

In the example that follows, the writer combines a formal definition with **classification, examples,** and **comparison** and **contrast.**

Formal definition: map
Classification: conventional picture
Characteristics: area of land, sea, or sky

A map is a conventional picture of an area of land, sea, or sky. Perhaps the maps most widely used are the road maps given away by the oil companies. They show the cultural features such as states, towns, parks, and roads, especially paved roads. They show also natural features, such as rivers and lakes, and sometimes mountains. As simple maps, most automobile drivers have on various occasions used sketches drawn by service station men, or by friends, to show the best automobile route from one town to another.   1

Example: road maps

Example: simple maps

Contrast: chart represents water; map represents land

The distinction usually made between "maps" and "charts" is that a chart is a representation of an area consisting chiefly of water; a map represents an area that is predominantly land. It is easy to see how this distinction arose in the days when there was no navigation over land, but a truer distinction is that charts are specially designed for use in navigation, whether at sea or in the air.   2

Contrast: chart for navigation

Example: use of maps

Maps have been used since the earliest civilizations, and explorers find that they are used in rather simple civilizations at the present time by people who are accustomed to traveling. For example, Arctic explorers have obtained considerable help from maps of the coast lines showing settlements, drawn by Eskimo people. Occasionally maps show not only the roads, but pictures of other features. One of the earliest such maps dates from about 1400 B.C. It shows not only roads, but also lakes with fish, and a canal with crocodiles and a bridge over the canal. This is somewhat similar to the modern maps of a state which show for each large town some feature of interest or the chief products of that town.   3

Example: features of some maps
Comparison: features of early maps with ones of modern maps

C. C. Wylie,
Astronomy, Maps, and Weather

As you can see, you may use any method of development that is appropriate when you need to extend the definition of a word or term.

Whether you are writing an extended definition or relying primarily on some other mode of development, always remember to define any words or terms you use that may be unfamiliar to your readers—particularly any words they must know to understand your meaning. You should also define words with any special or technical meaning.

Nostalgia

Richard Shelton

What is the crepuscular? Richard Shelton misses it, along with the bucolic and idyllic. Although he does not define the word, a careful reading tells us what it means.

Words to Know

bucolic   pastoral, rural, rustic
carnage   slaughter, bloodshed
gentility   politeness, refinement
idyllic   pleasing, simple, picturesque
mayhem   mutilation

Getting Started

Is there something that you remember from your childhood and now miss?

Whatever happened to the crepuscular? It's never mentioned anymore. Years since I heard any reference to the crepuscular. I wonder if anybody notices it now as we once did, creeping in and out with silent majesty, leaving some of us with lumps in our throats. It would be a relief from the carnage and mayhem. I remember sometimes at that time of day in the autumn when there was a chill in the air and somebody was burning leaves somewhere, I could nearly die of happiness. But I am older now and it's illegal to burn leaves. So I guess nobody notices the crepuscular anymore. Or the bucolic. Nobody ever says, "Let's go spend a bucolic weekend in the country." And nobody calls anything idyllic. Whatever became of idyllic afternoons beside the river? And grand passions? Passions don't seem to be grand anymore, just sort of everyday affairs. I guess it's hard to have a grand passion without idyllic afternoons and crepuscular evenings, and we are just too busy to take the time for such things. And nightingales? I never heard one myself, but I certainly read about them, and they seemed to be almost everywhere at one time. Perhaps they were no longer needed and they died out or somebody shot them. Might be a few left in a zoo somewhere, I wouldn't know about that. But surely gentility has survived. You mean gentility is gone too? Lord! But whatever happened to peace and quiet? Somewhere there still must be some peace and quiet. And whatever happened to kindness. . . .?

Questions About the Reading

1. According to the writer, how did people feel when they noticed the crepuscular?
2. How did the writer feel when somebody was burning leaves somewhere?
3. What would a bucolic weekend in the country be like?
4. What would an idyllic afternoon be like?

Questions About the Writer's Strategies

1. What is the main idea of the paragraph? Is it stated or implied?
2. What does *crepuscular* mean? How did you figure out the meaning?
3. What modes of development does the writer use?
4. What is the tone of the paragraph?

Writing Assignments

1. Write a paragraph in which you define one of the following terms: *democracy, religion, ethics.* Include a formal definition from an online dictionary such as yourDictionary.com (**http://www.yourdictionary.com/**), and use at least two other modes of development. Make a copy of the web page on which you find your definition and attach it to your paragraph.
2. Write a paragraph in which you define one of the following sports: baseball, football, basketball, soccer.
3. Write a paragraph about some holiday celebration that you remember and now miss.

Reliability

Dick DeVos

In this paragraph, Dick DeVos defines what he sees as an important human value.

Words to Know

affectionately   fondly
cherished   valued highly, cared for
integrity   honesty

Getting Started

Do you consider yourself a reliable person?

R eliability is a good, solid value to be cherished, encouraged, and re- 1
warded. The most obvious and easily understood form of reliability is
punctuality and dependability in our work—which means consistently
showing up and doing whatever we have agreed to do to the best of our
ability. Individuals of integrity are reliable, whether they are auto mechanics, bus drivers, doctors, businesspeople, short-order cooks, or
ballplayers.

One man who is famous for this kind of reliability is Cal Ripken Jr., the 2
baseball player with the Baltimore Orioles who broke Lou Gehrig's fifty-
six-year-old record by playing in 2,131 consecutive games. Little wonder
that he's known affectionately in the sport as "the Iron Man."

Questions About the Reading

1. What is reliability?
2. How do reliable people handle their work?
3. What kinds of individuals are reliable?
4. Why is Cal Ripken, Jr. considered reliable?

Questions About the Writer's Strategies

1. What modes of development does the writer use to define reliability?
2. How does the writer define punctuality and dependability?

Writing Assignments

1. Using several modes of development, write a paragraph in which you define one of the following terms: *ethics, morality, values, sincerity.*
2. Using several modes of development, write a paragraph in which you define one of the following terms: *politics, religion, political, religious.*

What Does It Mean to Be Creative?

S. I. Hayakawa

S. I. Hayakawa was a United States senator, the president of San Francisco State College, and an authority on semantics—the study of the development, structure, and changes of language. In this paragraph, he defines the creative person.

Word to Know

examining   investigating, looking at

Getting Started

What do you think it means to be creative?

A creative person, first, is not limited in his thinking to "what everyone knows." "Everyone knows" that trees are green. The creative artist is able to see that in certain lights some trees look blue or purple or yellow. The creative person looks at the world with his or her own eyes, not with the eyes of others. The creative individual also knows his or her own feelings better than the average person. Most people don't know the answer to the question, "How are you? How do you feel?" The reason they don't know is that they are so busy feeling what they are supposed to feel, thinking what they are supposed to think, that they never get down to examining their own deepest feelings.

Questions About the Reading

1. According to the writer, how does the creative person look at the world?
2. What distinguishes the creative individual from the average person?
3. Why do most people not know the answer to "How are you? How do you feel?"

Questions About the Writer's Strategies

1. What is the writer's definition of a creative person?
2. What are two transitional words the writer uses? Would the definition be clearer by changing one of the transitional words? What transitional words would you use in the definition?

Writing Assignments

1. Write a paragraph in which you define and give examples of a creative person.
2. Write a paragraph in which you explain how someone in a certain sport might be creative.

Grandparents

Nancy Merrell (student)

In the paragraph that follows, Nancy Merrell provides us with an extended definition of the word grandparents *by telling us what they do and how we feel about them at different times in our lives and theirs. By making us understand her feelings about grandparents, she makes us aware of our own attitudes and feelings.*

Words to Know

accomplishments achievements
appreciated valued

Getting Started

How would you define an excellent teacher?

Of all family members, grandparents are probably the least appreciated. They are just people who are always around. They make a fuss over the children in the family, brag to their friends about the accomplishments of this child or that child, and show countless pictures of new babies. Grandfathers can fix anything, and grandmothers always have homemade cookies around. When you are small, it's fun to stay with your grandparents because they always let you do things you can't do at home, and of course they buy you things. They are always available to babysit because they don't go out much and actually prefer to see their grandchildren. They are usually good for a small loan now and then that doesn't need to be paid back because they turn it into a gift. You respectfully listen to their advice but don't follow it because they are old and don't understand how things are in this day and age. You thank them politely for what they do for you, and then don't call or visit them until you need something else. And of course you never tell them how dear they are to you because they know how you feel about them anyway. Then all of a sudden, they are no longer there to do the things that only grandparents do, and you find yourself wishing that you had told them what they meant to you as people and not just as grandparents.

Questions About the Reading

1. What inferences can you draw about the writer's grandparents from the paragraph? Support your answer with statements from the paragraph.
2. What is the function of the last sentence of the paragraph?
3. What are some of the examples that the writer uses to define grandparents? What are some of the examples she uses to explain how we treat grandparents?

Questions About the Writer's Strategies

1. What is the main mode of development that the writer uses to define grandparents?
2. Does the writer use more than one mode? If so, which one(s)?
3. What is the point of view in the paragraph? Does it change? If so, could the writer have maintained the same point of view throughout the paragraph? If so, explain how this could be done.

Writing Assignments

1. Write a paragraph in which you define a true friend by giving examples of the person's behavior.
2. Write a paragraph in which you define a person or place by using descriptive details.
3. Write a paragraph in which you define what the word *parent* means to you. Use several modes of development: e.g., examples, description, narration. You might want to consider process in particular: how to be a good parent.

Baseball's Hot Dogs

Jim Kaplan

Baseball, the game of inches, requires precision performance and intense concentration. Do grandstanding and posturing constitute unfair psychological interference? In this definition of hot-dogging, Jim Kaplan presents some expert opinions on the question.

Words to Know

imperturbable   not easily disturbed
repertoire   a collection of dramatic skills

Getting Started

What is a nonedible definition for the term "hot dog"?

Here's Rickey Henderson at the plate. Taking forever to situate himself 1
in the batter's box, the New York Yankees outfielder crouches low and extends a shy left foot, like a man inching into a cold swimming pool. A pitch arrives on the inside corner. Henderson twists away and then looks shocked when the umpire calls it a strike. Finally, Rickey sees a pitch he likes and rides it out of the park.

Now the real fun begins. Playing shamelessly to the crowd and cam- 2
era, Henderson chucks his bat high over his head, ambles to first by way of the Yankee dugout, lowers his head and proceeds around the bases in an endless, mock-serious trot. The fans love it. The opponents do not.

Henderson is baseball's foremost "hot dog"—and his repertoire is so 3
varied and controversial that his employers have actually put pressure on him to modify his style. This spring, the Yankees proposed banning Henderson's famous "snatch," a one-handed catch in which he snaps his glove down like a teacher scrawling a semicircle on a blackboard and finishes with it pressed to his heart.

"They said, 'Rickey, the only snatch you can make is the last out of the 4
World Series,'" explained Henderson, adding that he thought he could still get away with it on occasion. "I want to show I can do more than catch. I want to show I can *catch*. To me, the snatch isn't hot-dogging; it's style. People say I'm a hot dog. What *is* a hot dog?"

Good question. "A hot dog is someone whose actions put down some- 5
one on another team," says Doug DeCinces, the former major-league third baseman now playing for Tokyo's Yakult Swallows.

"Hot-dogging is unnecessarily calling attention to yourself," adds Roy 6
Smalley, the well traveled former American League infielder.

But there's another point of view: that hot-dogging is flair and zest, 7
the very ingredients that make baseball so entertaining on the air or in
person. Hot dogs contribute to baseball science, strategy and style. Some
hot dogs show off; others motivate themselves; still others intimidate the
opposition; most are entertaining.

Henderson may qualify on every count. "I never try to put anyone 8
down," he says. "I take my time getting into the box because I'm thinking
of the pitches I'm going to get." But he knows only too well the effect his
apparent stalling has. Even as imperturbable a pitching pro as the now-
retired Tom Seaver got so flustered that he had to turn his back on the
mound until Henderson had set himself to hit.

"Rickey has always played with flair," says Milwaukee manager Tom 9
Trebelhorn, who handled Henderson in the minors. "When he played for
me, he drove the other side crazy. Now he drives *me* crazy."

National League managers echo those sentiments about the San Fran- 10
cisco Giants' Jeffrey "Hac-Man" Leonard, who showcased his trademark
"flap down" homerun trot (one arm pinned to his side) four times during
the 1987 League Championship Series.

"[One flap down] is entertaining, a guy having fun," the unflappable 11
Leonard has told reporters. "Anything that provides energy gets me up.
Like Muhammad Ali, we'll bring out the best in our opponents, and that'll
make us better."

Oh, there are many kinds of baseball hot dogs—kosher and otherwise. 12
Cleveland's Mel Hall used to round the bases with a batting glove in
each back pocket arranged to flap "bye-bye." He has since contained his
act. But there's no containing Dennis "Oil Can" Boyd, the Boston Red Sox
pitcher who celebrates good fortune by variously high-fiving and low-
fiving teammates, waving to the crowd, doing clenched-fist "out" calls
and Michael Jackson struts, and snapping his fingers as he walks off the
mound.

Oil Can (the nickname is Mississippi slang for beer can) grew up play- 13
ing with older men who had starred in the Negro leagues. "I had a lead-
off hitter who drag-bunted with the bat behind his back," says Boyd. "My
fielders would turn [the double play] by throwing the ball between their
legs. A first baseman named Bud Moore said to throw to him in the dirt
so he could pick it and look good. When I punched [struck] a guy out, I'd
say, 'Get outta here—next guy up.' To hot-dog was the way to play."

TV may be the biggest boon to hot-dogging since the invention of 14
mustard. Midway through the 1982 World Series, St. Louis pitcher Joaquin
Andujar was struck on the leg by a line drive and carried off in apparent
agony. NBC sportscaster Bob Costas raced down to the dugout expecting

to report on a broken leg. The Cardinals made faces and winked at him. "Television time," they were saying. Sure enough, Andujar returned to pitch and win the final game.

"These days there are fewer characters but more character-acting," says   15 Costas. "You can almost choreograph your own moment, and the camera will do the rest."

Hot *dog!*   16

Questions About the Reading

1. What *is* a hot dog? Fashion your own definition, based on the essay and your personal opinions.
2. What do you think the writer's opinion of hot-dogging is? Does he offer any conclusions about it?
3. In what forms do you think "hot-dogging" exists outside the world of sports? Explain your answer by describing nonsports "hot-dogs" you have known or read about.

Questions About the Writer's Strategies

1. What two similes does the writer use in his description of Rickey Henderson?
2. Identify the subjective elements in this essay.
3. What primary mode of development does the writer use to develop his definition?
4. What is the tone of the essay? What type of reader do you think the essay is aimed at?

Writing Assignments

1. Write an essay in which you define some other behavior in which people use different styles or about which they have various opinions, like flirting, arguing, dancing, or even walking. Try to talk with people about the behavior and use dialogue in developing your definition, as Kaplan does.
2. Write an essay defining the term *essay*. (Put this book aside and don't refer to it for help in composing your definition.)

The Underclass

Herbert J. Gans

Herbert Gans's essay was written in 1990, when unemployment and the welfare rolls were relatively high. The term underclass, *as Gans points out, unfairly assigns the poor and the unemployed—different people with different problems—to a single group.*

Words to Know

affluent   rich, well-off
consigned   assigned
patent   clear, plain
pejoratives   disparaging, downgrading, negative terms
quasi-fascist   seemingly believing in a dictatorship or
    totalitarian form of government

Getting Started

How would you define America's middle class?

Sticks and stones may break my bones, but names can never hurt me 1
goes the old proverb. But like many old proverbs, this one is patent nonsense, as anyone knows who has ever been hurt by ethnic, racist or sexist
insults and stereotypes.

The most frequent victims of insults and stereotypes have been the 2
poor, especially those thought to be undeserving of help because someone decided—justifiably or not—that they had not acted properly. America
has a long history of insults for the "undeserving" poor. In the past they
were bums, hoboes, vagrants and paupers; more recently they have been
culturally deprived and the hard-core poor. Now they are "the underclass."

Underclass was originally a nineteenth-century Swedish term for the 3
poor. In the early 1960s, the Swedish economist Gunnar Myrdal revived
it to describe the unemployed and unemployables being created by the
modern economy, people who, he predicted, would soon be driven out
of that economy unless it was reformed. Twenty years later, in Ronald
Reagan's America, the word sprang to life again, this time not only to
describe but also to condemn. Those normally consigned to the underclass
include: women who start their families before marriage and before the
end of adolescence, youngsters who fail to finish high school or find work,
and welfare "dependents"—whether or not the behavior of any of these

254

people is their own fault. The term is also applied to low-income delin-
quents and criminals—but not to affluent ones.

"Underclass" has become popular because it seems to grab people's   4
attention. What grabs is the image of a growing horde of beggars, muggers, robbers and lazy people who do not carry their part of the economic
load, all of them threatening nonpoor Americans and the stability of
American society. The image may be inaccurate, but then insults and
pejoratives don't have to be accurate. Moreover, underclass sounds technical, academic, and not overtly pejorative, so it can be used without
anyone's biases showing. Since it is now increasingly applied to blacks
and Hispanics, it is also a respectable substitute word with which to condemn them.

There are other things wrong with the word underclass. For one, it   5
lumps together in a single term very diverse poor people with diverse
problems. Imagine all children's illnesses being described with the same
word, and the difficulties doctors would have in curing them.

For example, a welfare recipient often requires little more than a de-   6
cent paying job—and a male breadwinner who also has such a job—to
make a normal go of it, while a high school dropout usually needs both a
better-equipped school, better teachers and fellow students—and a ration-
ale for going to school when he or she has no assurance that a decent job
will follow upon graduation. Neither the welfare recipient nor the high
school dropout deserves to be grouped with, or described by, the same
word as muggers or drug dealers.

Labeling poor people as underclass is to blame them for their poverty,   7
which enables the blamers to blow off the steam of self-righteousness.
That steam does not, however, reduce their poverty. Unfortunately,
underclass, like other buzzwords for calling the poor undeserving, is being used to avoid starting up needed antipoverty programs and other
economic reforms.

Still, the greatest danger of all lies not in the label itself but in the pos-   8
sibility that the underclass is a symptom of a possible, and dark, American future: that we are moving toward a "post-post-industrial" economy
in which there may not be enough decent jobs for all. Either too many
more jobs will move to Third World countries where wages are far lower
or they will be performed by ever more efficient computers and other
machines.

If this happens, the underclass label may turn out to be a signal that   9
the American economy, and our language, are preparing to get ready for
a future in which some people are going to be more or less permanently
jobless—and will be blamed for their joblessness to boot.

Needless to say, an American economy with a permanently jobless   10
population would be socially dangerous, for all of the country's current

social problems, from crime and addiction to mental illness would be sure to increase considerably. America would then also become politically more dangerous, for various kinds of new protests have to be expected, not to mention the rise of quasi-fascist movements. Such movements can already be found in France and other European countries.

Presumably, Americans—the citizenry and elected officials both—will 11 not let any of this happen here and will find new sources of decent jobs, as they have done in past generations, even if today this requires a new kind of New Deal. Perhaps there will be another instance of what always saved America in the past: new sources of economic growth that cannot even be imagined now.

The only problem is that in the past, America ruled the world eco- 12 nomically, and now it does not—and it shows in our lack of economic growth. Consequently, the term underclass could become a permanent entry in the dictionary of American pejoratives.

Questions About the Reading

1. What group of people does the writer say is most often the victim of stereotyping?
2. What is the origin of the term *underclass*? Who revived the term and when?
3. Why has the term become popular? What image does the term evoke?
4. What does the writer mean when he says that the term is possibly "a symptom of a possible, and dark, American future" (paragraph 8)?

Questions About the Writer's Strategies

1. What is the tone of the essay?
2. What predominant mode of development does the writer use to define the term *underclass*?
3. What other modes of development are used?
4. What is the thesis of the essay? Is it stated? If so, identify the statement(s); if not, state the thesis in your own words.
5. Does the writer explain the denotation or the connotation of the term *underclass*?

Writing Assignments

1. Write an essay in which you define the terms *liberal* and *conservative*.

2. ***Working Together***   Join with some classmates to write an essay in which you define the terms *underclass, middleclass,* and *upperclass.* Include formal definitions and at least two additional modes of development.

The Window

John Thorne

A window is not an ordinary, practical thing to John Thorne, and he finds an unusual way to tell us what a window means to him.

Words to Know

abhorrent causing fear or disgust
epithet name
harbinger omen, forewarning
hermetically airtight, sealed against air entering or escaping
licentious illicit, without moral or sexual restraint
opaque dull, not transparent
tactile can be felt or touched, tangible

Getting Started

Is the purpose of a window to shut the outside out or to let the outside in?

A window allows us to turn the inside out and let the outside in. It is a 1
rupture point between two separate realities, less a passageway than a
hole. To truly see out of one you must also be able to fall out of it; otherwise, no matter how much you look, you still won't know exactly where
you are.

Space and light, openness and closedness, are experienced most im- 2
mediately by our eyes, but their truth is finally tactile—they need to be
felt to be made real. Glass is visually transparent but sensually opaque; it
alone is not enough to make a window. What can't be opened is only
another kind of wall.

A French window is the most sensual of such openings, for it is wall, 3
door, and window, all at once. The epithet conveys the general suspicion
of such licentious access—and, even with that disclaimer, it still unnerves:
the general preference is to call it, instead, a door.

A glass door, at least, can be understood. A window that offers such 4
intimacy is abhorrent to the current puritanism which conspicuously designs windows to limit access: triple-paned, tinted, and sometimes even
hermetically sealed. Better, I think, to make do with blinds, shutters, shades
. . . window garments that casually fall open or get zipped up tight, depending on the season and the company.

The curtains are set aflutter by a sudden breeze, the cool, moist harbin- 5
ger of an approaching storm. Some jump at the touch and hurry through
the house, slamming windows shut. If, instead, it entices you to go fling
the nearest one wide open, you, too, know that there are times when a
window, like a piece of clothing, is most appealing when easiest to push
aside.

Questions About the Reading

1. What does the writer say you must be able to do to truly see out a
   window?
2. What is the writer's opinion of a French window? Does he think it is
   really a window?
3. What is the writer's opinion of a glass door?
4. Do you think the writer closes his windows when a storm approaches?

Questions About the Writer's Strategies

1. What is the tone of the essay?
2. Is the essay objective, subjective, or both? Give examples to support
   your answer.
3. What is the writer's definition of a window? State the definition in
   your own words.

Writing Assignments

1. Pick an ordinary object in your home and write an essay in which you
   define the object and its meaning to you.
2. Write an essay in which you define one of the following terms: *dog,
   home,* or *family.*

What Is Intelligence, Anyway?

Isaac Asimov

Many of us think that intelligence is something one is simply born with, or that it has to do with doing well in school or getting high scores on IQ tests. But did you ever stop to think about what IQ tests really measure? In the essay that follows, Isaac Asimov asks us to rethink our definition of intelligence.

Words to Know

aptitude   ability, talent
arbiter   someone who has the power to judge
complacent   self-satisfied
intricate   elaborate
KP   kitchen patrol
oracles   wise expressions or answers
raucously   loudly

Getting Started

Do you think that tests can ever really measure intelligence?

What is intelligence, anyway? When I was in the army I received a   1
kind of aptitude test that all soldiers took and, against a normal of 100, scored 160. No one at the base had ever seen a figure like that, and for two hours they made a big fuss over me. (It didn't mean anything. The next day I was still a buck private with KP as my highest duty.)

All my life I've been registering scores like that, so that I have the com-   2
placent feeling that I'm highly intelligent, and I expect other people to think so, too. Actually, though, don't such scores simply mean that I am very good at answering the type of academic questions that are considered worthy of answers by the people who make up the intelligence tests—people with intellectual bents similar to mine?

For instance, I had an auto-repair man once, who, on these intelligence   3
tests, could not possibly have scored more than 80, by my estimate. I always took it for granted that I was far more intelligent than he was. Yet, when anything went wrong with my car I hastened to him with it, watched him anxiously as he explored its vitals, and listened to his pronouncements as though they were divine oracles—and he always fixed my car.

Well, then, suppose my auto-repair man devised questions for an in-   4
telligence test. Or suppose a carpenter did, or a farmer, or, indeed, almost
anyone but an academician. By every one of those tests, I'd prove myself
a moron. And I'd *be* a moron, too. In a world where I could not use my
academic training and my verbal talents but had to do something intricate or hard, working with my hands, I would do poorly. My intelligence,
then, is not absolute but is a function of the society I live in and of the fact
that a small subsection of that society has managed to foist itself on the
rest as an arbiter of such matters.

Consider my auto-repair man, again. He had a habit of telling me jokes   5
whenever he saw me. One time he raised his head from under the automobile hood to say: "Doc, a deaf-and-dumb guy went into a hardware
store to ask for some nails. He put two fingers together on the counter
and made hammering motions with the other hand. The clerk brought
him a hammer. He shook his head and pointed to the two fingers he was
hammering. The clerk brought him nails. He picked out the sizes he
wanted, and left. Well, Doc, the next guy who came in was a blind man.
He wanted scissors. How do you suppose he asked for them?"

Indulgently, I lifted my right hand and made scissoring motions with   6
my first two fingers. Whereupon my auto-repair man laughed raucously
and said, "Why, you dumb jerk, he used his *voice* and asked for them."
Then he said, smugly, "I've been trying that on all my customers today."
"Did you catch many?" I asked. "Quite a few," he said, "but I knew for
sure I'd catch *you*." "Why is that?" I asked. "Because you're so goddamned
educated, Doc, I *knew* you couldn't be very smart."

And I have an uneasy feeling he had something there.   7

Questions About the Reading

1. What does the writer mean when he says, "My intelligence, then, is not
   absolute but is a function of the society I live in. . . ." (paragraph 4)?
2. What distinction does the writer make between being educated and
   being smart?
3. Do you think the repairman is smarter than the writer? Why or why
   not?

Questions About the Writer's Strategies

1. What mode of development does the writer use in paragraphs 5 and
   6? What is the purpose of these paragraphs?

2. Does the writer actually define *intelligence*? If so, state his definition in your own words. If not, explain why you think he didn't.
3. In paragraph 6, the writer says he made the scissoring motions "indulgently." What does this tell you about his attitude toward the joke? Why is his attitude ironic?
4. Does the essay contain a thesis statement? If so, where is it located? If not, state it in your own words.
5. Is the repairman a symbol? If so, what does he represent?

Writing Assignments

1. Imagine a society in which intelligence is measured by how well people can work with their hands and fix machinery. Write a definition of intelligence for that society.
2. Write an essay defining the term *joke*. Use examples to illustrate your definition.
3. Pick one of the following terms and define it in an essay: *beauty, truth, wisdom,* or *quality*.

Democracy

Amy Tan

Democracy is something Americans believe in, something many say they would fight and die for, and something the government tries to encourage in other parts of the world. As Amy Tan points out in this essay, those persons who can only dream of it define it differently.

Words to Know

bourgeoisie the middle class
entomology the study of insects
inalienable undeniable; not capable of being taken away
prestige honor, status

Getting Started

How do you imagine your life is different from that of a student living in a country that is not democratic?

How much we Americans take our freedoms for granted. We already 1 have the rights: freedom of expression, contracts and legal departments to protect them, the right to put differences of opinion to a vote. We put those rights in writing, carry them in our back pockets all over the world, pull them out as proof. We may be aliens in another country, but we still maintain that our rights are inalienable.

I try to imagine what democracy means to people in China who dream 2 of it. I don't think they are envisioning electoral colleges, First Amendment rights or civil lawsuits. I imagine that their dreams of democracy begin with a feeling in the chest, one that has been restrained for so long it grows larger and more insistent, until it bursts forth with a shout. Democracy is the right to shout, "Listen to us."

That is what I imagine because I was in China in 1987. I saw glimpses 3 of another way of life, a life that could have been mine. And along with many wonderful things I experienced in my heart, I also felt something uncomfortable in my chest.

In Shanghai in 1987, I attended the wedding of my niece. After the 4 ceremony, she and her husband went home to the three-room apartment shared with her mother, father and brother. "Now that you're married," I said with good humor, "you can't live at home anymore."

"The waiting list for government-assigned housing is sixteen years," 5
replied my niece's husband. "We will both be forty-eight years old when
we are assigned our own place."

My mouth dropped. He shrugged.   6

While on a boat trip down the Huangpu River, I asked a tour guide 7
how she had chosen her career. She told me matter-of-factly that people
in China did not choose careers. They had jobs assigned to them.

She saw my surprised expression. "Oh, but I'm lucky. So many people 8
can't get any kind of good job. If your family came from a bad background—the bourgeoisie—then, no college. Maybe only a job sweeping
the streets." At a family dinner in Beijing, I learned that my sister's husband could not attend our get-together. He was away at his job, said my
sister.

"When will he return?" I asked. My mother explained that his job was 9
in a city thousands of miles away. He had been living apart from my
sister for the past ten years. "That's terrible," I said to my sister. "Tell him
to ask for a transfer. Tell him you miss him."

"Miss, not miss!" my mother sniffed. "They can't even ask."   10

One of my sisters did ask. Several years ago, she asked for a visa to 11
leave China. Now she lives in Wisconsin. A former nurse, she now works
six days a week, managing a take-out Chinese restaurant. Her husband,
trained as a surgeon, works in the kitchen. And recently I've met others
who also asked, a waiter who was once a doctor in China, a taxi driver
who was formerly a professor of entomology, a housekeeper who was an
engineer. Why did they ask to leave? I found it hard to understand how
people could leave behind family, friends, their motherland and jobs of
growing prestige.

My sister in Wisconsin helped me understand. After my novel was 12
published, she wrote me a letter. "I was once like you," she said. "I wanted
to write stories as a young girl. But when I was growing up, they told me
I could not do so many things. And now my imagination is rusted and no
stories can move out of my brain."

My sister and I had the same dream. But my brain did not become 13
rusted. I became a writer. And later, we shared another dream, that China
and our family were on the verge of a better, more open life. We did not
imagine that the blood that is thicker than water would be running through
the streets of Beijing. We did not believe that one Chinese would kill another. We did not foresee that an invisible great wall would rise up, that
we would be cut off from our family, that letters would stop, that the
silence would become unbearable.

These days I can only imagine what has happened to my family in 14
China. And I think about the word democracy. It rolls so easily off my

English-speaking tongue. But in Beijing it is a foreign-sounding word, so many syllables, so many clashing sounds. In China, democracy is still not an easy word to say. Many cannot say it.

Hope then.   15

Questions About the Readings

1. What inspired Tan to write about democracy?
2. What is the writer expressing when she says, "I don't think they are envisioning electoral colleges, First Amendment rights, or civil lawsuits" (paragraph 2)?
3. Why did some of the writer's relatives and acquaintances leave their families, homes, and careers?
4. What does Tan mean when she states that the word *democracy* is so hard for the Chinese to say?

Questions About the Writer's Strategies

1. Does the writer actually define the word *democracy* in a formal way? Why do you think she chose to define it, or not define it?
2. What examples does the author use to describe the lack of freedom in China?
3. What parts of the essay are objective? What parts of the essay are subjective?
4. Is the writer emphasizing the connotation or the denotation of the word *democracy*?

Writing Assignments

1. Can you imagine being a student in another culture? Write an essay that compares your everyday life with the life of a student in a country with fewer freedoms.
2. Write an essay in which you define the word *dictatorship*. Use a mode of development that allows you to include examples from recent history.
3. Write an essay defining the term *immigrant,* using an extended example of someone in your own family background, someone you have known, or someone from American history.

—————————— Connections ——————————

1. Several selections in this chapter attempt to define words and ideas that are difficult to define. What is *intelligence*? What is the *underclass*? Choose two or more definitions found in the selections and add your own meanings to the writers' definitions.
2. Richard Shelton defines nostalgia, and John Thorne defines a window. What connections can you make between the two readings?
3. Choose two selections found in this chapter and discuss what you think might have been the writer's inspiration or purpose. Cite details and examples from the selections to support your ideas.

10

Argumentation and Persuasion

ALL EFFECTIVE WRITING involves, to some extent, argumentation or persuasion. As you have learned from the preceding chapters, writers use various kinds of information to develop a **topic** or **thesis.** Such information can be said to "argue" or "persuade" in the sense that it convinces the reader that the writer's idea is true or believable. However, as **modes of development,** argumentation and persuasion have some particular characteristics that you should know about and be able to use in your own writing.

Let's look first at **persuasion** in its most obvious form—the advertisement. You should not use sentence fragments in your writing assignments, as the advertisement below does; and of course you should continue to structure your writing according to a main (general) idea and to support it according to the various modes of development. But you will want to appeal to the emotions, qualities, or values that a reader is likely to share or find desirable, as advertisers do. One way to appeal to a reader is to use words for their **connotations**—explained in the preceding chapter as the feelings or qualities a reader may associate with a word—rather than for their **denotations,** or dictionary definitions.

In the following example, the advertiser uses the words *clean, smooth, fresh,* and *pure innocence.* We associate such words with highly desirable qualities, and the advertiser intends to persuade us that a particular soap will give our skin these qualities. The word *new* implies that the product has been improved and, therefore, is better or more desirable than its predecessor or a competing product. Notice, too, that the ad appeals to our senses when it describes the soap's lather as *silky* and *soft.*

Connotation ⌐ Now. Clean skin with the touch of <u>innocence</u>. The joy of it.

Connotation ⌐ Of having skin <u>so clean</u>, <u>so smooth</u>, <u>so fresh</u>, it has the touch
└ of <u>pure innocence</u>. Today, you can capture that feeling, sim-

Connotation ⌐ ply by <u>cleansing</u> with the extraordinary <u>new</u> Olay Beauty

Connotation ⌐ Bar. Its special Olay lather, <u>silky and soft</u>, <u>creams</u> up to clean

Connotation ⌐ when you work it in. The <u>tinier bubbles</u> work in <u>natural</u>
└ <u>harmony</u> with your skin. They lift out impurities, then <u>rinse</u>

Connotation ⌐ <u>cleanly</u> away, leaving <u>better skin</u> even before you raise your
└ eyes to the mirror—<u>fresher skin</u> each time, <u>smoother skin</u> at
every touch. Again and again, new Olay Beauty Bar cleanses

Connotation ⌐ <u>innocence</u> into your skin.

The purpose of persuasion is to make the reader accept the writer's
idea. That idea may be an opinion or judgment that the reader might not
ordinarily share or have knowledge of. The idea may be controversial—
as we shall see later, the idea of an argument must be—but it does not
have to be. The idea may even be humorous. Whatever the idea, the writer
will use words and information to appeal to the reader's emotions. Such
information may be biased in favor of the writer's idea, but it should be
honest and accurate. Notice the emotional strength of the writer's examples in the letter that follows.

R. J. Reynolds Tobacco Co.
4th and Main Street
Winston-Salem, N.C. 27102

Dear Sirs:

When my wife died of lung cancer in 1976, I wanted to
write you about her love affair with Camel cigarettes. I con-
cluded, however, that it would be an exercise in futility.

I take up the challenge now, because you have publicly
announced an advertising campaign to cast doubt on medical reports that cigarettes are a public-health hazard. You call
for an open debate. Okay, let's debate.

Example 1: wife ⌐ My wife died a painful death. She was just 56 and had
smoked at least a pack of Camels a day for 40 years. Coinci-
└ dentally, just 30 days before her demise her 47-year-old

Example 2: ⌐ brother died of the same illness. Both experienced unbear-
brother-in-law └ able pain. He, too, was a heavy smoker.

⌐ But there is more to this horror story. In 1958, my father
died suddenly of a cardiovascular ailment. He'd been a two-
pack-a-day man for years, and would "walk a mile for a

Example 3: Camel" when younger. Later in life, he could hardly walk at
father all. But he still puffed away, day and night, before breakfast
and with his meals. He endured continual nasal and respiratory problems, and never enjoyed a day free of a hacking
cough.

A popular pharmacist, he had many doctor friends who urged him to stop smoking. But he was firmly hooked and had been since 1909. Ill with lung disease (emphysema and chronic bronchitis), he had long suffered intensely painful attacks of near-suffocation. In 1955 he was forced to retire and spend his "golden years" either lying on our sofa or propped up in a lounge chair.

In late summer of 1957, I took him to a specialist at the University of Maryland Hospital in Baltimore. There he was told there was no cure for his condition. But he could help himself. "How?" he asked. "Stop smoking," was the reply.

That is a tall order for anyone who has smoked for almost 50 years. But my father did not want to live the life of an invalid, so he determined to try. That he succeeded—cold turkey—is nothing short of a miracle. But he really had no other choice, except to suffer.

Within weeks he was breathing easier, and it was not long before he was walking about and driving his car. He got to enjoy life a bit. I'm convinced that giving up smoking added that near-year to his life.

Example 4: daughter

Today, I have a daughter—a working mother of two—who has been addicted to cigarettes since peer pressure in high school encouraged her to smoke. She wants desperately to quit. In fact, she has done so several times, only to be lured back by the smoking of others in her workplace.

Having presented four powerful extended examples, this writer goes on to a thorough persuasive conclusion. You will see next that he uses **rhetorical questions** to introduce and structure his conclusion. A rhetorical question is a question to which no real answer is expected because only one obvious reply can be made—and that reply will either support or restate the writer's point. Rhetorical questions are fairly common in persuasive writing and in argumentation because they offer a way for writers to emphasize the correctness of their viewpoints.

Okay, R. J. Reynolds, that's my story. What's yours? Are you prepared to tell us that the National Institutes of Health, the Surgeon General and the various voluntary health agencies are all wrong? Are the many scientific studies indicting smoking just so much hogwash?

For the sake of debate, let's assume smoking's critics are wrong. Can you deny that cigarette smoking is addictive? Isn't that fact precisely the reason why you sell so many cigarettes? Is it moral to manufacture and sell *any* product that causes addiction—even if it might otherwise be harmless? As bad as alcohol abuse is, alcohol is addictive to only a relatively small number of consumers. You can't say that about cigarettes. Smoking hooks nearly every consumer. And once hooked it is difficult to stop; for some, it seems impossible.

In a free society, people can't be forbidden to smoke. But government does have the obligation to warn the public of the dangers involved. It has the responsibility to hold R. J. Reynolds Tobacco Co. and others accountable for luring impressionable people to smoke, while suggesting that medical findings establishing a relationship between smoking and cancer, cardiovascular diseases and respiratory ailments are inconclusive.

It's hard to fight the rich tobacco industry, but just maybe, through education, we non-smokers will eventually win. As a witness to so much tragedy caused by smoking, I feel compelled to hope so.

Sincerely,
Gil Crandall

In summary, then, a persuasive paragraph or essay, like the other modes of development, is based on a main (general) idea developed by one or more of the modes of development and is characterized by the use of words or information that appeals to the reader's emotions. The information or evidence used in persuasion may be one-sided, but it should be honest and accurate. The topic, or thesis, of persuasion may be controversial, but it does not have to be.

Argumentation, on the other hand, must be based on a controversial idea—an idea that people have conflicting views or opinions about. Although argumentation may include some persuasion, its appeal to the reader should be rational and logical, as opposed to emotional, and **objective,** rather than one-sided. A classic or formal argument includes five elements:

- **Statement of the problem**
- **Solution,** the writer's thesis or answer to the problem
- **Evidence,** the information the writer presents to support or prove the thesis
- **Refutation,** the writer's acknowledgment of and response to opposing views
- **Conclusion,** the writer's summation of the evidence and, generally, a restatement of the thesis

Although you may seldom need to write a paragraph-length argument, it is helpful to examine an example of one. Notice in the following example that the writer has explained the problem, stated a solution or answer to the problem—which is the topic of the paragraph—provided evidence in support of the solution, refuted the opposing view, and summarized the position taken on the topic.

During the late sixties and early seventies, political and social activism was rampant on college campuses. Student protests—which were sometimes peaceful and other times violent—addressed issues related to civil rights, the environment, war, nuclear arms, and consumer protection and rights.

Statement of the problem

In recent years, student protests have been much less frequent and, generally, peaceful, causing some writers and politicians to label present-day students as apathetic.

Solution

Nonsense! Today's students are not apathetic. They simply have different concerns from the ones of the sixties and seventies.

Evidence

They are more concerned about, for instance, employment and the quality of their own lives. They are assessing, confronting even, themselves—their hopes, plans, desires, ambitions, and values. They are fighting quietly for their causes—personal or otherwise—by pursuing training and retraining opportunities and by exercising their voting privileges.

Refutation

To say they are apathetic is to ignore the steadfastness with which they are pursuing their goals. To say they are apathetic is to imply that a person is not concerned about an issue unless that person takes to the streets or possibly engages in violent acts on behalf of that issue. The fact is, the current college population is older—the average age of community college students nationwide is about twenty-eight—more experienced, and in some ways wiser. As a consequence, they have perhaps learned that confrontation may win a battle but lose the war, that in the long run, they must live and work with those persons who hold opposing views.

Conclusion

Thus, while they are indeed quieter than their predecessors, they continue to be concerned about such important issues as employment (their own and others), nuclear arms, the environment, civil rights, and war. We make a mistake if we write off today's college students as apathetic simply because we do not see overt evidence of their concern.

In a full-length essay, you can develop your argument more fully and convincingly than you can in a paragraph. The order in which you present the elements of an argument may differ from the classic organization represented by the preceding paragraph. For instance, you may want to state the refutation before presenting the evidence for your argument. And sometimes one of the elements of your argument may be **implied** rather than stated, just as the topic sentence of a paragraph or the main idea of an essay may be implied.

No matter what method is used to develop an argument, however, always remember that the evidence presented to support the solution and the conclusion must be valid—true, supported by facts, accurately expressed, and based on sound reasoning. This is something to watch for not only in your own writing but also when you are reading arguments composed by others. When you read or write an argument, analyze not only the main conclusion but also all the ideas that support it. A conclusion may seem quite sensible based on the evidence the writer supplies, but if the evidence itself is not true and not presented logically, the conclusion will be viewed as faulty.

In the essay below, the writer follows the classic model in presenting her argument and supports her opinion with facts that give the reader sound reasons to accept her conclusion. Notice that she uses several modes of development, such as **contrast** and **examples.**

Statement of the problem

Each year, from late spring to early fall, thousands of high school students and their parents spend a great deal of time and money driving around the country to visit expensive and prestigious colleges that the students think they might like to attend. Each year, thousands of students go through the ritual of applying to and being rejected by these colleges.

Solution

Instead, they should go to a community college and, after earning their associate degree, transfer to a four-year university to complete their education.

Evidence

Most community colleges offer a wide choice of career or technical programs as well as a curriculum paralleling that offered by a university. If the student has already made a career choice, an associate degree prepares the student to enter the workforce or to continue his or her career study in a four-year university. If the student has not decided on a career, a community college is an excellent place to learn more about many different career possibilities and to complete the general education courses required by either a career or university-parallel program.

Evidence

Most community colleges also have a more diverse population than that of the student's high school. In a community college the student has the opportunity to meet persons of all ages, abilities, and ethnic and racial backgrounds and to improve his or her knowledge and understanding of others.

Evidence

A community college is also much less expensive than most colleges. In addition to the lower cost of tuition and fees, the student can usually live at home and commute to classes, which also saves the high cost of dorm or apartment fees.

Refutation

It is true, of course, that a community college does not offer the prestige of the more famous universities. But if prestige is significant, the student could complete a baccalaureate and graduate work at a better-known school. And whether the education the student receives at a community college is equal to that provided by a more prestigious university can be determined only on a case-by-case basis, since much of the success of any education depends on the individual student.

1

2

3

4

5

Conclusion

> The fact is, for most students a community college is a 6
> sound educational and economic choice. Instead of engag-
> ing in the expensive and time-consuming spring-to-fall ritual
> of college shopping, most students would be as well or bet-
> ter served by taking advantage of the educational opportu-
> nity offered by their local community college.

When you read an argument, remember too that a writer may present facts selectively. That is, the writer may not give you all the facts relating to an issue or problem. For this reason, it is advisable to read and consider arguments on both sides of the controversy and to carefully analyze the facts when you are trying to form an opinion about an important issue. It will then be up to you when writing an argumentation paper to interpret the facts and conclusions, to decide which ones are most valid, and to choose the ones you will use to support your own thesis.

Be alert, too, for fallacies in your reasoning. In addition to the fallacies identified in chapter 8 (p. 208), guard against the following:

- *False analogy.* A false analogy assumes that two things that are alike are alike in all respects. A Honda and a Cadillac are both cars, but they are not alike in all respects.
- *Circular argument.* A circular argument restates an idea in different words: "The airports are too crowded because too many people are travelling."
- *Argument to the man* (argument ad hominem). An argument to the man attacks the person rather than the issue: "He gets poor grades. After all, he's a computer nerd."
- *Bandwagon.* A bandwagon fallacy claims that something is true because the majority believe or act on it: "Everyone thinks she should be elected class president" or "We should go to the concert because everyone else is."
- *Either-or.* An either-or argument assumes that only two things are possible: "The submarine sank because of poor maintenance and personnel training."
- *Begging the question.* Begging the question presents as a fact an idea or premise that is not proven: "If we removed all chat rooms from the Internet, children would not be enticed to meet people who could do them harm."

In summary, although argumentation and persuasion have a common **purpose**—to convince the reader to accept the writer's opinion—they differ principally in the way the writer appeals to the reader. In argumentation, the writer supports the topic or thesis by presenting objective, logical evidence that appeals to the reader's reason. In persuasion, the writer does not necessarily abandon objectivity or logic, but uses words or other information that appeals to the reader's emotions. Also, although the thesis of persuasion *may* be controversial, the thesis of an argument *must* be. In both argumentation and persuasion, the writer makes use of whatever modes of development are effective and appropriate.

In school and beyond, there will be occasions when you will want to use argumentation or persuasion to make a point to your **audience.** Whether you are doing so orally or in writing, being familiar with techniques used in argumentation and persuasion will help you.

Ban All Handguns

Sallie Tisdale

In this paragraph from her essay "Zero Tolerance for Slaughter," Sallie Tisdale asks why we are willing to accept many regulations curtailing our freedoms but are reluctant to regulate the sale and ownership of handguns.

Word to Know

commodity   product, article for sale

Getting Started

Do you think more laws are needed to control the manufacture and sale of handguns?

In this strange, wonderful, unique democracy, we have freedoms no other people have enjoyed. Still, we regulate the swear words people say on the radio. We regulate toys. We regulate broccoli, aspirin and massage. We legislate which trees a homeowner can plant along their curb. We require motorcyclists to wear helmets. We insist on building permits, speed limits, and driver's licenses. We rate movies. We simply prohibit the use of marijuana. But we are afraid to say no to guns. Guns are, in fact, treated in a completely different way from any other commodity, any other choice. The American government and the American public—you and me—are peculiarly passive and even hopeless in the face of the gun lobby. In just the last 10 years, 35 million *new* guns have been added to the *200 million guns we've manufactured* in this country in the 20th century. They've been added to our daily lives, to our shopping malls, neighborhoods, city parks, street corners and schools. According to the *Coalition to Stop Gun Violence* there is now a gun for every single adult in this country *and* for every other child. A new handgun is made in this country every 20 *seconds.* Only the most outrageous weapons—machine guns and grenades—must be registered with the government. There are no federal safety standards for firearms. (There are clearly defined standards for stuffed animals, for Christmas tree lights and for cereal.) We allow people to buy lethal weapons at gun shows without even a swift background check. Imagine your worst nightmare, your scariest neighbor, your angriest employee or the most frightening student at your child's high school loading up on ammo this weekend at a convention center near you. It's perfectly legal. It happens all the time, and we act as though there is nothing we can do about it.

––––––––––––––

Questions About the Reading

1. What are some of the things for which we have accepted regulations or legislation?
2. According to the writer, how many new guns have been added in this country in the last ten years?
3. How many guns are there in this country for every adult and every other child?
4. How often is a new handgun made in this country?
5. What guns must be registered with the government?

Questions About the Writer's Strategies

1. What is the main idea of the paragraph? Is it stated or implied?
2. What modes of development does the writer use?
3. What is the tone of the paragraph?
4. What is the point of view of the paragraph in person and time? Is it consistent throughout? If not, is each change justified?

Writing Assignments

1. Write an argumentative or persuasive paragraph on the subject of gun control.
2. *Working Together*   Join with some classmates to write a paragraph on the subject of outlawing the manufacture of handguns.

The Measure of Our Success

Marian Wright Edelman

"Children—my own and other people's—became the passion of my personal and professional life. For it is they who are God's presence, promise, and hope for humankind." These are the words of Marian Wright Edelman, the African-American civil rights lawyer and founder of the Children's Defense League. In the following paragraph from her book, The Measure of Our Success: A Letter to My Children and Yours, *Edelman urges her readers to face the mounting crisis of our country's impoverished children and families by taking action themselves.*

Words to Know

empathy   understanding
mentoring   being a counselor or teacher
neonatal   having to do with children born prematurely

Getting Started

What are some things you can do to help build a stronger community for all our children and their children's children?

The place to begin is with ourselves. Care. As you read about or meet some of the children and families in this country who need your help, put yourself in their places as fellow Americans. Imagine you or your spouse being pregnant, and not being able to get enough to eat or see a doctor or know that you have a hospital for delivery. Imagine your child hungry or injured, and you cannot pay for food or find health care. Imagine losing your job and having no income, having your unemployment compensation run out, not being able to pay your note or rent, having no place to sleep with your children, having nothing. Imagine having to stand in a soup line at a church or Salvation Army station after you've worked all your life, or having to sleep in a shelter with strangers and get up and out early each morning, find some place to go with your children, and not know if you can sleep there again that night. If you take the time to imagine this, perhaps you can also take the time to do for them what you would want a fellow citizen to do for you. Volunteer in a homeless shelter or soup kitchen or an afterschool tutoring or mentoring program. Vote. Help to organize your community to speak out for the children who need you. Visit a hospital neonatal intensive care nursery or AIDS and boarder baby ward and spend time rocking and caring for an individual child. Adopt as a pen pal a lonely child who never gets a letter from anyone. Give a youth a summer job. Teach your child tolerance and empathy by your example.

Questions About the Reading

1. According to the writer, how can people begin to make a difference in this country? Do you agree or disagree with her argument? Why?
2. What different methods of action does Edelman describe? Pick out some of the examples she uses.
3. What do you think Edelman means by the last sentence? Do you agree or disagree with her statement? Why?
4. Think about all the different suggestions Edelman makes. Which have you tried? Which might you consider trying?

Questions About the Writer's Strategies

1. Is there a topic sentence in the paragraph? If so, where is it? If not, state the main idea in your own words.
2. Is this a paragraph of argumentation, persuasion, or both? Support your answer with details from the paragraph.
3. Besides persuasion, what other mode of development does the writer use? Support your answer with details from the text.
4. Edelman uses numerous powerful images to support her thesis that we all need to work together to rebuild this country. What are some of the images Edelman uses when she asks us to imagine trading places with our less fortunate fellow Americans? What impact do the images have on you?
5. What is the tone of the paragraph? Why does Edelman use this tone?

Writing Assignments

1. Do you agree or disagree with Edelman's argument that all responsible people need to be active in their communities and their nation? Write a persuasive paragraph on your answer.
2. Do you agree or disagree that children learn tolerance and empathy—or, for that matter, prejudice and hate—by the example of their parents? Write a paragraph in which you argue for or against that statement. Use examples and details to support your position.

The State of Our Health

Lewis Thomas

In this paragraph from his essay "The Health Care System," Lewis Thomas—medical doctor, teacher, and writer—praises the state of our health.

Words to Know

bicentennial   200th anniversary
gastrointestinal   having to do with the stomach and intestines
jeopardy   danger, risk
unimpeded   not obstructed

Getting Started

Is the nation concerned about the health care system because of its quality, its cost to the individual, or its cost to the nation?

It is extraordinary that we have just now become convinced of our bad health, our constant jeopardy of disease and death, at the very time when the facts should be telling us the opposite. In a more rational world, you'd think we would be staging bicentennial ceremonies for the celebration of our general good shape. In the year 1976, out of a population of around 220 million, only 1.9 million died, or just under 1 percent, not at all a discouraging record once you accept the fact of mortality itself. The life expectancy for the whole population rose to seventy-two years, the longest stretch ever achieved in this country. Despite the persisting roster of still-unsolved major diseases—cancer, heart disease, stroke, arthritis, and the rest—most of us have a clear, unimpeded run at a longer and healthier lifetime than could have been foreseen by any earlier generation. The illnesses that plague us the most, when you count up the numbers in the U.S. Vital Statistics reports, are respiratory and gastrointestinal infections, which are, by and large, transient, reversible affairs needing not much more than Grandmother's advice for getting through safely. Thanks in great part to the improved sanitary engineering, nutrition, and housing of the past century, and in real but less part to contemporary immunization and antibiotics, we are free of the great infectious diseases, especially tuberculosis and lobar pneumonia, which used to cut us down long before our time. We are even beginning to make progress in our understanding of the mechanisms underlying the chronic illnesses still with us, and sooner or later, depending on the quality and energy of biomedical research, we will learn to cope effectively with most of these, maybe all. We will still age away and die, but the aging, and even the dying, can become a healthy process. On balance, we ought to be more pleased with ourselves than we are, and more optimistic for the future.

Questions About the Reading

1. What does the writer think we should be celebrating?
2. What percentage of the population died in 1976?
3. What was the life expectancy for the whole population in 1976?
4. What illnesses plague us most?
5. What has contributed to freeing us from such infectious diseases as tuberculosis and lobar pneumonia?

Questions About the Writer's Strategies

1. What is the main idea of the paragraph? Is it stated or implied?
2. Is the paragraph argumentative or persuasive?
3. What modes of development does the writer use?
4. What is the point of view (person, time, tone)? Is the point of view consistent throughout?

Writing Assignments

1. Write a paragraph in which you argue for or against a government-funded health care system for everyone.
2. Write a persuasive paragraph on the health care available in different areas of your city or town.

Hunters

Joy Williams

Joy Williams, in this paragraph from her essay "The Killing Game," argues that sport hunting is immoral and should be made illegal. Wild animals, she says, "deserve our wonder and respect" and should not be killed for sport or recreation.

Words to Know

abattoirs   slaughterhouses
albeit   even though, although
indisputable   not arguable or doubtable
persecutors   people who harm or injure
prosecuted   punished
sentient   capable of feeling
stigmatize   brand, mark as unacceptable or disgraceful

Getting Started

Is killing a wild animal ever justified?

Hunters' self-serving arguments and lies are becoming more preposterous as nonhunters awake from their long, albeit troubled, sleep. Sport hunting is immoral; it should be made illegal. Hunters are persecutors of nature who should be prosecuted. They wield a disruptive power out of all proportion to their numbers, and pandering to their interests—the special interests of a group that just wants to kill things—is mad. It's preposterous that every year less than 7 percent of the population turns the skies into shooting galleries and the woods and fields into abattoirs. It's time to stop actively supporting and passively allowing hunting, and time to stigmatize it. It's time to stop being conned and cowed by hunters, time to stop pampering and coddling them, time to get them off the government's duck-and-deer dole, time to stop thinking of wild animals as "resources" and "game," and start thinking of them as sentient beings that deserve our wonder and respect, time to stop allowing hunting to be creditable by calling it "sport" and "recreation." Hunters make wildlife *dead, dead, dead*. It's time to wake up to this indisputable fact. As for the hunters, it's long past check-out time.

Questions About the Reading

1. What does the writer think should happen to hunters?
2. What percentage of the population are hunters?
3. What is the writer's opinion of sport hunting?
4. What does the writer mean by it's "time to get them off the government's duck-and-deer dole"?

Questions About the Writer's Strategies

1. Is the paragraph argumentative or persuasive?
2. Is the paragraph objective, subjective, or both?
3. What is the tone of the paragraph?

Writing Assignments

1. Write a persuasive paragraph on the subject of sport hunting.
2. *Working Together*   Join with some classmates to write a paragraph in which you argue for or against owning guns for the purpose of shooting wild animals.

The Death Penalty Is a Step Back

Coretta Scott King

Coretta Scott King has strong opinions about the death penalty. Despite the loss of two family members, including her husband, the Reverend Martin Luther King, Jr., by assassination, she remains firmly convinced that the death penalty is morally wrong and unjustifiable. A long-time civil rights activist, she believes that the practice of nonviolence is the way to make our society a more just and humane place to live. In the essay that follows, she argues passionately for her convictions.

Words to Know

abhor   detest, hate strongly
deterrent   something that prevents
inequitable   unfair
irrevocable   not reversible
legitimizing   making lawful
miscarriage   a failure
proponents   advocates, supporters
retaliation   act of revenge
sanctioned   approved
specter   ghost
unequivocally   clearly, without question
unwarranted   not supported by facts

Getting Started

Do you think the death penalty is a deterrent to murder?

When Steven Judy was executed in Indiana [in 1981] America took 1 another step backwards towards legitimizing murder as a way of dealing with evil in our society.

Although Judy was convicted of four of the most horrible and brutal 2 murders imaginable, and his case is probably the worst in recent memory for opponents of the death penalty, we still have to face the real issue squarely: Can we expect a decent society if the state is allowed to kill its own people?

In recent years, an increase of violence in America, both individual 3
and political, has prompted a backlash of public opinion on capital punishment. But however much we abhor violence, legally sanctioned ex-
ecutions are no deterrent and are, in fact, immoral and unconstitutional.

Although I have suffered the loss of two family members by assassina- 4
tion, I remain firmly and unequivocally opposed to the death penalty for
those convicted of capital offenses.

An evil deed is not redeemed by an evil deed of retaliation. Justice is 5
never advanced in the taking of a human life.

Morality is never upheld by legalized murder. Morality apart, there 6
are a number of practical reasons which form a powerful argument against
capital punishment.

First, capital punishment makes irrevocable any possible miscarriage 7
of justice. Time and again we have witnessed the specter of mistakenly
convicted people being put to death in the name of American criminal
justice. To those who say that, after all, this doesn't occur too often, I can
only reply that if it happens just once, that is too often. And it has occurred many times.

Second, the death penalty reflects an unwarranted assumption that 8
the wrongdoer is beyond rehabilitation. Perhaps some individuals cannot be rehabilitated; but who shall make that determination? Is any
amount of academic training sufficient to entitle one person to judge another incapable of rehabilitation?

Third, the death penalty is inequitable. Approximately half of the 711 9
persons now on death row are black. From 1930 through 1968, 53.5% of
those executed were black Americans, all too many of whom were represented by court-appointed attorneys and convicted after hasty trials.

The argument that this may be an accurate reflection of guilt, and hom- 10
icide trends, instead of a racist application of laws lacks credibility in
light of a recent Florida survey which showed that persons convicted of
killing whites were four times more likely to receive a death sentence
than those convicted of killing blacks.

Proponents of capital punishment often cite a "deterrent effect" as the 11
main benefit of the death penalty. Not only is there no hard evidence that
murdering murderers will deter other potential killers, but even the "logic"
of this argument defies comprehension.

Numerous studies show that the majority of homicides committed in 12
this country are the acts of the victim's relatives, friends and acquaintances in the "heat of passion."

What this strongly suggests is that rational consideration of future con- 13
sequences is seldom a part of the killer's attitude at the time he commits
a crime.

The only way to break the chain of violent reaction is to practice non- 14
violence as individuals and collectively through our laws and institutions.

Questions About the Reading

1. What does the writer think we should do instead of enforcing the death penalty?
2. According to the writer, who commits the majority of homicides?
3. What three "practical reasons" does the writer give as an argument against capital punishment?

Questions About the Writer's Strategies

1. Is this essay an example of argument, persuasion, or both? Support your answer with examples.
2. Why does the writer state that she has lost two family members by assassination? How does this contribute to the effectiveness of her argument?
3. What modes of development does the writer use to develop her argument?
4. Where is the thesis most clearly stated?

Writing Assignments

1. Write an essay that argues either for or against the death penalty.
2. Some states have enacted laws that mandate jail sentences for people who are convicted of drunk driving. Do you agree with such laws? Write an essay in which you provide evidence for your position.

Death to the Killers

Mike Royko

*In the following essay, Mike Royko (1932–1997), a syndicated colum-
nist, takes the opposing view of the death penalty from that of Coretta
Scott King. He tells the stories of the families of several murder victims
and says, "Opponents of the death penalty should try explaining to these
people just how cruel it is to kill someone."*

Words to Know

decomposed   rotting
delegate   to give duties to another
deter   to keep from acting
dispatching   getting rid of (in this context, putting to death)
retribution   punishment

Getting Started

Do you think the justice system ensures that innocent people will
not be put to death for crimes they did not commit?

Some recent columns on the death penalty have brought some interest-   1
ing responses from readers all over the country.

There were, of course, expressions of horror and disgust that I would   2
favor the quick dispatching of convicted murderers.

I really don't like to make fun of people who oppose the death penalty   3
because they are so sincere. But I wish they would come up with some
new arguments to replace the worn-out ones.

For example, many said something like this: "Wouldn't it be better to   4
keep the killers alive so psychiatrists can study them in order to find out
what makes them the way they are?"

It takes the average psychiatrist about five years to figure why a guy   5
wants to stop for two drinks after work and won't quit smoking. So how
long do you think it will take him to determine why somebody with an
IQ of 92 decided to rape and murder the little old lady who lives next
door?

Besides, we have an abundance of killers in our prisons—more than   6
enough to keep all the nation's shrinks busy for the next 20 years. But shrinks
aren't stupid. Why would they want to spend all that time listening

to Willie the Wolfman describe his ax murders when they can get $75 an hour for listening to an executive's fantasies about the secretarial pool?

Another standard is: "The purpose of the law should be to protect so- 7 ciety, not to inflict cruel retribution, such as the death penalty."

In that case, we should tear down all the prisons and let all the crimi- 8 nals go because most people would consider a long imprisonment to be cruel retribution—especially those who are locked up. Even 30 days in the Cook County Jail is no picnic.

And: "What gives society the right to take a life if an individual can't?" 9 The individuals who make up society give it that right. Societies perform many functions that individuals can't. We can't carry guns and shoot people, but we delegate that right to police.

Finally: "The death penalty doesn't deter crime." I heard from a num- 10 ber of people who have a less detached view of the death penalty than many of the sensitive souls who oppose it.

For instance, Doris Porch wrote me about a man on Death Row in Ten- 11 nessee. He hired men to murder his wife. One threw in a rape, free of charge.

Porch wrote: "My family had the misfortune of knowing this man (the 12 husband) intimately. The victim was my niece. After her decomposed body was found in the trunk of her car, I made the trip to homicide with my sister."

Sharon Rosenfeldt of Canada wrote: "We know exactly what you are 13 talking about because our son was brutally murdered and sexually abused by mass murderer Clifford Olson in Vancouver.

"Words can't explain the suffering the families of murder victims are 14 left to live with. After two years, we're still trying to piece our lives back together mentally and spiritually."

Eleanor Lulenski of Cleveland said: "I'm the mother of one of the in- 15 nocent victims. My son was a registered nurse on duty in an emergency room. A man walked in demanding a shot of penicillin. When he was told he would have to be evaluated by a physician, he stomped out, went to his car, came back with a shotgun and killed my son.

"He was sentenced to life, but after several years the sentence was re- 16 versed on a technicality—it being that at the time of his trial it was mentioned that this was his second murder."

And Susie James of Greenville, Miss.: "My tax dollars are putting bread 17 into the mouth of at least one murderer from Mississippi who showed no mercy to his innocent victim.

"He caught a ride with her one cold February night. She was returning 18 to her home from her job in a nursing home. She was a widow. The murderer, whom she had befriended, struck her on the head with a can of oil.

Ignoring her pleas, he forced her through a barbed wire fence into the woods at knifepoint. He stabbed her repeatedly, raped her and left her for dead.

"When the victim's son walked down the stairs to leave the courthouse 19 after the guilty sentence had been uttered, he happened to look at the killer's mother.

"She said: 'You buzzard, watching me.'   20

"The murder victim was my mother."   21

There are many others. The mother of the boy who angered some 22 drunken street thugs. They shot him and then ran him over repeatedly with a car. The mother whose son and daughter were beaten to death. The brother who remembers how his little sister would laugh as they played—until she was butchered.

They have many things in common. They suffered a terrible loss, and 23 they live with terrible memories.

One other thing they share: The knowledge that the killers are alive 24 and will probably remain alive and cared for by society.

Opponents of the death penalty should try explaining to these people 25 just how cruel it is to kill someone.

Questions About the Reading

1. Why does Royko think that psychiatrists are not interested in finding out why people kill?
2. What do the families and friends of homicide victims have in common?
3. How does the writer refute the argument that the death penalty won't deter criminals?

Questions About the Writer's Strategies

1. What is the predominant mode of development used to develop the argument?
2. Locate the writer's statement of the problem.
3. Is this essay an example of argumentation, persuasion, or a mixture of the two? Explain your answer.
4. Why does Royko refer to opponents of the death penalty as "sensitive souls" in paragraph 10?
5. Locate the writer's conclusion. Is it effective? Do you think it could have been expanded? Why or why not?

Writing Assignments

1. Write an essay in which you argue for or against the death penalty. Support your argument with information from at least three web sites, and include a list of their addresses. To find helpful sites, use a search engine such as AltaVista (**http://www.altavista.com/**), Yahoo! (**http://www.yahoo.com/**), or Excite (**http://www.excite.com/**) and type in keywords such as "death penalty" or "capital punishment."

2. Some people support mandatory sentencing: people who commit certain crimes are automatically given prison sentences of a certain length. What purpose do you think mandatory sentencing would serve? Write an essay in which you support or reject the concept?

Do We Need These Laws?

Andrew Sullivan

Andrew Sullivan, author of Virtually Normal: An Argument About
Homosexuality *and* Love Undetectable, *maintains that getting jobs
and keeping them are not the most pressing issues that homosexuals face.
He argues that focusing on equal rights—for example, in marriage and
the military—should be the group's agenda.*

Words to Know

bigotry   prejudice, intolerance
irreparably   beyond repair, unchangeable
minuscule   tiny, very small
nexus   group connection or bond

Getting Started

Do you think homosexual people are discriminated against in the
workplace?

Before I make myself irreparably unpopular, I might as well start with   1
a concession. Almost all the arguments the fundamentalist right uses
against gay "special rights" are phony ones. If there's legal protection for
blacks, whites, Jews, Latinos, women, the disabled, and now men in the
workplace, then it's hard to see why homosexuals should be excluded.

It's also true that such laws would ban discrimination against straights   2
as well as gays, and so they target no single group for "special" protection. Nevertheless, there's a reason the special rights rhetoric works, and
that is because it contains a germ of truth. However evenhanded antidiscrimination laws are in principle, in practice they're designed to protect
the oppressed. So while the laws pretend to ban discrimination on the
neutral grounds of sex, race, ethnicity, or disability, they really exist to
protect women, blacks, Latinos, the disabled, and so on. They are laws
that create a class of victims and a battery of lawyers and lobbyists to
protect them.

The real question, then, is this: Are gay people generally victims in   3
employment? Have we historically been systematically barred from jobs
in the same way that, say, women, blacks, and the disabled have? And is
a remedy therefore necessary? My own view is that, while there are some
particular cases of discrimination against homosexuals, for the most part

getting and keeping jobs is hardly the most pressing issue we face. Aided by our talents, by the ability of each generation to avoid handing on poverty to the next, and by the two-edged weapon of the closet, we have, by and large, avoided becoming economic victims. Even in those states where job-protection laws have been enacted, sexual orientation cases have made up a minuscule proportion of the whole caseload.

Most people—gay and straight—know this to be true; and so they sense 4 that the push for gay employment rights is unconvincing and whiny. I think they're right. The truth is, most gay people are not victims, at least not in the economic sense. We may not be much richer than most Americans, but there's little evidence that we are much poorer. Despite intense psychological, social, and cultural hostility, we have managed to fare pretty well economically in the past few generations. Instead of continually whining that we need job protection, we should be touting our economic achievements, defending the free market that makes them possible, investing our resources in our churches and charities and social institutions, and politically focusing on the areas where we clearly are discriminated against by our own government.

The problems of gay and lesbian Americans are not, after all, system- 5 atic exclusion from employment. They are (to name a few off the top of my head): a recourse to the closet, a lack of self-esteem, an inability to form lasting relationships, the threat of another epidemic, exclusion from our own churches, and our own government's denial of basic rights, such as marriage, immigration, and military service. In this sense, employment discrimination is a red herring. National gay rights groups love it because they are part of the lobbyist-lawyer nexus that will gain from it and because their polls tell them it's the least objectionable of our aims. But anyone could tell them it's the least objectionable because it's the least relevant.

Of course, we're told that until we're protected from discrimination in 6 employment, we'll never be able to come out of the closet and effect the deeper changes we all want. But this is more victim-mongering. Who says gay people can't risk something for their own integrity? Who says a civil rights revolution can only occur when every single protection is already in place? If African-Americans in the 1980s had waited for such a moment, there would still be segregation in Alabama.

Our national leaders should spend less time making excuses for us 7 and more time challenging us to risk our own lives and, yes, if necessary, jobs to come out and make a difference for the next generation. An "equal rights" rather than "special rights" agenda would focus on those areas in which gay people really are discriminated against. After all, have you heard any fundamentalist "special rights" rhetoric in the marriage debate? Or in the military battle? Not a squeak. What you hear instead is a revealing mumble of bigotry in opposition. And in these areas of clear government discrimination, we stand on firm, moral ground instead of the muddy bog of interest-group politics. In an equal-rights politics, we reverse the self-defeating logic of victim culture. We are proud and pro-active instead of defensive and cowed. And we stop framing a move-ment around the tired 1970s mantra of "what we want" and start build-ing one around the 1990s vision of "who we actually want to be."

Questions About the Reading

1. Whom are the equal-rights laws designed to protect?
2. Does the writer think homosexuals are economic victims? Are they richer or poorer than most Americans?
3. What does the writer say homosexuals should be "touting"?
4. What does the writer say are the problems of gay and lesbian Ameri-cans?

Questions About the Writer's Strategies

1. What is the main idea (thesis) of the essay? Is it stated or implied?
2. Is the essay argumentative or persuasive? Explain your answer.
3. Does the essay contain all the elements of a formal argument? If so, identify the elements.
4. Who is the audience for the essay?

Writing Assignments

1. Write an argument for or against special rights for homosexuals.
2. *Working Together*   Join with some classmates to write a formal argu-ment for or against antidiscrimination laws.

Earth to Andrew

Elizabeth Birch

Elizabeth Birch, executive director of the Human Rights Campaign, dis-
agrees strongly with Andrew Sullivan. She argues that discrimination
against homosexuals in the workplace is a serious problem that requires
antidiscrimination laws to protect them.

Words to Know

cavalier   arrogant, haughty
disseminated   distributed, handed out
distraught   upset, concerned
ostensibly   supposedly
traumatic   emotional, wounding
trivializing   making unimportant or insignificant

Getting Started

Do you agree with Andrew Sullivan or Elizabeth Birch about the
need for antidiscrimination laws?

Each morning when the alarm clock rings, thousands of lesbian and 1
gay Americans wake up with knots in their stomachs. From line workers
to executives, from short-order cooks to engineers, they fear this may be
the day when their livelihoods are ripped away from them and their families.

Like other organizations, the Human Rights Campaign receives a steady 2
stream of phone calls from distraught individuals who were fired from
their jobs simply because of their sexual orientation. It is distressing to
realize that in 40 states, it is perfectly legal to discriminate against gay
Americans in the workplace. We also know that for every person who
calls us with a horror story, there are just as many people who don't call
us because they know they are not legally protected.

Based on our numerous experiences, we were amazed when Andrew 3
Sullivan questioned, in the April 14 edition of *The Advocate*, the need for
antidiscrimination laws such as the Employment Non-Discrimination
Act, which is pending federal legislation that would protect lesbians,
gay men, and bisexuals from job discrimination. Perhaps even more
puzzling was his questioning of whether job discrimination against lesbians and gay men was even a problem. It is possible that Sullivan has

never experienced job discrimination, but we can assure him there are thousands of gay people who have.

According to a 1996 poll conducted by the ICR Survey Group for Lake 4 Research, 82% of the gay people surveyed cited a law to protect gay people from discrimination in employment as "one of the most important issues" facing the community.

A complete disconnect in logic occurs when Sullivan denies this is a 5 problem, then turns around and says that he recognizes that gays endure "intense psychological, social, and cultural hostility." If this hostile climate exists as he says it does, how can he believe that these hostile attitudes simply disappear when a gay person punches the time clock? Take Mark Anderson's experience, for instance.

Anderson, who worked for a high-powered consulting firm in Califor- 6 nia, arrived home from a business trip one afternoon to confront a chilling sight. His car had been stolen and returned, repainted as a police car, covered with antigay epithets like "Rump Ranger" and "1-800-BUTT-BOY." What really made this incident scar, however, was that it was not street thugs who were responsible for this crime but Anderson's coworkers. To complete his nightmare, the makeover on his car was videotaped and disseminated at his company's biennial sales meeting. Shortly after this episode, Anderson was terminated.

Many discrimination cases are not this dramatic. A more typical case is 7 that of Sue Kirchofer, a three-year employee of a Seattle-based distributor, who had received annual raises and praise from management for her job performance. For her annual vacation, Kirchofer went to compete in the Gay Games. Before she left she told a few coworkers of her plans. Two days after returning from the games, she was fired, ostensibly for low quarterly earnings.

Incredibly, Sullivan accuses those hurt by discrimination, such as 8 Anderson and Kirchofer, and the national organizations who try to assist them of engaging in the "self-defeating logic" of "victim-mongering." He goes on to say, "Who says gay people can't risk something [their jobs] for their own integrity?" HRC agrees with Sullivan that people should "come out," and we help thousands take this difficult step each year through our National Coming Out Project. However, it is cavalier to suggest that people who may be raising children or caring for a partner lack integrity. When he flippantly suggests that people abort their careers, is he thinking of the lesbian couple with average jobs who are trying to put their children through school?

Fortunately, according to a bipartisan 1997 poll, the majority of Ameri- 9 cans recognize what Sullivan does not. The poll found that 68% of Americans support ENDA. It is also clear that we must work toward protections based on gender identity. In 1996 ENDA was one vote short of passage in the Senate, and it has a solid chance of passing this year. That is, if people such as Andrew Sullivan would stop trivializing the traumatic workplace experiences that many lesbians and gay men have endured.

Questions About the Reading

1. According to the writer, is it legal to discriminate against gays in the workplace?
2. What is the antidiscrimination act that the writer says should be passed?
3. Who was responsible for painting Mark Anderson's car?
4. What percentage of Americans, according to the writer, support the Employment Non-Discrimination Act?

Questions About the Writer's Strategies

1. What is the main idea (thesis) of the essay? Is it stated or implied?
2. What modes of development does the writer use to support her thesis?
3. What is the point of view (person, time, tone) of the essay? Is it consistent throughout?

Writing Assignments

1. Many female athletes argue that colleges and universities discriminate against women by providing less funding for women's sports than for men's. Write an argumentative or persuasive essay on the subject.
2. *Working Together*   Join with some classmates to write a formal argument for or against the rating given to a current movie.

Addicted to Violence

Stanley Crouch

In his essay, Stanley Crouch argues that the movies have contributed to the rise of street gangs, to distrust of government and the army, and to the idea that violence is a reasonable solution to major social problems.

Words to Know

blaxploitation   movies made in the early 1970s to exploit the market for films about blacks
consensus   agreement
ethos   attitudes, habits, characteristics of a group
maudlin   very foolishly sentimental
naif   innocent person
retrospect   looking back, thinking about

Getting Started

Do you think the violence depicted in movies has influenced people to behave violently toward each other?

Our society has gotten to the point where we might soon become less 1
and less shocked by any kind of violence. A little girl is shot to death after
arguing with a little boy who has grown up in a world of drugs and disorder, one in which he could get an illegal firearm and take it to school
with him. A fireman goes mad and shoots a couple of people to death.
Before that, the country was wringing its hands because a couple of Col-
umbine oddballs felt that they had taken enough criticism from their peers.
Then, while walking the yard in the federal "supermax" prison in Florence, Colorado, where they both were held until last summer, the Oklahoma City bomber and the Unabomber discovered that, politics aside,
they had a lot in common.

What all of these people have in common is a set of ideas that have 2
been pumped into society for quite some time now, from every direction
imaginable. When I was living in Los Angeles 30 years ago, gang violence had largely simmered down, until *The Godfather*, a masterpiece, arrived in movie houses and did for street gangs the same thing that *Birth
of a Nation* did for the Ku Klux Klan five-and-a-half decades earlier. (One
of the street gangs that came into existence after the film was called "The

Family.") That was far from what Francis Ford Coppola had in mind, but such are the odd twists of a society in which the idea of the metaphor seems to have no weight. Too, too much is taken literally.

This and the many other gangster films that formed a trend helped 3 create the ethos out of which rose the Crips and the Bloods and the many, many drive-by murders that eventually became a national crisis. Kids started joining gangs and parents started trying to move them out of that gang environment if they could. The blaxploitation films that kicked off with *Sweet Sweetback's Badass Song* in 1971 were also important because they glamorized Negro criminal types and elevated the idea that violence was fine and dandy because the rules of the system didn't apply to people who weren't white.

On the other side of the lane, as with the Oklahoma City bomber and 4 the Unabomber, there was consensus. It didn't matter if one got a right- or left-wing reading: The police, the FBI, the CIA and local and federal government were all too corrupt to depend on. In the South, during the civil rights movement years, underground tapes were circulated with titles like "For Segregationists Only"; they depicted those who attempted to bring constitutional rights below the Mason Dixon Line as invaders who had to be dealt with very, very firmly. That firmness took three dimensions in the form of assassinations, bombings, beatings, hosings and the killing, mutilating and bruising of men, women and children. In the North, Malcolm X, always a heckler of the nonviolent movement, was calling for rifle clubs and "busting them redneck crackers in the head."

In the wake of the Negro riots that moved along, almost summer to 5 summer, from 1964 to 1968, the Black Panther Party and the Weather Underground picked up on all of that Malcolm X rhetoric. During the anti-war years they put those ideas about self-defense and revolution into some thin Marxist wrappers and went to market calling for "offing the pig" and "bringing the war home." There were plenty of shootouts between the Panthers and the police, as well as between them and rival cultural nationalists who thought African cultural retention and reassertion were more sturdy than alliances with white people and using texts by Europeans like Karl Marx. The Weather Underground attacked people in the street, bombed police stations and robbed banks. The Wild West, Bonnie and Clyde and dreams of overthrowing the government came together.

In retrospect, there wasn't much actual difference between the violence 6 of those reactionaries in the South and those purported revolutionaries in the North. Because violence was the common reaction of greatest intensity, a new level of it became popular in the mass medium of film. Violence was a seat that could fit every rump. Once Arthur Penn's *Bonnie and Clyde* and Sam Peckinpah's *The Wild Bunch* cranked up the scale and realistic depiction of violence higher than ever, two kinds of things began to happen. From the right, there were the lone vigilante types, such as Charles Bronson's *Death Wish* character and Clint Eastwood's Dirty Harry. They had to break the rules because the system neither could nor would protect society from the demons who were rising from below. These men took the law into their own hands and blew away the riffraff. It had to be done. They had no choice. This made them heroes in rebellion against the system.

From the left end of the spectrum came all of the movies, culminating 7 in *JFK* that said, over and over and over, that the federal government and the army were corrupt, that most problems could be traced back to the CIA and that anyone who had faith in the system was, at best, a naif. The only thing one could have faith in was the fact that these institutions would forever play dirty tricks, try to cover them up and, when discovered, murder those who came across the muddy tracks that led to the powers that be.

The grand irony, however, is that Southern segregation was not brought 8 to an end, nor redneck violence dramatically reduced, by violence. They were taken care of by the passage of civil rights laws, the election of local black mayors and other officials and the imprisoning of whites for violent crimes against black people that were once ignored by the local police. Richard Nixon was not felled by bullets or mail bombs but by the freedom of the press and Senate hearings. Big business, for all its lobbying, is often put in line by investigative reporting, public scandals and multi-million-dollar judgments in court against those who put products on the market that are dangerous to their buyers.

But the myth of violent solutions as the ultimate solutions maintains 9 itself in much of popular media.

It is not, therefore, surprising that the Oklahoma City bomber and the 10 Unabomber would find that they have much in common. It is not, therefore, surprising that the marauding street gangs who have made receiving respect a life or death game would listen to rap recordings thick with references to blaxploitation, gangster and horror films in which blood is the sticky unit of exchange. It is not, therefore, surprising that anyone, no matter their color, their station in life, their religion, even their sex, might decide that the time has come to let the world know that things have gone too far, that the insults and indignities must be put to a stop and bullets and bombs alone can make clear just how reprehensible things are.

Does this mean that we have to go after the gun makers and demand 11 more of them? Sure. Does it mean that there should be a ban on violent films? In our world, bans only send things underground, where child pornography is bought and sold. What this society has to do now is re-create an image of civilization that is neither painfully repressed nor maud-lin. That's pretty clear. When a violent minority that crosses color lines comes to believe that killing those you know or do not know is a reason-able solution to problems, we are in need of another vision. Blowing up federal buildings, shooting other school kids because they make you an-gry and sending out bombs to express your rage against technology are the result of a brutal attitude toward difficulty, one that has been cel-ebrated in our popular culture for far too long.

Questions About the Reading

1. What does the writer seem to think is the main cause for violence in our society?
2. Besides using bombs to commit their crimes, what do you think the Oklahoma City bomber and the Unabomber have in common?
3. What does the writer say would be the effect of banning violent films?
4. According to the writer, what does society have to do to counter the belief that violence is a solution to problems?

Questions About the Writer's Strategies

1. What is the main idea of the essay? Is it stated or implied?
2. Is the essay argumentative or persuasive? Explain your answer.
3. What other modes of development does the writer use?

Writing Assignments

1. Write an argumentative or persuasive essay about the influence of the media on violent behavior.
2. *Working Together*   Join with some classmates to write a formal argu-ment on the subject of media violence and its influence on society.

Getting the Facts Straight on Media Violence

Paul McMasters

Before we blame the violence depicted in the media, says Paul McMasters, we should get the facts and the social science straight and use some common sense.

Words to Know

demographic   populations relating to statistics
ideology   creed, philosophy, body of doctrine
inevitable   certain, cannot be escaped
pandering   catering to or giving in to
perception   belief, impression
phenomenon   unusual occurrence
punditry   philosophy, interpretation
pundits   authorities
saturated   soaked, absorbed
surcease   pause, relief from
vagaries   uncertainties, oddities

Getting Started

What do you think causes violence?

Following closely on any tragedy involving human violence will be the   1
inevitable procession of experts and officials placing the blame on violence in the media. To gauge the reach of this phenomenon, consider the
reaction last week after a teen-ager was accidentally shot to death by a
friend in the northern French town of Tourcoing. "I don't want America
to export its civilization of violence," intoned Claude Allegre, minister of
education. "Freedom of creation is fine, but America cannot impose this
on us. We are not a country of cowboys, we are not a country of gang-
sters."

After reflecting on the shooting horror in Jonesboro, Arkansas, the   2
French newspaper *Le Figaro* added: "What happens across the Atlantic
often foreshadows what will happen to us. Rather than smile at American errors, we should keep them at a distance. A society that lets children
arm themselves—whether through ideology or through weakness—can't

claim to give morality lessons." We are to understand, of course, that in this instance the disdain is directed not at Americans in general but at American media. In that, the French join cause with a substantial chunk of American punditry.

When a community is wracked by a tragedy of violence, we yearn to 3 find a cause, something or someone to blame. Therefore, it is only natural, if not exactly rational, that a gaggle of psycho-babblists will waddle forth with their denunciations of "violence in the media." These days, the culprit of choice most often is television, but other targets include the movies, music, books, comics, video games and, yes, even the newspapers. It does seem that popular culture today is saturated with violent images and action, making it easier for the pundits to point the finger of blame at the media. Some have learned to call for "responsibility" rather than "regulation."

And that's fair enough. But while we're at it, how about a little more 4 responsibility all around? For the media, for the pundits, for the regulators lurking in the background, and for the public itself.

Her are some thinking points: 5

First, get the facts straight.   6

Violence on network television has been declining steadily over the 7 past three years, according to a report released in January by the Center for Communication Policy at the University of California at Los Angeles.

Public perception, largely the result of media emphasis, is that almost 8 half of all violent crime is committed by juveniles; in fact, the figure is 19%.

Public perception is that violent crime among juveniles is increasing 9 dramatically; actually, it has remained at about 20% for more than 100 years.

After a terrifying spike beginning in the 80s, the murder rate among 10 young people declined 31% between 1993 and 1996, according to the National Center for Juvenile Justice.

Next, get the social science straight.   11

Studies that indicate a link between viewing violence and doing vio- 12 lence turn out to be either quite qualified in their conclusions or quite clumsy in their methodology.

Children form basic values at a very young age based primarily on 13 family influence.

There is no way to safely predict whether a given stimulus will pro- 14 voke positive, negative or neutral behavior, given the vagaries of human personality.

Finally, add a dose of common sense.   15

If juvenile crime and violence were a function of watching television, 16 then incidents of violence and crime would be more evenly distributed across demographic and geographic boundaries according to the availability of television. As a matter of fact, the rates vary greatly from community to community, class to class.

For the media, being more responsible means taking care with both   17
depictions of violence and discussions of violence as a social problem. For the pundits, being responsible means acknowledging that blaming the media can be a dangerous game as well as a zero-sum game. For the policy-makers, being responsible means resolving to quit pandering to fear and to start addressing the clearly demonstrable causes of violence in our society: poverty, guns, drugs, gangs and the declining influence of the family. For the rest of us, we must resist the impulse to take isolated events, such as the Jonesboro shootings, and turn them into a national trend. And we must recognize that, while blaming violence on the media may give us comfort, it will give us neither surcease nor solutions.

Questions About the Reading

1. According to the writer, why do we want to blame the media when there is a violent tragedy?
2. What do we most often blame for violence?
3. According to the writer, what should we consider in determining the cause or causes of violence?
4. What does the writer think are the causes of violence in our society?

Questions About the Writer's Strategies

1. The writer uses many single-sentence paragraphs, as in journalistic or newspaper-style writing. How would you revise paragraphs 6 through 17 to conform to the style used in academic essays?
2. What is the main idea of the essay?
3. What metaphor does the writer use in paragraph 3?

Writing Assignments

1. Write an argumentative or persuasive essay about the effects of the media on social attitudes toward business people, doctors, lawyers, bartenders, or another group of professionals.
2. *Working Together*   Join with some classmates to write a formal argument about the positive or negative influence of media advertising on social values.

Connections

1. The purpose of some of the selections in this chapter is to persuade the reader to take action. What do the writers want you to do? Discuss at least two of the selections. What are their messages? Do they appeal to your emotions or to your logical reasoning? What is your reaction to the selections?
2. What connections can you make between Marian Wright Edelman's call to action and Nelliejean Smith's cause-and-effect paragraph ("On Being Unemployed," Chapter 8)?
3. What connections can you make between the essays on violence and the popularity of Stephen King's books and movies and reader interest in him? (See "Ever Et Raw Meat?" in chapter 5.)

11

Combining the Strategies

IN THIS CHAPTER, you will find some additional reading selections. Although some of the readings have one dominant **mode of development,** most of them illustrate combinations of the different modes.

As you read, keep in mind what we have stressed in earlier chapters. Determine the

- topic of each paragraph
- thesis of each essay
- structure of the reading (introduction, development, conclusion)
- supporting details
- modes of development
- point of view (person, time, tone)
- method of organization (time, space, order of importance)
- transitional words
- effective words and sentences

Then, make use of these same strategies to write paragraphs and essays that are as clear and effective as those you have read.

The Dare

Roger Hoffmann

*Roger Hoffmann recounts an episode from his adolescence when approval
from his peers was more important than his personal safety. No matter
our age or particular adolescent experience, we are able to relate to the
pressure Hoffmann felt as a child. The desire for acceptance by friends
and colleagues is something we never outgrow.*

Words to Know

ambiguous   not clear; having many interpretations
escalated   increased
guerrilla act   warfare carried out by an independent military
  force
implicit   understood although not directly stated
provoke   to cause anger or resentment
silhouette   an outline of something that appears dark against a
  light background; a shadow

Getting Started

Have you ever taken a risk because of a dare?

The secret to diving under a moving freight train and rolling out the   1
other side with all your parts attached lies in picking the right spot between the tracks to hit with your back. Ideally, you want soft dirt or pea
gravel, clear of glass shards and railroad spikes that could cause you instinctively, and fatally, to sit up. Today, at thirty-eight I couldn't be threat-
ened or baited enough to attempt that dive. But as a seventh grader struggling to make the cut in a tough Atlanta grammar school, all it took was a
dare.

  I coasted through my first years of school as a fussed-over smart kid,   2
the teacher's pet who finished his work first and then strutted around
the room tutoring other students. By the seventh grade, I had more A's
than friends. Even my old cronies, Dwayne and O.T., made it clear I'd
never be one of the guys in junior high if I didn't dirty up my act. They
challenged me to break the rules, and I did. The I-dare-you's escalated:
shoplifting, sugaring teachers' gas tanks, dropping lighted matches into
public mailboxes. Each guerrilla act won me the approval I never got for
just being smart.

306

Walking home by the railroad tracks after school, we started playing   3
chicken with oncoming trains. O.T., who was failing that year, always
won. One afternoon he charged a boxcar from the side, stopping just short
of throwing himself between the wheels. I was stunned. After the train
disappeared, we debated whether someone could dive under a moving
car, stay put for a 10-count, then scramble out the other side. I thought it
could be done and said so. O.T. immediately stepped in front of me and
smiled. Not by me, I added quickly, I certainly didn't mean that I could
do it. "A smart guy like you," he said, his smile evaporating, "you could
figure it out easy." And then, squeezing each word for effect, "I . . . DARE
. . . you." I'd just turned twelve. The monkey clawing my back was
Teacher's Pet. And I'd been dared.

As an adult, I've been on both ends of life's implicit business and so-   4
cial I-dare-you's, although adults don't use those words. We provoke with
body language, tone of voice, ambiguous phrases. I dare you to: argue
with the boss, tell Fred what you think of him, send the wine back. Only
rarely are the risks physical. How we respond to dares when we are young
may have something to do with which of the truly hazardous male inner
dares—attacking mountains, tempting bulls at Pamplona—we embrace
or ignore as men.

For two weeks, I scouted trains and tracks. I studied moving boxcars   5
close up, memorizing how they squatted on their axles, never getting
used to the squeal or the way the air felt hot from the sides. I created an
imaginary, friendly train and ran next to it. I mastered a shallow, head-
first dive with a simple half-twist. I'd land on my back, count to ten, imagine wheels and, locking both hands on the rail to my left, heave myself
over and out. Even under pure sky, though, I had to fight to keep my eyes
open and my shoulders between the rails.

The next Saturday, O.T., Dwayne and three eighth graders met me be-   6
low the hill that backed up to the lumberyard. The track followed a slow
bend there and opened to a straight, slightly uphill climb for a solid third
of a mile. My run started two hundred yards after the bend. The train
would have its tongue hanging out.

The other boys huddled off to one side, a circle on another planet, and   7
watched quietly as I double-knotted my shoelace. My hands trembled.
O.T. broke the circle and came over to me. He kept his hands hidden in
the pockets of his jacket. We looked at each other. BB's of sweat appeared
beneath his nose. I stuffed my wallet in one of his pockets, rubbing it
against his knuckles on the way in, and slid my house key, wired to a red-
and-white fishing bobber, into the other. We backed away from each other,
and he turned and ran to join the four already climbing up the hill.

I watched them all the way to the top. They clustered together as if I   8
were taking their picture. Their silhouette resembled a round shouldered

tombstone. They waved down to me, and I dropped them from my mind and sat down on the rail. Immediately, I jumped back. The steel was vibrating.

The train sounded like a cow going short of breath. I pulled my shirt-   9
tail out and looked down at my spot, then up the incline of track ahead of me. Suddenly the air went hot, and the engine was by me. I hadn't pictured it moving that fast. A man's bare head leaned out and stared at me. I waved to him with my left hand and turned into the train, burying my face into the incredible noise. When I looked up, the head was gone.

I started running alongside the boxcars. Quickly, I found their pace,   10
held it, and then eased off, concentrating on each thick wheel that cut past me. I slowed another notch. Over my shoulder, I picked my car as it came off the bend, locking in the image of the white mountain goat painted on its side. I waited, leaning forward like the anchor in a 440-relay, wishing the baton up the track behind me. Then the big goat fired by me, and I was flying and then tucking my shoulder as I dipped under the train.

A heavy blanket of red dust settled over me. I felt bolted to the earth.   11
Sheet-metal bellies thundered and shook above my face. Count to ten, a voice said, watch the axles and look to your left for daylight. But I couldn't count, and I couldn't find left if my life depended on it, which it did. The colors overhead went from brown to red to black to red again. Finally, I ripped my hands free, forced them to the rail, and, in one convulsive jerk, threw myself into the blue light.

I lay there face down until there was no more noise, and I could feel   12
the sun against the back of my neck. I sat up. The last ribbon of train was slipping away in the distance. Across the tracks, O.T. was leading a cavalry charge down the hill, five very small, galloping boys, their fists whirling above them. I pulled my knees to my chest. My corduroy pants puckered wet across my thighs. I didn't care.

Dawn Watch

John Ciardi

*How many things do we not see because we do not look? In this essay,
poet and critic John Ciardi describes in rich detail exactly what happens
when the sun comes up in the morning.*

Words to Know

bedraggled   to be wet and limp

braggarts   persons given to boasting

buffet   a meal at which guests serve themselves

crease   a line made by a fold or a wrinkle

grackles   blackbirds

grate   to make a rasping sound

inured   to become used to something undesirable

laurel   a shrub or tree having aromatic evergreen leaves

mulched   covered with a protective covering of leaves, manure,
and so on

pincer   to work together in a clawlike way

spectrum   a broad sequence or range of colors

sprawl   to spread out awkwardly

thickets   dense growths of scrub or underbrush

Getting Started

What is your favorite time of the day?

Unless a man is up for the dawn and for the half hour or so of first 1
light, he has missed the best of the day.

The traffic has just started, not yet a roar and a stink. One car at a time 2
goes by, the tires humming almost like the sound of a brook a half mile
down in the crease of a mountain I know—a sound that carries not because it is loud but because everything else is still.

It isn't exactly a mist that hangs in the thickets but more nearly the 3
ghost of a mist—a phenomenon like side vision. Look hard and it isn't
there, but glance without focusing and something registers, an exhala-
tion that will be gone three minutes after the sun comes over the treetops.

The lawns shine with a dew not exactly dew. There is a rabbit bobbing 4
about on the lawn and then freezing. If it were truly a dew, his tracks

would shine black on the grass, and he leaves no visible track. Yet, there is something on the grass that makes it glow a depth of green it will not show again all day. Or is that something in the dawn air?

Our cardinals know what time it is. They drop pure tones from the hemlock tops. The black gang of grackles that makes a slum of the pin oak also knows the time but can only grate at it. They sound like a convention of broken universal joints grating uphill. The grackles creak and squeak, and the cardinals form tones that only occasionally sound through the noise. I scatter sunflower seeds by the birdbath for the cardinals and hope the grackles won't find them. 5

My neighbor's tomcat comes across the lawn, probably on his way home from passion, or only acting as if he had had a big night. I suspect him of being one of those poolroom braggarts who can't get next to a girl but who likes to let on that he is a hot stud. This one is too can-fed and too lazy to hunt for anything. Here he comes now, ignoring the rabbit. And there he goes. 6

As soon as he has hopped the fence, I let my dog out. The dog charges the rabbit, watches it jump the fence, shakes himself in a self-satisfied way, then trots dutifully into the thicket for his morning service, stopping to sniff everything on the way back. 7

There is an old mountain laurel on the island of the driveway turnaround. From somewhere on the wind a white morning-glory rooted next to it and has climbed it. Now the laurel is woven full of white bells tinged pink by the first rays through the not quite mist. Only in earliest morning can they be seen. Come out two hours from now and there will be no morning-glories. 8

Dawn, too, is the hour of a weed I know only as day flower—a bright blue button that closes in full sunlight. I have weeded bales of it out of my flower beds, its one daytime virtue being the shallowness of its root system that allows it to be pulled out effortlessly in great handfuls. Yet, now it shines. Had it a few more hours of such shining in its cycle. I would cultivate it as a ground cover, but dawn is its one hour, and a garden is for whole days. 9

There is another blue morning weed whose name I do not know. This one grows from a bulb to pulpy stems and a bedraggled daytime sprawl. Only a shovel will dig it out. Try weeding it by hand and the stems will break off to be replaced by new ones and to sprawl over the chosen plants in the flower bed. Yet, now and for another hour it outshines its betters, its flowers about the size of a quarter and paler than those of the day flower but somehow more brilliant, perhaps because of the contrast of its paler foliage. 10

And now the sun is slanting in full. It is bright enough to make the leaves of the Japanese red maple seem a transparent red bronze when the 11 tree is between me and the light. There must be others, but this is the only tree I know whose leaves let the sun through in this way—except, that is, when the fall colors start. Aspen leaves, when they first yellow and before they dry, are transparent in this way. I tell myself it must have something to do with the red-yellow range of the spectrum. Green takes sunlight and holds it, but red and yellow let it through.

The damned crabgrass is wrestling with the zinnias, and I stop to weed 12 it out. The stuff weaves too close to the zinnias to make the iron claw usable. And it won't do to pull at the stalks. Crabgrass (at least in a mulched bed) can be weeded only with dirty fingers. Thumb and forefinger have to pincer into the dirt and grab the root-center. Weeding, of course, is an illusion of hope. Pulling out the root only stirs the soil and brings new crabgrass seeds into germinating position. Take a walk around the block and a new clump will have sprouted by the time you get back. But I am not ready to walk around the block. I fill a small basket with the plucked clumps, and for the instant I look at them, the zinnias are weedless.

Don't look back. I dump the weeds in the thicket where they will be 13 smothered by the grass clippings I will pile on at the next cutting. On the way back I see the cardinals come down for the sunflower seeds, and the jays join them, and then the grackles start ganging in, gate-crashing the buffet and clattering all over it. The dog stops chewing his rawhide and makes a dash into the puddle of birds, which splashes away from him.

I hear a brake-squeak I have been waiting for and know the paper has 14 arrived. As usual, the news turns out to be another disaster count. The function of the wire services is to bring us tragedies faster than we can pity. In the end we shall all be inured, numb, and ready for emotionless programming. I sit on the patio and read until the sun grows too bright on the page. The cardinals have stopped singing, and the grackles have flown off. It's the end of birdsong again.

Then suddenly—better than song for its instant—a hummingbird the 15 color of green crushed velvet hovers in the throat of my favorite lily, a lovely high-bloomer I got the bulbs for but not the name. The lily is a crest of white horns with red dots and red velvet tongues along the insides of the petals and with an odor that drowns the patio. The hummingbird darts in and out of each horn in turn, then hovers an instant, and disappears.

Even without the sun, I have had enough of the paper. I'll take that 16 hummingbird as my news for this dawn. It is over now. I smoke one more cigarette too many and decide that, if I go to bed now, no one in the family need know I have stayed up for it again. Why do they insist on shaking their heads when they find me still up for breakfast, after having scribbled through the dark hours? They always do. They seem compelled to express pity for an old loony who can't find his own way to bed. Why won't they understand that this is the one hour of any day that must not be missed, as it is the one hour I couldn't imagine getting up for, though I can still get to it by staying up? It makes sense to me. There comes a time when the windows lighten and the twittering starts. I look up and know it's time to leave the papers in their mess. I could slip quietly into bed and avoid the family's headshakes, but this stroll-around first hour is too good to miss. Even my dog, still sniffing and circling, knows what hour this is.

Come on, boy. It's time to go in. The rabbit won't come back till tomor- 17 row, and the birds have work to do. The dawn's over. It's time to call it a day.

A Very Basic Decision

Mary Mebane

Mary E. Mebane discovered that prejudice can exist within as well as between races when she attended a North Carolina college for blacks in the 1950s. The light-skinned, urban, middle-class blacks who made up the faculty and most of the student body could not believe that a dark-skinned black girl from a poor rural family could be a superior student. In "A Very Basic Decision," a passage from Mary: An Autobiography, *Mebane tells of two meetings she had with the wife of the English department's chairman, a light-skinned woman who was convinced that Mebane could not be as talented as her test scores and grades showed. But Mebane decided not to give up her quest for a college degree. She graduated at the top of her class and is now a college English professor.*

Words to Know

appalled   dismayed
bolstered   supported, propped up
criteria   standards
defer   submit, yield
indistinguishable   not able to be recognized or seen as different
noncommittal   to show no opinion or preference
nonplussed   confused, perplexed, baffled
pinnacle   peak, top
recourse   choice, option

Getting Started

What experiences have influenced your choice of a school program?

North Carolina College at Durham (it used to carry the words "for Ne-   1
groes" in its official title—it said so on the sign right on the lawn) is located in the southern part of the town. Its immaculately groomed lawns and neat, squarish, redbrick classroom buildings and dormitories mark it as an oasis of privilege and ease. Looking at the postcard scenes through the low-hanging branches of the surrounding trees, one would not have believed that this was six minutes away from some of the worst slums in the South. The college hadn't forgotten their existence; it simply never acknowledged that they were there. The black dispossessed murmured against the "big dogs," and bided their time. I often thought that if and

313

when "the revolution" came and the black masses in American awakened from their long sleep, their first target was going to be the black professional class and it would be a horrendous bloodbath. . . .

During my first week of classes as a freshman, I was stopped one day 2 in the hall by the chairman's wife, who was indistinguishable in color from a white woman. She wanted to see me, she said.

This woman had no official position on the faculty, except that she was 3 an instructor in English; nevertheless, her summons had to be obeyed. In the segregated world there were (and remain) gross abuses of authority because those at the pinnacle, and even their spouses, felt that the people "under" them had no recourse except to submit—and they were right, except that sometimes a black who got sick and tired of it would go to the whites and complain. This course of action was severely condemned by the blacks, but an interesting thing happened—such action always got positive results. Power was thought of in negative terms: I can deny someone something, I can strike at someone who can't strike back, I can ride someone down; that proves I am powerful. The concept of power as a force for good, for affirmative response to people or situations, was not in evidence.

When I went to her office, she greeted me with a big smile. "You know," 4 she said, "you made the highest mark on the verbal part of the examination." She was referring to the examination that the entire freshman class took upon entering the college. I looked at her but I didn't feel warmth, for in spite of her smile her eyes and tone of voice were saying, "How could this black-skinned girl score higher on the verbal than some of the students who've had more advantages than she? It must be some sort of fluke. Let me talk to her." I felt it, but I managed to smile my thanks and back off. For here at North Carolina College at Durham, as it had been since the beginning, social class and color were the primary criteria used in determining status on the campus.

First came the children of doctors, lawyer, and college teachers. Next 5 came the children of public-school teachers, businessmen, and anybody else who had access to more money than the poor black working class. After that came the bulk of the student population, the children of the working class, most of whom were the first in their families to go beyond high school. The attitude toward them was: You're here because we need the numbers, but in all other things defer to your betters.

The faculty assumed that light-skinned students were more intelligent, 6 and they were always a bit nonplussed when a dark-skinned student did well, especially if she was a girl. They had reason to be appalled when they discovered that I planned to do not only well but better than my light-skinned peers. . . .

When the grades for that first quarter came out, I had the highest aver- 7
age in the freshman class. The chairman's wife called me into her office
again. We did a replay of the same scene we had played during the first
week of the term. She complimented me on my grades, but her eyes and
voice were telling me something different. She asked me to sit down;
then she reached into a drawer and pulled out a copy of the freshman
English final examination. She asked me to take the exam over again.

At first I couldn't believe what she was saying. I had taken the course 8
under another teacher, and it was so incredible to her that I should have
made the highest score in the class that she was trying to test me again
personally. For a few moments I knew rage so intense that I wanted to
take my fists and start punching her. I have seldom hated anyone so deeply.
I handed the examination back to her and walked out.

She had felt quite safe in doing that to me. After all, she was the 9
chairman's wife, and so didn't that give her the right to treat the black
farm girl as she chose? (Life is strange. When in the mid-1960s the department started hiring native-born whites, it was she who most bitterly
resented their presence.)

It was that incident which caused me to make a very basic decision. I 10
was in the world alone; no one bolstered my ambitions, fed my dreams. I
could not quit now, for if I did I would have no future. . . . If I was going
to get through college, I would have to be bland, noncommittal. I would
simply hang on. I needed a degree and I would stay until I got it.

By Earth Obsessed

Esther Iverem

For some people, the trend toward recycling is an infringement on their freedom; for others, like journalist and poet Esther Iverem, recycling is an obsession. In this column from Essence *magazine, she argues that people should do everything they can to protect the planet from the ravages of garbage.*

Words to Know

chauvinistic   belief in the superiority of one's own group
countered   opposed
indigenous   native to an area
legions   large numbers of something
tangible   concrete, real

Getting Started

What is your opinion about the ultimate usefulness of recycling?

Lunchtime left me with pangs of guilt. Each day I was throwing away a 1
clear-plastic salad container, a plastic fork, a napkin, a juice bottle and the
plastic bag it all came in. I mentally multiplied the trash I had created by
the number of people in my office, in my office building and in the New
York City work force, and I felt sickened by this tangible example of why
landfills are filling up so quickly.

So I started recycling bottles and cans. Then I began reusing the plastic 2
bag from my lunch by taking it back to the salad bar each day. Then I
washed and reused the container and fork. The store owners began to
look at me funny. I began to feel funny. Then I started to feel just a little
brave.

In part because it is healthier and cheaper, I finally decided to start 3
bringing my lunch from home every day. But I soon realized that, with
my sandwich wrappings and brown paper bags, I was simply substitut-
ing home trash for store-bought trash. So now I'm looking for a lunch
box with a thermos.

My internal debates and decisions about the environment sometimes 4
leave me feeling obsessed. And when I can't live up to the standards I've
set for myself, I feel guilty—like the church deacon who tips to the corner
bar, the feminist who loves a chauvinistic man, the Black nationalist who

secretly dates white women. But I hardly ever feel embarrassed when
friends poke fun at me. With all the coolness and superiority I can mus-
ter, I tell them that if everyone continues to disregard the earth, there
won't be much of an earth left.

I confess that I sometimes wonder how I got to the point of lugging 5
home chin-high piles of newspapers to recycle and apologizing to passengers in my car about the recyclable bottles and cans that clatter around
in the backseat. I do know that I feel a great kinship with the earth. I trace
these feelings back to my childhood, which took place during the birth
of the modern environmental movement. On Earth Day 1970 I was an
elementary-school student, alarmed to learn the side effects of our throwaway society: toxic dumps, choking air, polluted waterways and a di-
minishing animal kingdom. Soon I began to link civil rights and environmental sanity. The environment is not a white people's issue. People of
color, more than three quarters of the world's population, are indigenous
to continents where the world's beauty and natural resources remain.
Surely we, descendants of those who came from these unspoiled continents, should not treat the world like a giant Hefty bag. Because in 1970
Black folks were vocally fighting for their rightful share of the pie, the
logical question for me became "What kind of shape will that pie be in?"
I have never forgotten those early feelings. Although I know that the biggest sins against the environment are committed by multinational corpo-
rations, I nevertheless believe that one person can make a difference, especially when she joins with others.

Thus I spent $100 on a trash can because it has a removable bin for 6
recyclable goods. I carry my own reusable sack to the grocery store. And
I have had heated discussions with my husband about whether it is environmentally correct to buy plastic garbage bags, which keep garbage from
decomposing naturally.

Recently we were in a supermarket, standing in the paper-products 7
aisle. As people around us plucked everything from toilet paper to sanitary napkins off the shelves, I stood with my arms crossed and my brow
knitted, refusing to buy paper towels and napkins.

"But we need them," he said, slowly and calmly, as if talking to some- 8
one from another planet.

"We should buy dishcloths instead," I countered, imagining forests 9
cut down to make towels that boast super-absorbency. "And we should
buy cloth napkins."

We argued every week for a while. Sometimes I won, triumphantly 10
pushing the cart away with a haughty whip of my head. At other times
(usually after a week when I had failed to show the superiority of my
choice), he prevailed, swishing paper towels into the cart like Michael
Jordan nailing a short baseline jumper.

We now compromise. We use dishcloths and have put a large set of 11 cloth napkins on our shopping list. But we also buy either paper towels or napkins if they are made with recycled paper.

Solutions aren't always this easy, and I still, shamefully, do things that 12 I know aren't good for the planet. It took months of nudging by my husband before I remembered to turn off the water while brushing my teeth. I write for a newspaper that requires me to have a car. I love having a new ride for the first time in my life, but I know that I am yet another motorist filling the city air—the earth's air—with exhaust fumes.

Despite my revulsion at the idea of trees cut down and discarded for 13 the Christmas holiday, I was overwhelmed by sentiment last Christmas and bought a tree (a small one) for the first time. I convinced myself that the cut tree would still be dead whether I bought it or not. As I carried the tree to the car, I took in its sweet smell and was momentarily happy, but then I began to feel as if I were carrying a corpse. I had already decided that I would not discard the tree; it would not join the legions of dried-out evergreens tossed on street corners with pitiful wisps of tinsel still dangling from their branches. So after New Year's I stuffed the tree into my trunk and drove to a park where they grind Christmas trees into mulch, a protective covering for the soil. I felt a sense of accomplishment driving back home. Then I started wondering if my car ride had canceled out the environmental benefits of returning the tree to nature.

But despite my ecological anxieties, I have learned important lessons. 14 I've become far more appreciative of my mother's wisdom. I realize now that she and many of our mothers were environmentally correct, even if motivated primarily by thrift. Every time they made meals from scratch rather than from processed food in boxes and cans, they were cutting down on trash. As a child I didn't appreciate this. All I knew was that our food seemed old-fashioned compared with that of other families who ate "modern" food—packaged macaroni and cheese, hamburgers from fast-food joints. I learned to appreciate the superior nutrition my mother's meals provided. Now I see how her approach also helped save the earth.

Doing things the old-fashioned way is sometimes more modern than 15 we think. Even though doing simple things, like bringing lunch from home, is more time-consuming, we need to stop and think about how much time the earth has left if we keep treating our oceans like dumpsters, chopping down our rain forests and breaking the chain of life that keeps us connected to the planet.

We can't give up. I haven't. I'm as confident as ever that the earth's 16 problems, which are as big as the world itself, can be solved by one person at a time. So I have made changes in my life. For my sake. For my earth's sake.

The Pie

Gary Soto

Childhood pranks and misdeameanors often become bigger than life in the retelling. In this selection, Gary Soto recalls the day he gave in to temptation and committed a sin.

Words to Know

proximity closeness
retrieve to get back

Getting Started

Can you describe an incident from your childhood that involved a petty crime?

I knew enough about hell to stop me from stealing. I was holy in almost   1
every bone. Some days I recognized the shadows of angels flopping on the backyard grass, and other days I heard faraway messages in the plumbing that howled underneath the house when I crawled there looking for something to do.

But boredom made me sin. Once, at the German Market, I stood before   2
a rack of pies, my sweet tooth gleaming and the juice of guilt wetting my underarms. I gazed at the nine kinds of pie, pecan and apple being my favorites, although cherry looked good, and my dear, fat-faced chocolate was always a good bet. I nearly wept trying to decide which to steal and, forgetting the flowery dust priests give off, the shadow of angels and the proximity of God howling in the plumbing underneath the house, sneaked a pie behind my coffee-lid frisbee and walked to the door, grinning to the bald grocer whose forehead shone with a window of light.

"No one saw," I muttered to myself, the pie like a discus in my hand,   3
and hurried across the street, where I sat on someone's lawn. The sun wavered between the branches of a yellowish sycamore. A squirrel nailed itself high on the trunk, where it forked into two large bark-scabbed limbs. Just as I was going to work my cleanest finger into the pie, a neighbor came out to the porch for his mail. He looked at me, and I got up and headed for home. I raced on skinny legs to my block, but slowed to a

quick walk when I couldn't wait any longer. I held the pie to my nose and breathed in its sweetness. I licked some of the crust and closed my eyes as I took a small bite.

In my front yard, I leaned against a car fender and panicked about 4 stealing the apple pie. I knew an apple got Eve in deep trouble with snakes because Sister Marie had shown us a film about Adam and Eve being cast into the desert, and what scared me more than falling from grace was being thirsty for the rest of my life. But even that didn't stop me from clawing a chunk from the pie tin and pushing it into the cavern of my mouth. The slop was sweet and gold-colored in the afternoon sun. I laid more pieces on my tongue, wet finger-dripping pieces, until I was finished and felt like crying because it was about the best thing I had ever tasted. I realized right there and then, in my sixth year, in my tiny body of two hundred bones and three or four sins, that the best things in life came stolen. I wiped my sticky fingers on the grass and rolled my tongue over the corners of my mouth. A burp perfumed the air.

I felt bad not sharing with Cross-Eyed Johnny, a neighbor kid. He stood 5 over my shoulder and asked, "Can I have some?" Crust fell from my mouth, and my teeth were bathed with the jam-like filling. Tears blurred my eyes as I remembered the grocer's forehead. I remembered the other pies on the rack, the warm air of the fan above the door and the car that honked as I crossed the street without looking.

"Get away," I had answered Cross-Eyed Johnny. He watched my fin- 6 gers greedily push big chunks of pie down my throat. He swallowed and said in a whisper, "Your hands are dirty," then returned home to climb his roof and sit watching me eat the pie by myself. After a while, he jumped off and hobbled away because the fall had hurt him.

I sat on the curb. The pie tin glared at me and rolled away when the 7 wind picked up. My face was sticky with guilt. A car honked, and the driver knew. Mrs. Hancock stood on her lawn, hands on hip, and she knew. My mom, peeling a mountain of potatoes at the Redi-Spud factory, knew. I got to my feet, stomach taut, mouth tired of chewing, and flung my frisbee across the street, its shadow like the shadow of an angel fleeing bad deeds. I retrieved it, jogging slowly. I flung it again until I was bored and thirsty.

I returned home to drink water and help my sister glue bottle caps 8 onto cardboard, a project for summer school. But the bottle caps bored me, and the water soon filled me up more than the pie. With the kitchen stifling with heat and lunatic flies, I decided to crawl underneath our house and lie in the cool shadows listening to the howling sound of plumbing. Was it God? Was it Father, speaking from death, or Uncle with his last shiny dime? I listened, ear pressed to a cold pipe, and heard a howl like the sea. I lay until I was cold and then crawled back to the light, rising from one knee, then another, to dust off my pants and squint in the harsh light. I looked and saw the glare of a pie tin on a hot day. I knew sin was what you take and didn't give back.

Time to Look and Listen

Magdoline Asfahani (student)

Magdoline Asfahani, an Arab and a Muslim, gives us a sensitive and thoughtful account of the effect of discrimination on her life. Asfahani is a student at the University of Texas, El Paso.

Words to Know

alluding   referring, suggesting
incompatible   not in agreement
medley   mixture, assortment
monotheistic   having a belief in one God
nuances   subtleties, slight variations or differences

Getting Started

Do you feel that you discriminate against a group of people?

———————————

I love my country as many who have been here for generations cannot. 1
Perhaps that's because I'm the child of immigrants, raised with a conscious respect for America that many people take for granted. My parents chose this country because it offered them a new life, freedom and possibilities. But I learned at a young age that the country we loved so much did not feel the same way about us.

Discrimination is not unique to America. It occurs in any country that 2
allows immigration. Anyone who is unlike the majority is looked at a little suspiciously, dealt with a little differently. The fact that I wasn't part of the majority never occurred to me. I knew that I was an Arab and a Muslim. This meant nothing to me. At school I stood up to say the Pledge of Allegiance every day. These things did not seem incompatible at all. Then everything changed for me, suddenly and permanently, in 1985. I was only in seventh grade, but that was the beginning of my political education.

That year a TWA plane originating in Athens was diverted to Beirut. 3
Two years earlier the U.S. Marine barracks in Beirut had been bombed. That seemed to start a chain of events that would forever link Arabs with terrorism. After the hijacking, I faced classmates who taunted me with cruel names, attacking my heritage and my religion. I became an outcast and had to apologize for myself constantly.

322

After a while, I tried to forget my heritage. No matter what race, relig- 4
ion or ethnicity, a child who is attacked often retreats. I was the only Arab
I knew of in my class, so I had no one in my peer group as an ally. No
matter what my parents tried to tell me about my proud cultural history,
I would ignore it. My classmates told me I came from an uncivilized,
brutal place, that Arabs were by nature anti-American, and I believed
them. They did not know the hours my parents spent studying, working,
trying to preserve part of their old lives while embracing, willingly, the
new.

I tried to forget the Arabic I knew, because if I didn't I'd be forever 5
linked to murderers. I stopped inviting friends over for dinner, because I
thought the food we ate was "weird." I lied about where my parents had
come from. Their accents (although they spoke English perfectly) humili-
ated me. Though Islam is a major monotheistic religion with many similarities to Judaism and Christianity, there were no holidays near Chanukah
or Christmas, nothing to tie me to the "Judeo-Christian" tradition. I felt
more excluded. I slowly began to turn into someone without a past.

Civil war was raging in Lebanon, and all that Americans saw of that 6
country was destruction and violence. Every other movie seemed to feature Arab terrorists. The most common questions I was asked were if I
had ever ridden a camel or if my family lived in tents. I felt burdened
with responsibility. Why should an adolescent be asked questions like
"Is it true you hate Jews and you want Israel destroyed?" I didn't hate
anybody. My parents had never said anything even alluding to such sentiments. I was confused and hurt.

As I grew older and began to form my own opinions, my embarrass- 7
ment lessened and my anger grew. The turning point came in high school.
My grandmother had become very ill, and it was necessary for me to
leave school a few days before Christmas vacation. My chemistry teacher
was very sympathetic until I said I was going to the Middle East. "Don't
come back in a body bag," he said cheerfully. The class laughed. Suddenly, those years of watching movies that mocked me and listening to
others who knew nothing about Arabs and Muslims except what they
saw on television seemed like a bad dream. I knew then that I would
never be silent again.

I've tried to reclaim those lost years. I realize now that I come from a 8
culture that has a rich history. The Arab world is a medley of people of
different religions; not every Arab is a Muslim, and vice versa. The Arabs
brought tremendous advances in the sciences and mathematics, as well
as creating a literary tradition that has never been surpassed. The language itself is flexible and beautiful, with nuances and shades of meaning unparalleled in any language. Though many find it hard to believe,

Islam has made progress in women's rights. There is a specific provision in the Koran that permits women to own property and ensures that their inheritance is protected—although recent events have shown that interpretation of these laws can vary.

My youngest brother, who is 12, is now at the crossroads I faced. When   9 initial reports of the Oklahoma City bombing pointed to "Arab-looking individuals" as the culprits, he came home from school crying. "Mom, why do Muslims kill people? Why are the Arabs so bad?" She was angry and brokenhearted, but tried to handle the situation in the best way possible: through education. She went to his class, armed with Arabic music, pictures, traditional dress and cookies. She brought a chapter of the social-studies book to life, and the children asked intelligent, thoughtful questions, even after the class was over. Some even asked if she was coming back. When my brother came home, he was excited and proud instead of ashamed.

I only recently told my mother about my past experience. Maybe if I 10 had told her then, I would have been better equipped to deal with the thoughtless teasing. But, fortunately, the world is changing. Although discrimination and stereotyping still exist, many people are trying to lessen and end it. Teachers, schools and the media are showing greater sensitivity to cultural issues. However, there is still much that needs to be done, not for the sake of any particular ethnic or cultural group but for the sake of our country.

The America that I love is one that values freedom and the differences 11 of its people. Education is the key to understanding. As Americans we need to take a little time to look and listen carefully to what is around us and not rush to judgment without knowing all the facts. And we must never be ashamed of our pasts. It is our collective differences that unite us and make us unique as a nation. It's what determines our present and our future.

Glossary

Various terms are used throughout this edition of *Patterns Plus* to explain the basic strategies of writing. These terms are boldfaced in the chapter introductions, and they are boldfaced and defined here in the following pages. Terms in bold type within the definitions are also defined in the Glossary.

Alternating Method   The alternating method of **comparison** and **contrast,** also called point-by-point method, compares and contrasts two subjects item by item. (See also **Block Method** and **Mixed Method.)**

Antonym   An antonym is a word that has a meaning *opposite* that of another word. For example, *pleasure* is an antonym of *pain.* Using an antonym is one method writers use to define an unfamiliar word.

Argumentation   Argumentation is a **mode of development** used to express a controversial idea. A classic or formal argument includes five elements: statement of the problem, solution, evidence, refutation, and conclusion. Argumentation may or may not include some persuasion, but should be rational, logical, and objective rather than emotional. (See also **Persuasion.)**

Audience   A reader or readers of a piece of writing. More specifically, an audience is that reader or group of readers toward which a particular piece of writing is aimed. (See also **Purpose** and **Occasion.)**

Block Method   In the block method of **comparison** and **contrast,** the writer first explains the characteristics of the first item in a block and then explains the characteristics of the second item in a block. (See also **Alternating Method** and **Mixed Method.)**

Body   The body is the development of the **thesis** in a group of related paragraphs in an **essay.** (See also **Introduction** and **Conclusion.)**

Brainstorming   A prewriting technique that many writers use to generate ideas for writing. In brainstorming, a writer jots down as many details and ideas on a subject as come to mind.

Cause   A cause is a reason why something happens or an explanation of why some effect occurs. Writers explain why an **effect** (or result) comes about by explaining its causes. See chapter 8, "Cause and Effect," for further discussion.

Chronological Order   See **Order.**

Class   In **classification** and **division,** a writer can classify or divide items if they are of the same type; that is, if they belong to the same class.

Classification   Classification is the process of sorting a group of items into categories on the basis of some characteristic or quality that the items have in common. As a **mode of development,** classification is used by writers to organize and develop information included in a **paragraph** or **essay.** Classification is sometimes combined with **division** to develop a **topic** or **thesis.** See chapter 5, "Classification and Division," for further discussion.

Cliché   Clichés are words or phrases that have become so overused they have lost their expressive power. Examples of clichés are "rosy red," "silly goose," "bull in a china shop," and "works like a horse."

Coherence   Coherence refers to the logical flow of a piece of writing. Writing is coherent when the **main idea** is clearly stated and the connections between the supporting **details** and the main idea are obvious. (See also **Unified/Unity.**)

Collaboration/Collaborative Writing   Collaboration or collaborative writing is the working together of two or more persons in developing and producing a piece of writing.

Comparison/Compare   When making a comparison, the writer discusses the similarities of objects or ideas. Writers sometimes combine comparison with **contrast** in developing their **main idea.** See chapter 6, "Comparison and Contrast," for further discussion.

Conclusion   In writing, the term *conclusion* is used to refer to the sentence or **paragraph** that completes the composition. Within the conclusion, the writer may restate the **main idea** of the composition or sum up its important points.
   In reading, the term *conclusion* refers to the idea the reader can draw from the information in the reading selection. Drawing a conclusion involves making an **inference;** that is, deriving an idea that is implied by the information stated within a composition.

Connotation   Connotation refers to the feelings or qualities a reader associates with a word. In **persuasion,** writers often use the connotations of words to appeal to their readers. (See also **Denotation.**)

Contrast When making a contrast, the writer discusses the differences among objects or ideas. Writers sometimes combine contrast with **comparison** in developing an idea. See chapter 6, "Comparison and Contrast," for further discussion.

Deductive Order In deductive order—also called general-to-specific order—the writer presents the argument or discussion by beginning with a general statement, such as the **topic** of a **paragraph** or **thesis** of an **essay,** and proceeding to the specific information that supports the statement.

Definition A definition explains the meaning of a word or term. Writers frequently use a variety of methods for defining the words and terms they use. They may use a dictionary definition, a **synonym,** or an **antonym.** They may also use any combination of the **modes of development** explained in this text.

An **extended definition** is one composed of several sentences or paragraphs. It is often used to define complex objects or concepts. See chapter 9, "Definition," for further discussion.

Denotation Denotation refers to the exact definition, or dictionary definition, of a word. (See also **Connotation.**)

Description In a description, the writer discusses the appearance of a person, place, or object. In descriptions, writers use words and details that appeal to the senses in order to create the **impression** they want the reader to have about what is being described.

Details Details are specific pieces of information—examples, incidents, dates, and so forth—that explain and support the general ideas in a composition. Writers use details to make their general ideas clearer and more understandable to the reader.

Development Development refers to the detailed explanation of the main—and usually more general—ideas in a composition. The **main idea** (or **topic**) of a paragraph is developed by providing specific information in the sentences within the paragraph. The main idea or **thesis** of an **essay** is explained or developed through **paragraphs**.

Dialogue Dialogue is conversation, usually between two or more persons. It is used by writers to give the exact words spoken by people and is always set off by quotation marks. The writer usually uses a new paragraph to indicate a change of speaker. Dialogue is commonly found in **narration.**

Division In division, the writer breaks down or sorts a single object or idea into its components or parts and then gives detailed information about each of the parts. Division is sometimes used in combination with **classification.** See chapter 5, "Classification and Division," for further discussion.

Draft A draft is the first version of a piece of writing. Preparation of a draft follows prewriting in the writing process. A draft requires rewriting, revising, and editing. (See also **Edit, Prewriting, Revising,** and **Rewriting.**)

Edit   Editing is the final step in the writing process and involves checking the piece of writing for accuracy of spelling, sentence structure, grammar, and punctuation. (See also **Draft, Prewriting, Revising,** and **Rewriting.**)

Effect   An effect is the result of certain events or **causes.** An effect may be the result of one or more causes. Writers often combine cause and effect to explain why something happens. See chapter 8, "Cause and Effect," for further discussion.

Essay   An essay is a written composition based on an idea, which is called its **thesis.** An essay usually consists of at least three **paragraphs.** In the paragraphs, writers usually introduce and state the **thesis,** develop or explain the thesis, and conclude the essay. See chapter 1, "The Basics of Writing: Process and Strategies," for further discussion.

Event   An occurrence or happening that a writer wishes to portray, often as part of a **fictional** or **nonfictional narrative.**

Example   An example is a specific illustration of a general idea or statement. Writers may use one or more examples and may extend a single example over an entire essay in order to illustrate and support their ideas.

Extended Definition   See **Definition.**

Extended Example   An extended example is described in several sentences or paragraphs. It is used as a way of providing additional support for a **topic sentence** or **thesis statement.** See chapter 4, "Examples," for further discussion.

Fact(s)   Any thing or things known with certainty. Writers often present facts as a way of showing they are **objective** about a subject. (See also **Opinion.**)

Fallacy   A fallacy is an error in the writer's reasoning or logic. Types of fallacies include the post hoc (meaning "after this, therefore because of this"), hasty generalization, non sequitur (claiming an effect that does not follow from the cause), false analogy, circular argument, argument to the man (argument ad hominem), bandwagon, either-or, and begging the question. See chapters 8, "Cause and Effect," and 10, "Argumentation and Persuasion," for further discussion.

Fiction/Fictional Narrative   A **paragraph** or an **essay** that presents a story or event that did not occur or that differs significantly from a real or true event is called fiction. (By contrast, see **Nonfiction/Nonfictional Narrative.**)

Figure of Speech   A word or phrase used to compare unlike things to create an image or **impression.** Examples are "He fought like a tiger" and "A little girl is sugar and spice." (See also **Metaphor** and **Simile.**)

First Person   See **Person.**

Formal Definition   A formal definition assigns the word or term being defined to the **class** or **classification** of items to which it belongs and then describes the characteristics that distinguish it from other items in that class.

Freewriting   Freewriting is a prewriting exercise that involves writing without stopping for a set period of time, often five to ten minutes. Freewriting is an effective way to start writing and to generate ideas.

General Idea/General Statement   A general idea or statement is broad and sweeping and therefore must usually be explained with more specific information. The **main idea** of a **paragraph** or an **essay** is a relatively general idea, involving only the main features of the thought. In a paragraph or an essay, the general ideas and statements must be supported by more specific information.

Imply/Implied   To imply is to hint at or indicate indirectly. Writers sometimes only imply their ideas rather than state them directly. An implied idea requires the reader to draw **conclusions** or make **inferences** in order to determine the idea.

Impression   The effect, feeling, or image that an author tries to create through **description.**

Incidents   Incidents are the more specific, detailed happenings that make up a particular event. The **narration** of an event will include an account of the specific incidents that occurred as part of the event.

Inductive Order   In inductive order—also called specific-to-general order—the writer presents the argument or discussion by beginning with specific supporting information and proceeding to the **general statement,** such as the **topic** of a **paragraph** or **thesis** of an **essay.**

Infer/Inference   An inference is a conclusion drawn by the reader based on information known or **implied**. Writers sometimes imply their ideas rather than state them. Readers must make inferences and use the information that is known or stated to determine the writer's ideas.

Inform   Inform means to relate or tell about something. Writers often use **process** as a **mode of development** to inform their readers, though any of the modes discussed in this text can be used to inform.

Instruct   Instruct means to teach or educate. Writers often use **process** as a **mode of development** to instruct their readers.

Introduction   The introduction of a **paragraph** or **essay** is at its beginning. The introduction of an essay is often where the writer places the **thesis statement.** (See also **Body** and **Conclusion.**)

Irony   The use of a relationship that is contradictory or unexpected. Writers often use irony to amuse, sadden, instruct, or anger their readers.

Main Idea   The main idea of a composition is the general concept, broad **opinion,** or argument on which the composition is based. The main idea of a **paragraph** is called the **topic.** The main idea of an **essay** is called the **thesis.**

Metaphor   A metaphor is a **figure of speech** that compares unlike items by attributing the qualities or characteristics of one item to the other. A metaphor compares the items without the use of the words *like* or *as*. (See also **Simile**.)

Mixed Method   The mixed method of **comparison** and **contrast** explains similarities and then differences, or differences first and then similarities. (See also **Alternating Method** and **Block Method**.)

Mode of Development   The mode of development refers to the kind of information used to support and explain the **main idea** of a paragraph or essay. Writers commonly use, either singly or in combination, the modes discussed in this text: **narration, description, examples, classification** and **division, comparison** and **contrast, process, cause** and **effect, definition,** and **argumentation** and **persuasion.**

Narration/Narrative Writing   Narration is a **mode of development** used by writers to tell a story or give an account of a historical or fictional event. See chapter 2, "Narration," for further discussion.

Nonfiction/Nonfictional Narrative   A paragraph or essay that presents a story or event that actually happened. (By contrast, see **Fiction/Fictional Narrative**.)

Objective   A paragraph or essay that presents the facts without including the writer's interpretation of those facts is said to be objective. (By contrast, see **Subjective**.)

Occasion   An occasion is a set of circumstances under which a particular piece of writing occurs. The writing assignments in this text are occasions for writing **paragraphs** and **essays.**

Opinion   An opinion is a belief or conclusion that may or may not be based on fact. Writers often use opinion as a way of presenting a subjective description of an event or object. (By contrast, see **Fact[s]**.)

Order   Order refers to the sequence in which the information in a composition is organized or arranged. Information is commonly organized in chronological order, order of importance, or spatial order. In **chronological order,** the information is arranged according to time. In **order of importance,** the information may be arranged from the least to the most important—or from the most to the least important. In **spatial order,** the information is presented from a particular vantage point: the door to a room, front to back, floor to ceiling, and so forth.

Order of Importance   See **Order.**

Paragraph   A paragraph is usually a set of two or more sentences that help explain an idea. The major use of a paragraph is to mark a division of the information within a composition. Another use of the paragraph is to set off **dialogue**. In this text, a paragraph is considered as a unit. The first word of a paragraph is usually indented a few spaces from the left margin of the printed page.

Person   Person is indicated by the personal pronouns used in a composition. Writers use the first person (*I, we*) to represent themselves as participants or firsthand observers of their subject. They use the second person (*you*) to address the reader directly. They use the third person (*he, she, it, one, they*) to provide the reader with a less limited and more objective view of the subject than may be possible by using first or second person. (See also **Point of View.**)

Persuasion   Persuasion is a **mode of development** in which the writer appeals to the reader's emotions in an attempt to convince the reader to accept the writer's **opinion** or judgment. The writer's **thesis** may or may not be controversial. (See also **Argumentation.**)

Point-by-Point Method   See **Alternating Method.**

Point of View   Point of view refers to the way writers present their ideas. Point of view is determined by the **person, time,** and **tone** used in a composition. Person is indicated by personal pronouns. Time is determined by the words that indicate when the action discussed in the composition takes place (past, present, or future). Tone refers to the attitude that writers take toward their subjects. The tone may be serious, humorous, formal, informal, cynical, sarcastic, ironic, sympathetic, and so forth.

Prewriting   Prewriting may involve **freewriting** and **brainstorming**. The purpose of prewriting is to get the writer started on defining the **main idea.** (See also **Brainstorming, Draft,** and **Freewriting.**)

Process   Process is a **mode of development** used by writers to explain the method of performing a task, making or preparing something, or achieving a particular result. See chapter 7, "Process," for further discussion.

Purpose   Purpose refers to a writer's reason for writing. Writers usually want to **inform** and to **instruct.**

Quotation Marks   Quotation marks are a pair of punctuation marks (" ") used to indicate the beginning and end of **dialogue** or information cited verbatim from a source.

Revising   The process of evaluating, reworking, and **rewriting** a **draft,** keeping **audience, purpose, thesis, development,** and, finally, mechanics (sentence structure, punctuation) in mind.

Rewriting   Rewriting involves reworking and clarifying the **draft** of a piece of writing. (See also **Draft, Edit, Prewriting,** and **Revising.**)

Second Person   See **Person.**

Sentence   A sentence is a group of words that expresses a thought. A sentence usually contains a word or words that express who is doing an action or is being acted upon (the *subject* of the sentence) and a word or words that express the action that is taking place (the *verb* of the sentence). The first word of a sentence begins with a capital letter. The end of a sentence is marked by a period (.), a question mark (?), or an exclamation point (!).

Simile   A simile is a **figure of speech** in which unlike items are compared. A simile is usually introduced by *like* or *as*, as in "He worked *like a horse* on the project" or "The chicken was as tasteless *as a piece of cardboard.*" (See also **Metaphor.**)

Spatial Order   See **Order.**

Subjective   Subjective writing is that in which the writer's own feelings about the topic are expressed. (By contrast, see **Objective.**)

Support   Support refers to the information—specific details, **examples,** and so forth—used to develop or explain the **general idea** in a composition.

Symbol   A symbol is a person, place, or object that represents something other than itself, usually something immaterial or abstract.

Synonym   A synonym is a word or phrase that has the same meaning as another word or phrase. Writers sometimes use a synonym to clarify an unfamiliar word or phrase used in their compositions.

Thesis   The thesis is the **main idea** of an essay. The thesis may be stated directly (see **Thesis Statement**) or only implied (see **Imply/Implied**).

Thesis Statement   The thesis statement is the sentence or sentences in which the **main idea** of an **essay** is stated. The thesis statement is generally placed at or near the beginning of an essay.

Third Person   See **Person.**

Time   Time refers to the period (past, present, future) when the action discussed in the composition took place. Time is indicated by action words (verbs) and such words as *tomorrow, yesterday, next week,* and so on. (See also **Point of View.**)

Tone   Tone refers to the attitude writers take toward their subjects. The attitude in a composition may be formal, informal, serious, humorous, and so forth. (See also **Point of View.**)

Topic   The main idea of a **paragraph** is called its topic. The topic of a paragraph may be stated directly (see **Topic Sentence**) or only implied (see **Imply/Implied**).

Topic Sentence   The topic sentence is the sentence (or sentences) in which the **main idea** of a **paragraph** is stated. The topic sentence is commonly placed at or near the beginning of a paragraph, but it may appear at any point in the paragraph.

Transitions   Transitions are words and phrases such as *for example, on the other hand, first, second,* or *to illustrate* that help the reader identify the relationships among ideas in a composition.

Unified/Unity   A **paragraph** or **essay** must be unified to be effective, which means each must deal with a single idea, and the information included in the paragraph or essay must be related to that idea. (See also **Main Idea** and **Coherence.**)

Acknowledgments

Jack Agueros: "Halfway to Dick and Jane" by Jack Agueros, copyright © 1971 by Doubleday, a division of Bantam Doubleday Dell Publishing Group, Inc. from *The Immigrant Experience* by Thomas C. Wheeler. Used by permission of Doubleday, a division of Bantam Doubleday Dell Publishing Group, Inc.

Kurt Anderson: "Hush, Timmy—This is Like a Church," *Time,* 4/15/85. © 1985 Time Inc. Reprinted by permission.

L. O. Anderson: From *Wood-Frame House Construction* by L. O. Anderson (Dover, 1973). Reprinted by permission.

Magdoline Asfahani: "Time to Look and Listen," by Magdoline Asfahani from *Newsweek,* December 2, 1996. All rights reserved. Reprinted by permission.

Isaac Asimov: From *Please Explain* by Isaac Asimov. Copyright © 1973 by Isaac Asimov. Reprinted by permission of Houghton Mifflin Company. All rights reserved.

Russell Baker: "Learning to Write," from *Growing Up* by Russell Baker. Copyright © 1982 by Russell Baker. Published by agreement with Congdon & Weed, Inc.

James Baldwin: From *Notes of a Native Son* by James Baldwin. Copyright © 1955, renewed 1983, by James Baldwin. Reprinted by permission of Beacon Press, Boston.

Elizabeth Birch: "Earth to Andrew" is reprinted from *The Advocate,* May 26, 1998. © 1998 by Elizabeth Birch. All rights reserved.

Suzanne Britt: Suzanne Britt, "Neat People vs. Sloppy People," from *Show and Tell.* Reprinted by permission of Glencoe/McGraw-Hill.

Leo Buscaglia: Reprinted by permission of the author.

Karel Čapek: "On Literature" excerpted from *Toward the Radical Center: A Karel Čapek Reader,* edited by Peter Kussi, Catbird Press, by permission. © 1990 Peter Kussi and Catbird Press.

John Ciardi: "Dawn Watch." Copyright 1972 Rutgers University Press. Reprinted by permission of the author.

John Ciardi: "The Pencil Rack." Copyright 1972 Rutgers University Press. Reprinted by permission of the author.

Jacques Cousteau: Selection from *The Bounty of the Sea*. Reprinted by permission of the Cousteau Society, Inc.

Gil Crandall: From "Letter to a Tobacco Company," by Gil Crandall in *Reader's Digest* Vol. 125, July 1984, pp. 64–65. Reprinted by permission of the author.

Stanley Crouch: "Addicted to Violence," by Stanley Crouch. Copyright © 2000 by Stanley Crouch. Reprinted by permission of Georges Borchardt, Inc., for the author.

Richard Ford: "The Marion," by Richard Ford is reprinted by permission of the author.

Herbert J. Gans: "The Underclass," by Herbert J. Gans, *Washington Post*, September 10, 1990. (Original title: "So Much for the Underclass.") © The Washington Post. Reprinted with permission.

Bob Greene: "It Took This Night To Make Us Know," from *Johnny Deadline: Reporter* by Bob Greene. Copyright © 1976 Nelson-Hall Inc. Reprinted by permission of the publisher.

Mark Harris: Mark Harris, "Each Game Was a Crusade" from *Short Work of It*, 1979, The University of Pittsburgh Press. Reprinted by permission of The Fox Chase Agency, Inc.

S. I. Hayakawa: "How Dictionaries Are Made" adapted from *Language in Thought and Action*, Fourth Edition by S. I. Hayakawa and Alan R. Hayakawa, copyright © 1978 by Harcourt, Inc., reprinted by permission of the publisher.

L. Rust Hills: "How to Eat An Ice Cream Cone" from *How to Do Things Right: The Revelations of a Fussy Man* (New York: Doubleday, 1972). Reprinted by permission of the author.

Suzanne Hilton: Excerpt from *How Do They Get Rid of It?* by Suzanne Hilton. Reprinted by permission of Ray Lincoln Literary Agency, Elkins Park House, 107–B, Elkins Park, Pa. as agent for author.

Roger Hoffman: "The Dare," by Roger Hoffman, *The New York Times*, March 23, 1986. Copyright © 1986 by the New York Times Co. Reprinted by permission.

Sue Hubbell: Excerpt from *A Book of Bees* by Sue Hubbell. Copyright © 1988 by Sue Hubbell. Reprinted by permission of Houghton Mifflin Company/Mariner Books. All rights reserved.

Esther Iverem: Esther Iverem, "By Earth Obsessed," from *Essence*, September 1991, pp. 37–38. Reprinted by permission of the author.

E. J. Kahn, Jr.: "The Discovery of Coca-Cola" from *The Big Drink: The Story of Coca-Cola* by E. J. Kahn, Jr. Copyright © 1950, 1959, 1960 by E. J. Kahn, Jr. Used by permission of Random House, Inc.

Jim Kaplan: "Baseball's Hot Dogs," by Jim Kaplan, from "Baseball's Hot Dogs—Do They Spice Up the Game—or Leave a Bad Taste in Your Mouth?," by Jim Kaplan, from *TV Guide*, 5/28/88, pp. 14–15. Reprinted with permission from *TV Guide* ® Magazine. Copyright © 1988 by News America Publications Inc.

Garrison Keillor: "How to Write a Personal Letter," by Garrison Keillor, *Reader's Digest*, November 1987, pp. 129–131. Copyright © 1987 by International Paper Company. Reprinted by permission of International Paper Company.

Coretta Scott King: Coretta Scott King, "The Death Penalty is a Step Back." Reprinted by arrangement with Coretta Scott King c/o Writers House as agent.

Stephen King: Stephen King, "Ever Et Raw Meat," *The New York Times Book Review,* December 6, 1987. Copyright © 1987 by the New York Times Co. Reprinted by permission.

Brian Manning: "The Thirsty Animal," by Brian Manning, *The New York Times,* October 13, 1985. Copyright © 1985 by The New York Times Co. Reprinted by permission.

David Mazie: Excerpted with permission from "Keep Your Teen-Age Driver Alive" by David Mazie, *Reader's Digest,* June 1991. Copyright © 1991 by The Reader's Digest Assn., Inc.

Frank McCourt: "Angela's Ashes." Reprinted with the permission of Scribner, a Division of Simon & Schuster from *Angela's Ashes: A Memoir* by Frank McCourt. Copyright © 1996 by Frank McCourt.

Paul McMasters: Paul McMasters, "Getting the Facts Straight on Media Violence," The Freedom Forum Online, 4/9/98. Reprinted by permission of the author.

Mary Mebane: From *Mary* by Mary Mebane, copyright © 1981 by Mary Elizabeth Mebane. Used by permission of Viking Penguin, a division of Penguin Putnam Inc.

Alcestis "Cooky" Oberg: Alcestis "Cooky" Oberg, "The Internet Instills Family Values—Really," *USA Today,* 3/13/00 is reprinted by permission of the author. Alcestis Oberg © 2000. All rights reserved.

Marvin Olasky: "Aiming for Success" by Marvin Olasky originally published in *USA Today,* August 14, 1997. Reprinted by permission of the author.

Jeanne Park: Jeanne Park, "Eggs, Twinkies and Ethnic Stereotypes," *The New York Times,* April 20, 1990. Copyright © 1990 by The New York Times Co. Reprinted by permission.

Anna Quindlen: "Homeless" from *Living Out Loud* by Anna Quindlen, copyright © 1987 by Anna Quindlen. Used by permission of Random House, Inc.

Carin C. Quinn: "The Jeaning of America—and the World," by Carin C. Quinn, *American Heritage,* Volume 30, number 3. Reprinted by permission of *American Heritage* Magazine, a division of Forbes Inc. © Forbes Inc., 1978.

Peggy Robbins: "The Kickapoo Indian Medicine Company," by Peggy Robbins in *American History Illustrated,* Vol. XV, #2, May 1980. Reprinted through the courtesy of Cowles Magazine, publishers of *American History Illustrated.*

Anne Roiphe: Excerpt from *Fruitful* by Anne Roiphe. Copyright © 1996 by Anne Roiphe. Reprinted by permission of Houghton Mifflin Company. All rights reserved.

Andy Rooney: "Types" by Andy Rooney. Reprinted with the permission of Scribner, a Division of Simon & Schuster from *A Few Minutes With Andy Rooney* by Andrew A. Rooney. Copyright © 1981, 1986 Essay Productions, Inc.

Mike Royko: Mike Royko, "Death to the Killers," *Chicago Sun Times,* 1983. Reprinted with special permission from the Chicago Sun-Times, © 2001.

Nancy M. Sakamoto:　"Conversational Ballgames" from *Polite Fictions* by Nancy Masterson Sakamoto. Reprinted by permission of the author.

Scott Russell Sanders:　Excerpts from *Secrets of the Universe* by Scott Russell Sanders. Copyright © 1991 Scott Russell Sanders. Reprinted by permission of Beacon Press, Boston.

Jonathan Schell:　From *The Fate of the Earth* by Jonathan Schell. Copyright © 1982 by Jonathan Schell. Reprinted by permission of Alfred A. Knopf, Inc. Originally appeared in *The New Yorker.*

Bonnie Smith-Yackel:　"My Mother Never Worked," by Bonnie Smith-Yackel. Reprinted with permission from *Women: A Journal of Liberation*, Vol. 4, No. 2, Spring 1975.

Gary Soto:　Gary Soto, "The Pie." Reprinted from *A Summer Life*, by permission of the author. Copyright 1990.

Brent Staples:　Brent Staples, "Black Men and Public Space." *Ms.*, September 1986, pp. 54, 86. Reprinted with permission of the author.

Andrew Sullivan:　Andrew Sullivan, "Do We Need These Laws?" Reprinted from *The Advocate*, April 14, 1998. © 1998 by Andrew Sullivan. All rights reserved. Used by permission.

Amy Tan:　Excerpted from "Watching China" by Amy Tan as first appeared in *Glamour*, September 1990. Copyright by Amy Tan.

Clifton L. Taulbert:　Reprinted with permission of Council Oak Books from *Once Upon A Time When We Were Colored*, by Clifton L. Taulbert; copyright © 1989 by Clifton L. Taulbert. (pp. 1–7)

Edward Tenner:　From *Why Things Bite Back* by Edward Tenner, copyright © 1996 by Edward Tenner. Used by permission of Alfred A. Knopf, a division of Random House, Inc.

Lewis Thomas:　"The Health-Care System," from *The Medusa and The Snail* by Lewis Thomas, copyright © 1974, 1975, 1976, 1977, 1978, 1979 by Lewis Thomas. Used by permission of Viking Penguin, a division of Penguin Putnam Inc.

Sallie Tisdale:　Sallie Tisdale, "Ban All Handguns" from the essay "Zero Tolerance for Slaughter," Salon.com, 5/6/99. Reprinted by permission of the author.

James Tuite:　"The Sounds of the City" by James Tuite. From *The New York Times*, August 6, 1966. Copyright © 1966 by The New York Times Co. Reprinted by permission.

Eliot Wigginton:　From *The Foxfire Book* by Eliot Wigginton. Copyright © 1968, 1969, 1970, 1971, 1972 by The Foxfire Fund, Inc. Used by permission of Doubleday, a division of Bantam Doubleday Dell Publishing Group, Inc.

Joy Williams:　Excerpt from Joy Williams, "The Killing Game." First published in *Esquire Magazine*, October 1990. Reprinted courtesy of Esquire and the Hearst Corporation.

Index